GENIE

A Psycholinguistic Study of a
Modern-Day "Wild Child"

PERSPECTIVES IN
NEUROLINGUISTICS and PSYCHOLINGUISTICS

Harry A. Whitaker, Series Editor
DEPARTMENT OF PSYCHOLOGY
THE UNIVERSITY OF ROCHESTER
ROCHESTER, NEW YORK

HAIGANOOSH WHITAKER and HARRY A. WHITAKER (Eds.).
  Studies in Neurolinguistics, Volumes 1 and 2; Volume 3. In preparation
NORMAN J. LASS (Ed.). Contemporary Issues in Experimental Phonetics
JASON W. BROWN. Mind, Brain, and Consciousness: The Neuropsychology
  of Cognition
S. J. SEGALOWITZ and F. A. GRUBER (Eds.). Language Development and
  Neurological Theory
SUSAN CURTISS. Genie: A Psycholinguistic Study of a Modern-Day "Wild
  Child"

In preparation

I. M. SCHLESINGER and LILA NAMIR (Eds.). Sign Language of the Deaf:
  Psychological, Linguistic, and Sociological Perspectives
JOHN MACNAMARA (Ed.). Language Learning and Thought

GENIE

A Psycholinguistic Study of
a Modern-Day "Wild Child"

SUSAN CURTISS

University of California
Los Angeles, California

ACADEMIC PRESS   New York   San Francisco   London   1977

A Subsidiary of Harcourt Brace Jovanovich, Publishers

ACADEMIC PRESS, INC.
111 Fifth Avenue, New York, New York 10003

United Kingdom Edition published by
ACADEMIC PRESS, INC. (LONDON) LTD.
24/28 Oval Road, London NW1

Library of Congress Cataloging in Publication Data

Curtiss, Susan
    Genie : a psycholinguistic study of a modern-day
"wild child."

    (Perspectives in neurolinguistics and psycholinguistics
series)
    Originally presented as the author's thesis, University
of California, Los Angeles, 1976.
    Bibliography: p.
    1.   Children—Language—Case studies.   2.   Psycho-
linguistics—Case studies.   3.   Speech disorders in
children—Case studies.   4.   Languages—Physiological
aspects—Case studies.   I.   Title.
P118.C8 1976   401'.9   76-55968
ISBN 0-12-196350-0

PRINTED IN THE UNITED STATES OF AMERICA

To Genie

This drawing is testimony to the importance and strength of the mother-child relationship for all human beings, and to Genie's need for a sense of her own history. Early in 1977, filled with loneliness and longing, Genie drew this picture. At first she drew only the picture of her mother and then labeled it "I miss Mama." She then suddenly began to draw more. The moment she finished she took my hand, placed it next to what she had just drawn, motioning me to write, and said "Baby Genie." Then she pointed under her drawing and said, "Mama hand." I dictated all the letters. Satisfied, she sat back and stared at the picture. There she was, a baby in her mother's arms. She had created her own reality.

Contents

PART II LINGUISTIC DEVELOPMENT

PART III NEUROLINGUISTIC ASPECTS

Preface

Scholars have long been fascinated with cases of feral and isolated children, hoping to learn through the study of such individuals, the possibilities for man's development apart from societal input and influences. Questions concerning the development of cognitive and intellectual faculties in such cases have been of particular interest. The scholarly writings of Professor Itard on Victor (the child discovered in France at the turn of the nineteenth century, popularly known as the "Wild Child") are fascinating and represent the most reputable and widely known first-hand reporting of such a case, although others have also been reported (cf. Singh & Zingg, 1942).

The opportunities that such cases present for studying human behavior and development and the nature of the human mind are great and challenging.

> If it were proposed to solve the following problem of metaphysics: *to determine what would be the degree of intelligence and the nature of the ideas of an adolescent who, deprived from his childhood of all education, had lived entirely separated from individuals of his own species* . . . the mental picture of this adolescent would be of the Wild Boy of Aveyron, and the solution of the problem would consist in exhibiting the extent and the cause of his intellectual state.*

* From Itard, J.M.G. 1801. *De l'Education d'un homme sauvage or des premiers developpements physiques et moraux du jeune sauvage de l'Aveyron.* Paris: Gouyon. Reprinted in *The Wild Boy of Aveyron,* Humphrey, G. and Humphrey, M. 1932. New York: Appleton-Century-Crofts, p. 7.

The Wild Boy of Aveyron died over a century ago, but another adolescent who affords us equally rich opportunities for study has been discovered in our own time: Genie.

Genie was discovered in 1970. Deprived and isolated to an unprecedented degree, she was not discovered until she was an adolescent. An inhuman childhood had prevented her from learning language, and she knew little about the world in any respect save abuse, neglect, isolation, and deprivation. Since that time, Genie has been rehabilitated and educated to the fullest extent possible and studied in an attempt to answer questions of interest to linguists, neuroscientists, psychologists, and others. This work reports on the linguistic research carried out through studying and working with Genie.

Through in-depth psycholinguistic and neurolinguistic research, I have attempted to explore just what this case can tell us about some of the questions of interest for linguists and psycholinguists: Is there a critical period for language acquisition? If so, what kind of language development is possible beyond the critical period? Are language acquisition and language lateralization interrelated? Will language be lateralized if acquired after puberty? If so, will it be lateralized to the left hemisphere as it is in normal human brains? What happens to cerebral organization in general when one of the brain's basic functions fails to develop? These questions are addressed in Parts II and III.

Part I (Chapters 1–5) provides a case history and background material on Genie's personality and language behavior. Much of what I have written in Part I does not follow the normal canons of scientific writing. To some extent it is an account of the interaction between this remarkable girl and myself. Since these circumstances will hopefully never be repeated, our interaction is itself part of the data which other scientific observers must consider.

Part II (Chapters 6–10) details Genie's linguistic development and overall language abilities. Chapter 6 describes the sources and kinds of data analyzed in the ensuing chapters. Chapter 7 describes and discusses Genie's phonological development. Chapter 8 details the extent of Genie's receptive knowledge of syntax, morphology, and semantics. Chapter 9 discusses Genie's productive grammatical abilities in syntax, morphology, and semantics. Chapter 10 provides a comparison between her linguistic development and the language acquisition of other children.

Part III (Chapter 11) presents a full description of the neurolinguistic work carried out on Genie and discusses the implications of this aspect of the case.

To protect Genie's identity, the names presented in the text are largely fictitious. Only the names or initials of a few individuals are factual. Most important, *Genie* is not this child's real name. It is a name given to protect her privacy, chosen because it captures, to a small measure, the fact that she emerged into human society past childhood, having existed previously as something other than fully human.

Acknowledgments

This research was supported, in part, by a grant from the National Institutes of Mental Health. U.S. Department of Health, Education and Welfare, No. MH-21191-03.

A large number of people have contributed to this book and the work it represents. To all those whom I inadvertently fail to mention, please accept my apologies and thanks.

First and foremost, I am indebted to Victoria Fromkin. Her encouragement, criticism, time, and ideas all played a major role in my writing and completing this work. In addition to all her other help, she drew several of the pictures for the tests used with Genie.

I am also indebted to Richard Harshman, who helped me with statistics and suggested and made available to me many test materials to use with Genie. In addition, our many discussions were extremely helpful and stimulating.

I am grateful to Stephen Krashen not only for designing and administering all of the dichotic listening tests and for helpful and encouraging discussion, but most of all for serving as an example of the unselfish pursuit of scientific truth in his constant willingness to share ideas and credit.

There are several others to whom I owe thanks: to Warren Brown, who offered his time and help to design and run the evoked potential studies on Genie; to James Marsh and Roger Sperry for making their labs available to us; to Eran and Dahlia Zaidel for sharing materials and helpful discussion; to Peter Ladefoged for helpful comments and criticisms; to James Kent for sharing his notes and other professional observations with me; to David and Marilyn Rigler for sharing data of many kinds on Genie and making me part of the family; to Caroline Carr for telling me things that Genie said when I wasn't there; to Margie Lifflander for her beautiful test drawings; and to Phil Hanff for some key help at a crucial time.

I owe thanks to John Gresham for many hours of help in proofreading the manuscript, to Judy Rozzen for all the time and work she contributed in helping me fieldtest normal children, to the Lawrence School for Early Years for providing me with an enriching educational experience as well as children to fieldtest, and the Michael Adam Rozzen, first for serving as guinea pig for new test ideas, and second for providing me with love and joy during otherwise difficult times.

Finally, I am indebted to Genie, herself. She has enriched my life beyond measure.

Part I

CASE HISTORY

1

Family Background and
Early Childhood

To understand this case history, one must understand Genie's family background. Genie's mother said that when she married, her life ended. She had a stormy marriage, during which she was frequently beaten by her husband. He repeatedly threatened to kill her, and she lived in fear, reinforced by the recurrent beatings over the years.

Despite the fact that her husband disliked children and was adamant about not having any, after 5 years of marriage, Genie's mother became pregnant. Very late into the pregnancy, the father-to-be viciously beat and tried to kill his wife by strangling her. Nonetheless, their first daughter was born, evidently healthy and thriving. As babies often do, this infant cried considerably. Exasperated and irritated by her crying, the father had his new daughter put into the garage so that he would not have to listen to her. At the age of $2\frac{1}{2}$ months this child died of pneumonia and overexposure.

The following year, a second child was born. A boy, this infant had an RH blood type incompatibility. He died when he was 2 days old, allegedly from choking on his own mucous.

Three years later, another son was born. Delivered by Caesarian section (as were the first two infants) with an RH blood incompatibility as well, he was nonetheless an apparently healthy baby. Because the father had very rigid ideas about obedience and discipline, the mother was under great pressure to keep her new son from "acting up" or crying. Perhaps not surprisingly, then, this young boy began to manifest early developmental problems. He was reportedly late to walk, had eating problems, was late to talk, and was still not toilet-trained at the age of three. At that point his paternal grandmother took the boy into her own home. Under her care, he thrived, rapidly became toilet-trained, and, finally, in much better developmental condition, was returned to his parents.

Three years later Genie was born. A full-term baby, she, too, was delivered by Caesarian section, and suffered from an RH blood incompatibility for which she received an exchange transfusion 1 day after birth. Her birth weight (7 pounds, $1\frac{1}{4}$ ounces) was in the 50th percentile on the Iowa Growth Chart (i.e., completely normal). Genie was first taken to a pediatrician at the age of 3 months. He noticed a congenital dislocation of the hip for which he prescribed a Frejka pillow splint to hold both legs in abduction. At this visit, Genie's weight was 12 pounds, $2\frac{1}{4}$ ounces, her height was 23 inches—again, normal for her age and sex. At 4 months she was noted to have "good head control." At $4\frac{1}{2}$ months Genie began wearing the Frejka splint. At the age of 5 months, when she was brought in for a routine follow-up examination, she was noted to be alert and engaged in hand-to-mouth movements. On a return examination at 6 months, she weighed 14 pounds, $7\frac{1}{2}$ ounces, and was $25\frac{1}{2}$ inches tall. At that visit, the doctor asked that she be returned again in a month. Genie was not brought back for 5 months, however, until she was 11 months old. At that time she weighed only 17 pounds—below the 16th percentile for her age and sex; thus, within the first year of life, her weight had fallen drastically. Nonetheless, at that visit, Genie could sit alone, was described as alert, and had normal primary dentition for her age. Soon after this visit, the Frejka splint was removed. Her physician recommended physiotherapy following removal of the splint, but Genie's father refused to permit it.

We do not know many other details of Genie's life during her first year and a half. Her mother reports that Genie was a noncuddly baby, that she didn't coo or babble very much, that she resisted any solid food, even Junior foods. Genie reportedly, then, was manifesting similar developmental problems and lags to those her brother had shown—reluctance to chew, resistance to most foods, lateness in walking. We do not know the cause of these early problems, but we do know that Genie's father disliked his daughter and did not allow his wife to devote too much time or attention to her. Thus, her life may not have provided the nurturing that aids development.

At 14 months, Genie developed an acute illness (pneumonitis) and was taken to a different pediatrician. Feverish, she was listless and unresponsive; this physician stated that she showed signs of possible retardation but because of the fever, it was difficult to assess her development. The doctor's statement— that Genie showed signs of possible retardation—proved to have disastrous consequences for Genie. Genie's father, who was already intensely jealous of the attention the mother paid to Genie, used this statement as justification for the subsequent isolation and abuse Genie suffered.

At the age of 20 months, Genie's life worsened tragically. Her paternal grandmother was hit by a truck and killed while crossing the street. Although his mother had been in her late seventies, Genie's father considered her death untimely, and although he had not had a very close relationship with her when she was alive, he become outraged and embittered when the truck driver who had hit her was acquitted of all charges. His response was to move his family into his dead mother's home and to isolate them from the outside world.

Living in fear of the father, this move was the beginning of imprisonment and seclusion for the whole family; but for Genie it was the beginning of her extreme abuse, neglect, and isolation. Genie was increasingly confined to the smaller of two bedrooms. It is reported by her mother that, at first, Genie was occasionally allowed to go outside, to sit on the back steps or play in a playpen in the backyard. When discussing these backyard "excursions," however, the mother revealed that even these were often times of neglect and confinement. She reports that Genie was a "bad girl," that left in her playpen to play, Genie would take it apart with her fingernails. One wonders how long Genie, a tiny toddler, must have been left in that playpen, how long she must have been neglected or forgotten, to resort to this action.

In the house Genie was confined to a small bedroom, harnessed to an infant's potty seat. Genie's father sewed the harness, himself; unclad except for the harness, Genie was left to sit on that chair. Unable to move anything except her fingers and hands, feet and toes, Genie was left to sit, tied-up, hour after hour, often into the night, day after day, month after month, year after year. At night, when Genie was not forgotten, she was removed from her harness only to be placed into another restraining garment—a sleeping bag which her father had fashioned to hold Genie's arms stationary (allegedly to prevent her from taking it off). In effect, it was a straight jacket. Therein constrained, Genie was put into an infant's crib with wire mesh sides and a wire mesh cover overhead. Caged by night, harnessed by day, Genie was left to somehow endure the hours and years of her life.

There was little for her to listen to; there was no TV or radio in the house. Genie's bedroom was in the back of the house next to a bedroom and a bathroom. The adjacent bedroom was left unoccupied the entire time the family lived in the house. It was (the father's) "mother's" room. Not wishing to "defile" it, Genie's father permitted no one to enter it, not even to dust. The father had an intolerance for noise, so what little conversation there was between family members in the rest of the house was kept at a low volume. Except for moments of anger, when her father swore, Genie did not hear any language outside her door, and thus received practically no auditory stimulation of any kind, aside from bathroom noises. There were two windows in her room, and one of them was kept open several inches. She may, therefore, have occasionally heard an airplane overhead or some other traffic or environmental noises; but set in the back of the house, Genie would not have heard much noise from the street.

Hungry and forgotten, Genie would sometimes attempt to attract attention by making noise. Angered, her father would often beat her for doing so. In fact, there was a large piece of wood left in the corner of Genie's room which her father used solely to beat her whenever she made any sound. Genie learned to keep silent and to suppress all vocalization; but sometimes, desperate for attention or food, Genie would use her body or some object to make noise. Her father would not tolerate this either, and he often beat her with his wooden stick on these occasions as well. During these times, and on all other occasions that her father dealt with Genie, he never spoke to her. Instead, he acted like a wild dog. He made barking sounds, he growled at her, he let his nails grow long and scratched her, he bared his teeth at her; and if he wished to merely threaten her with his presence, he stood outside the door and made his dog-like noises— to warn her that he was there and that if she persisted in whatever she was doing, he would come in and beat her. That terrible noise, the sound of her father standing outside her door growling or barking or both, was almost the only sound Genie heard during those years she was imprisoned in her room.

At first, Genie's mother did manage to spend a few moments with Genie each day. But as she was fast becoming blind, and finding it harder and harder to even minimally care for Genie, Genie's brother increasingly became the principal caretaker. The father taught the brother to imitate his own dog-like behavior, so that Genie's brother did not speak to her either. In the fashion of his father, her brother only barked and growled at her.

Just as there was little to listen to, there was not much for Genie to touch or look at. The only pieces of furniture in her room were the crib and the potty seat. There was no carpet on the floor, no pictures on the walls. There were two windows, but they were covered up except for a few inches at the top out of which Genie could see the sky from one and the side of a neighboring house from the other. There was one dim, bare ceiling light bulb, a wall of closets, and another wall with the bedroom door. The room was a dirty salmon color. Occasionally, two plastic raincoats, one clear and one yellow, hung outside the closet in the room, and once in a while Genie was allowed to "play" with them. In addition, Genie was sometimes given "partly edited" copies of the TV log, with pictures that her father considered too suggestive removed (like women advertising swimming pools, etc.). She was also given an occasional empty cottage cheese container, empty thread spools, and the like. These were Genie's toys; and together with the floor, her harness, and her body, they were her primary sources of visual and tactile stimulation.

Genie's diet was equally limited. She was given baby foods, cereals, an occasional soft-boiled egg. Under pressure from the father to keep contact with Genie to a minimum, she was fed hurriedly, usually by having food stuffed into her mouth. Should Genie choke and spit out some of her food, she would have her face rubbed in it. Her mother reports that Genie was fed three times a day, but from the mother's recalling how through the years Genie would attempt to attract attention (and risk being beaten for it), it is probable that she was often left to go hungry.

This was Genie's life—isolated, often forgotten, frequently abused (many details of horrible abuse are omitted here), physically restrained, starved for sensory stimulation. Thus minimally exposed to humanity, and most of that the most hideous of human behavior, Genie grew into a pitiful creature.

Genie's father was convinced that Genie would die. He was positive that she would not live past the age of twelve. He was so convinced of this that he promised his wife that if the child did live beyond twelve, the mother could seek help for Genie. But age twelve came and went; Genie survived, but the father reneged on his promise. The mother, too blind to even dial the phone and forbidden under threat of death to contact her own parents (who lived in the area), felt helpless to do anything.

Finally, when Genie was $13\frac{1}{2}$-years-old, Genie's mother, after a violent argument with her husband in which she threatened to leave unless he called her parents, succeeded in getting her husband to telephone her mother. Later that day Genie's mother took Genie and left her home and her husband.

They escaped to the grandmother's home, where she and Genie stayed for three more weeks. During the third week, Genie's mother was advised to apply for aid to the blind. Taking Genie with her, she inadvertently went to the family aids building, where an eligibility worker, upon seeing Genie, sensed that something was terribly wrong. The worker alerted her supervisor immediately, and the two of them questioned the mother. What they saw and heard caused them to call the police. The police took Genie into custody; charges were brought against the parents. On the day of the trial the father killed himself. He left a suicide note stating, "The world will never understand."

Genie was admitted into the hospital for extreme malnutrition. She had been discovered, at last.

2

November 1970–January 1971

Genie was pitiful. Hardly ever having worn clothing, she did not react to temperature, heat or cold.[1] Never having eaten solid food, Genie did not know how to chew, and had great difficulty in swallowing. Having been strapped down and left sitting on a potty chair, she could not stand erect, could not straighten her arms or legs, could not run, hop, jump, or climb; in fact, she could only walk with difficulty, shuffling her feet, swaying from side to side. Hardly ever having seen more than a space of 10 feet in front of her (the distance from her potty chair to the door), she had become nearsighted exactly to that distance. Having been beaten for making noise, she had learned to suppress almost all vocalization save a whimper. Suffering from malnutrition, she weighed only 59 pounds and stood only 54 inches tall. She was incontinent of feces and urine. Her hair was sparse and stringy. She salivated copiously, spitting onto anything at hand. Genie was unsocialized, primitive, hardly human.

Surprisingly, however, Genie was alert and curious. She maintained good eye contact and avidly explored her new surroundings. She was intensely eager for human contact and attention. In the face of her hunger for contact with her new world, her almost total silence had an eerie quality. Except for a high-pitched whimpering and a few words she is reported to have imitated when she was first admitted to the hospital, she was a silent child who did not vocalize in any way, who did not even sob when she cried. Her silence was complete even in the face of frenzied emotion. Sometimes, frightened and frustrated by

---

[1] Singh and Zingg (1942) reported that the "wolf girls" did not react to changes in temperature and seemed oblivious to heat or cold. The wild boy of Aveyron also displayed this imperviousness to temperature.

both her former life and her new surroundings, Genie would erupt and have a raging tantrum, flailing about, scratching, spitting, blowing her nose, and frantically rubbing her face and hair with her own mucous, all the time trying to gouge or otherwise inflict pain on herself—all in silence. Unable to vocalize, Genie would use objects and parts of her body to make noise and help express her frenzy: a chair scratching against the floor, her fingers scratching against a balloon, furniture falling, objects thrown or slammed against other objects, her feet shuffling. These were Genie's noises during her sobless silent tantrum. At long last, physically exhausted, her rage would subside, and Genie would silently return to her undemonstrative self.

There was no real language during her placid times either. Except for a few words, Genie never spoke. She was a bizarre, unsocialized, silent human being. But what lay beneath the surface? For us, the primary question was what, if any, language abilities lay unrevealed in her eerie silence. Could she understand language? Did she know how to speak but not do so because she had conditioned herself not to speak aloud? If so, the task ahead of her was surely a difficult one, but one that therapy and recovery might achieve. If she had a passive knowledge of language, it would mean that she would have only to learn to use in performance what she already knew. Was Genie, instead, a pubescent adolescent over $13\frac{1}{2}$-years-old who did not understand or speak? If that was the case, then she was faced with the task of learning her first language as an adolescent, long past the time when children ordinarily learn language, possibly past the time when the brain can do so. (See Part III, 11.1 for further discussion of this question.)

It was several months after her admission into the hospital before careful linguistic observation, documentation, and investigation were begun. Thus, in order to determine that state of Genie's linguistic knowledge at the point when she was first discovered, we had to find out all we could from those who had had contact with her and from any and all records that were made regarding Genie during that first period at the hospital.

In tracing back we discovered that Genie understood a few words but had not acquired language. Our evidence came from a variety of sources. Reports from Genie's mother conflicted. One version was that Genie had begun to speak words, but stopped shortly thereafter. In another version, she reported that Genie never spoke at all. We didn't know which was true.

The hospital staff had the general impression that Genie could understand a fair amount based on the fact that she maintained good eye contact and seemed to pay special attention to faces when people spoke to her. Yet all the staff interviewed admitted on questioning that they tended to point and demonstrate when relating to Genie, and thus a fair amount of gesturing most probably accompanied their speech to her. They also stated that often Genie did not respond to very common, simple commands or questions.

The careful observations made by Dr. K (Genie's primary therapist while she was at the hospital) in his notes were very revealing. Although his notes were based on daily visits with Genie, there was reference to language only once in November and six times in December of 1970. These notes reflect, first of all, then, the scarcity of linguistic responses that Genie exhibited in those months. More importantly, his notes reveal that Genie understood little more than a few single words and negative command intonation. His notes demonstrate that Genie zeroed in on single words and ignored the sentences in which they occurred. If someone used a word she understood, she responded to it in a uniform fashion, regardless of its grammatical or semantic context.

Dr. K's notes also reveal that at times Genie imitated words that were spoken to her, thereby showing that she attended to speech directed to her and was motivated to interact and behave linguistically.

The videotapes further supported our conclusions. (See Part II, Chapter 8, Section 8.1 for a detailed look at these data.) From over 30 hours of tape, the evidence is very strong that Genie comprehended several individual words (namely, "rattle," "bunny," "red," "blue," "green," and "brown") and a few names (including "mother"), and, in addition, was able to extract the information NEG and WARNING from negative commands, and possibly the information QUESTION from yes/no question intonation. Moreover, it may be that some words were used spontaneously, but it is unclear because of Genie's poor articulation. There is no evidence, however, that Genie had any additional knowledge of English. On the contrary, there is convincing evidence that Genie could not process a sentence of English on the basis of its linguistic content alone, but rather that she depended critically on gestures and other nonlinguistic cues to successfully make any sense of speech directed to her. She readily responded to gestures alone, yet failed to respond to speech without accompanying gestures or nonlinguistic cues. What is more, her failure to respond often occurred at times when she was visibly tuned in to the speech around her and motivated sufficiently to attempt vocalizations of her own—both imitative and spontaneous. The observations from Dr. K parallel the 30 hours of videotape.

Genie was faced with learning her first language when she was 13 years, 7 months of age. Though it might be true, as her mother suggested, that Genie had begun to acquire some vocabulary and speak some words as a baby, words which may even have remained with her through her years of isolation, it was apparent that her linguistic environment had not provided sufficient stimulation or exposure to primary linguistic data for true language to emerge.

It was also necessary to determine whether her environment had permitted sufficient cognitive development for language acquisition. The evidence indicated that it had.

In November 1970 Genie was given the Vineland Social Maturity Scale and the Preschool Attainment Record, the scores of which were mental age (MA) 1.05 years and MA 13 months, respectively. In January 1971 Genie was given the Leiter International Performance Scale, achieving an MA of 4.9. Her performance on these tests placed her somewhere around the 2-year-old level with a wide scatter in subtest scores (see Part III). Although we were to conclude that these first test performances were not at all reliable measures of her cognitive abilities (underrepresenting her abilities), her performance was, notwithstanding, sufficient to judge her to be at least as advanced as normal children are when they begin to acquire language (Sinclair-de Zwart, 1971).

There were also linguistic indicators of her preparedness for the language learning task ahead. Her comprehension of single words implied an ability to scan and segment the speech stream for familiar sounds and groups of sounds and showed, in addition, an ability to parse the stream of incoming speech into linguistic units, e.g., words. Moreover, her receptive abilities were in some sense paralleled by what was probably the most persuasive indicator of all that Genie was ready for language—her imitation and spontaneous production of words— the same phenomenon that marks the onset of language in normal children.

Thus it appeared that Genie was ready, cognitively and linguistically. But was it too late? Was this girl, already 13 years and 7 months old, too old to learn language?

3

January 1971–June 1971

As of January 1971, Genie appeared to have a small receptive vocabulary and an even smaller productive vocabulary. Her receptive vocabulary included the following:

Proper nouns	Verbs	Negatives	Common nouns	Color adjectives
Genie	walk	no	door	red
Mother	go	don't	jewelry box	blue
Other names			rattle	green
			bunny	brown

There may have been a few other words she understood for which we have no record. Her receptive knowledge of language may have included some knowledge of intonation cues, most probably negative imperative intonation.

Her spontaneous productive vocabulary included *stopit* and *nomore*. Again, there may have been a few other utterances which were neither identifiable nor documented.

Genie also manifested an interest in watching a speaker's articulating mouth and imitating words, a hopeful sign for the emergence of speech.

These appeared to be the extent of Genie's linguistic abilities as of January 1971. We could not tell to what extent these meager indications of language already represented growth and development since Genie's emergence.

The prognosis for recovery or significant growth in any and every area of her development was poor. But we didn't know Genie, a child who would refuse to stand still, who refused to "listen" to the pessimistic prognoses regarding her chances for growth and development. Despite our pessimism, Genie began to change and grow.

In December she was moved to the hospital Rehabilitation Center because it offered greater opportunities for socialization, a richer activity program, and better access to the outdoors than did the hospital ward. While there, Genie began to change physically, to gain weight and to grow taller. Breast development signaled the onset of sexual maturation. Her walk became steadier, her carriage more erect. After several months, she was able to take long walks through the area surrounding the Rehabilitation Center, usually tiring out her adult companions long before she was ready to return.

Slowly, but noticeably, during the months from January through June of 1971, Genie changed socially as well. She began to differentiate the adults around her and to devlop closer dependent relationships with some of the hospital staff. She began to differentiate affect and respond more appropriately. Dr. K's description (Kent, 1972), found in Appendix III, elucidates the quality of change in Genie during this period. Physically, socially, and emotionally, Genie was changing, growing, and developing, and beginning to realize a small portion of her human potential.

Genie was developing cognitively and intellectually as well. Her visibly increasing cognitive awareness and functioning were reflected in her test performances, even though testing Genie was extremely difficult and in many ways not comparable to testing a normal child (see Part II, Chapter 6).

In January, Genie received a score of 4 years, 9 months on the Leiter International Performance Scale, a nonverbal test of cognitive abilities. In February, an attempt was made to give her the Illinois Test of Psycholinguistic Abilities (ITPA). Although most subsections were unscorable, she did score at the level of 3 years, 1 month on the visual sequential memory subsection and at the level of 2 years, 6 months on the visual association subsection. In April, when the Leiter was repeated, she passed all items through the 4-year level, half at the 5-year level and half at the 6-year level.

Observations by psychologists who were called in as consultants showed that Genie was demonstrating increasing cognitive abilities. They also noted a surprising scatter in her abilities. Dr. Jeanne Block, in February of 1971, noted that while Genie failed some items on the Vineland Scale at the 2-year level (masticates food, uses names for familiar objects, talks in short sentences), she passed other items at the 8 to 9-year level (does routine tasks, cleans up, bathes self). Dr. Jack Block, also in February of 1971, noted that in some ways her behavior was that of a 2-year-old, in others like a 5-year-old, and in still others like a 12- or 13-year-old. Dr. Elkind, in May of 1971, described Genie as being in the stage of concrete operations, that is, in the 6- to 7-year-old range. This striking disparate scatter in ability noted as early as February of 1971, became more and more apparent as time went on, and will be discussed further in Part III.

Genie's growing knowledge and cognitive ability were evident in less formal situations as well as on tests. Her interest and performance in classroom activities involving numbers, letters, colors, puzzles, and fine motor skills revealed in her a continuous curiosity about her new world and the capacity to learn and retain skills and concepts she was exposed to. An anecdotal example captured on videotape demonstrates a little of the focus and knowledge she was beginning to reveal: In May, in the classroom with Genie and others, the teacher asked a child who had two balloons how many he had. He said, *Three*. Genie looked startled and gave him another balloon.

This anecdote reveals more than Genie's new awareness and understanding of her environment. It reveals her new linguistic knowledge as well. And so it was that as other aspects of Genie's physical and psychological being began to develop, language began to emerge. From the barest rudiments of a vocabulary, she began—at first slowly, then toward May, much more rapidly—to learn the names for almost everything around her. When she wanted to learn the word for something, she would take the hand of someone nearby and place it on the object or point it toward the object of her attention as best she could. Hungry to learn the words for all the new items filling her senses, she would at times point to the whole outdoors and become frustrated and angry when someone failed to immediately identify the particular object she was focused on. The number of words she recognized grew sizably, probably totaling hundreds of words by June, 1971.

As her receptive vocabulary grew, her productive vocabulary increased as well. From *stopit*, which was nothing more than a ritualized expression of play, Genie began to speak words spontaneously, purposefully, and appropriately. She began to say *Mama*, *spit*, and *back*; by May 1971 she was spontaneously saying numbers from one through five, color words, the verbs *open*, *blow*, and others, and many, many nouns. If asked the name for something in her surroundings, she could almost always provide it.

The examples of Genie's spontaneous use of vocabulary during this period in the following set of examples are taken mostly from notes made by Dr. K, with a few additional samples from my own notes when I began working with Genie in June 1971.

3/3/71   K: *We have to put it away now.*
               G: *Back.*

4/23/71   G: *Put back.* (Probably one word, said when she wanted the teacher to put things back on the bulletin board.)

6/2/71   G: *balloon*; *ball*; *turtle*; *store.* (Spoken upon seeing the articles.)

6/3/71   G: *Open.* (Said when she wanted K to open the cage and give the rabbit some carrots, pushing K's hand to the door of the cage as she spoke.)

6/9/71   K: *That's hot.*
             G: *Burn.*

6/14/71   G: *Spit* (grabbing K's coat and spitting).
             G: *Car* (seeing K's car in the lot).

6/16/71   G: *Dish*; *pan*; *basket.*

6/22/71   G: *Mirror*; *come*; *dog*; *box*; *bulb.*

6/23/71   a. G: *Doctor*, . . . *come.* (to K)
             b. G: *Big* (looking at a big turtle).
             c. G: *Balloon*; *gone* (referring to lemonade that was gone).
                     get; *back*; *bracelet*; *doll*; *dog.*

6/28/71   G: *Fall.* (Spoken as she walked to a railing, apparently concerned about the height.)

6/30/71   G: *Store.* (Pulling on K to take her out of the workroom.)

             G: *Shower.* (Spoken to the nurse after she had gotten her things together to take a shower.)

It is apparent from these examples that Genie was developing a sizable productive vocabulary, especially toward the end of this period (April, May, and June). But language is not simply knowledge of words; it is, more importantly, knowledge of the grammar. More significant than the development of vocabulary, then, was the emergence of comprehension of sentences spoken to her. In contrast with the first months, several incidents reported in Dr. K's notes or documented on videotape from this second period suggest such comprehension. Although as before, many, probably most, documented situations during this period demonstrate a lack of comprehension, a few reported events, as given below, point to the emergence of comprehension.

4/23/71   Her teacher asked another child with two balloons how many he had. He said three. Genie looked startled and gave him another balloon.

5/4/71   a. Genie took one necklace. K said, *You can have two.* Genie took another one.
             b. K said, *Show me the bracelets.* Genie "showed" them to him. (She didn't give them to him.)

5/18/71   a.   J (teacher at Rehabilitation Center): *Leave the pan in the car.*
Genie did so. (There was a pan, a balloon, and a bracelet. She took the items about which nothing was said with her.)

         b.   Genie tried to pull a plastic bag off a roll in the store.
J: *Pull hard.*
G: *Pull.* (She pulled harder than before.)
Genie said *Pull* spontaneously when she found another roll.

5/24/71   a.   J: *What's this?* (referring to a frying pan).
G: *Pan.*

         b.   J: *Scrub them with the brush.*
Genie made the appropriate response.

         c.   J: *Flush the toilet.*
Genie did so.

         d.   Genie found some trays and couldn't reach them.
K: *How many do you want?*
G: *Three. Four. Five. Ten.*
(She made appropriate gestures with her fingers to indicate the numbers. There were pauses between each response.)

5/25/71   a.   K phoned Genie and said he'd come at 5:00. J gave Genie a play clock and told her to set it at 5:00. Genie did so. J then said, *Four.* Genie changed the hands to 4:00. J said, *Later.* Genie said, *Now.*

         b.   K: *What is that?* (referring to a chaise lounge in a store).
G: *Bed.*

5/29/71   a.   K: *The zipper is broken, Genie.*
Genie went to the nurses' station and got a safety pin from a drawer, without assistance.

         b.   There was a picture of a dog on a dogfood bowl.
K: *Is that a bird?*
G: *No. Dog.*

6/14/71   a.   Genie threw her glasses up on the roof.
K: *Where are your glasses?*
Genie took him outside and looked at the roof and laughed.

         b.   Genie seemed to make a distinction between a "pail" and a "bucket."
K: *What's this?*
G: *Pail*
K: *What's this?* (Pointing to what he thought was another pail.)
G: *Bucket.*

These examples show that Genie was beginning to learn language. She was beginning to comprehend more than one word at a time, and she was beginning to speak. Her production appeared to lag behind her comprehension, but exactly what and how much she understood we still did not know, as there was no systematic investigation of her knowledge of language until after this period.

Genie had changed from the painfully small, thin, pitiful creature that was admitted to the hospital months before. She had grown taller, heavier, more self-assured, more aware of herself, more physically developed, more knowledgeable in the social–psychological aspects of normal human life. But Genie remained a severely disturbed and underdeveloped human being, her human potential yet untapped. And she was past fourteen. Time was not on her side.

4

June 1971–August 1971

I first met Genie in June 1971. I remember how small she was, so little, so thin, so completely unlike a normal 14-year-old girl.

I was apprehensive about meeting her, and so at first examined her from a distance. Her dress was too long for her, and she was barefoot, both somehow stressing how painfully small she was for her age. Her movements were slow, yet syncopated rather than even. Her walk was stiff-legged and jerky. Even her stationary stance appeared uneven in the sense that though she was standing still one instinctively knew that she was not a normal person.

I ventured closer. Her hair was mousy and thin; her teeth were jagged, or fanged, and terribly discolored. And yet she was pretty. Considering all of the pitiful and strange aspects of her appearance, it seems remarkable that she could have seemed pretty, but she did. Her skin was beautiful—soft, white, with a faint touch of pink on each cheek, almost as if an artist had painted each one of them carefully and delicately. Her nose was small and beautifully shaped, turned up ever so slightly, finely drawn like that of a china doll.

Most of all, though, her beauty lay in her eyes—big, gray, deep. The whole story of her past, all of the neglect, abuse, pain, and misery, seemed to lie within.

There was a softness about Genie, a softness in her expression, a softness in her manner, a softness in the way she looked at everything, and despite her stiffness and jerkiness, a softness in the way she carried herself and moved. Perhaps it was really timidity. Whatever the reason, despite her peculiarity, she projected an appealing softness.

Such was her appearance. As I got to know her, I learned that not everything about her was soft and appealing. Her behavior was quite another matter.

Genie had many distasteful mannerisms and her behavior was often disconcerting and unpalatable. She salivated copiously, and spit out her saliva onto anything near her—her body, her clothing, even (as I unfortunately learned rather quickly) onto a companion's clothing or body. Since her body and clothing were filled with spit, she reeked of a foul odor.

Her eating habits were also disturbing. Never having had solid foods, she did not know how to chew. When given solid foods Genie would typically stuff her mouth with food and wait—cheeks puffed out like a chipmunk storing nuts—until her saliva could break down the food. Often, when she got tired of waiting, she would spit out the food in her mouth onto her plate, and then play with it and the rest of her food with her fingers, usually making circles of mush out of the food on her plate.

Genie had a habit of walking around during mealtime, stopping at other children's places at the table, sometimes attempting to take their portions of foods she especially liked (applesauce, milk, ice cream, etc.). She often walked around with her mouth stuffed with food, and during her journey around the dining room she would sometimes spit it out onto the nearest plate. Perhaps, in her bizarre unsocialized way, she was giving the other children an "offering" of food, to make up for the (unwilling and unoffered) offering of what she was about to take from them. In any case, her "offering" was never welcome, and mealtime with Genie was usually not a pleasant event.

Genie had other personal habits that were not socially acceptable. She blew her nose onto anything or nothing, often making a mess of her clothing. At times, when excited or agitated, she would urinate in inappropriate places—leaving her companion to deal with the results. But it was her lack of socialization that was most difficult to deal with, especially in public. Genie had a special fondness for certain things—anything made of plastic, certain foods, certain articles of clothing or accessories. If anyone she encountered in the street or in a store or other public place had something she liked, she was uncontrollably drawn to him or her, and without obeying any rules of psychological distance or social mores, she would go right up to the person and put her hands on the desired item. It was bad enough when she went up to someone else's shopping cart to reach in to take something out; but when the object of attention was an article of clothing, and Genie would simply attach herself to the person wearing that clothing and refuse to let go, the situations were extremely trying.

Even when Genie did not attach herself in quite such an embarrassing manner, she still went right up to strangers, stood directly in front of them, without any accepted distance between them, and peered into their faces with her face directly in front of theirs, pointing (without looking) at whatever possession of theirs held her interest. Other times, she very simply walked up to them and linked her arm through theirs or put her arm around them and was ready to walk on. All of this behavior, though charming and even endearing in the abstract, was quite embarrassing.

Genie masturbated excessively, which proved to be the most serious antisocial behavior problem of all. Despite admonishments, she continued to masturbate as often as possible, anywhere and everywhere. We have no knowledge of whether she had been sexually abused by her father or brother, but she preferred the company of men and when in their company usually tried to get them involved. Many of the items she coveted were objects with which to masturbate, and she would attempt to do so, regardless of where she was. She was drawn to chair backs, chair arms, counter edges, door knobs, door edges, table corners, car handles, car mirrors, and so forth; in essence, indoors and outdoors she was continually attempting to masturbate. Learning to control these desires has been terribly difficult for Genie, and now, 4 years later, it is still a problem.[1]

Despite all of these difficulties, going out with Genie was fascinating. To see her explore and hungrily take in the colors, textures, and sights of everything around her was a moving experience, but one of the most enriching aspects of being in public with Genie was to witness people's reactions and responses to her. Many people were unkind or attempted to ignore her and move themselves away from her. But many others were remarkably patient and sensitive to her.

One remarkable individual was a man who worked behind the meat counter at a Safeway store. Genie was fascinated by the meat section and used to spend quite a long time there, touching and examining all of the packages. This man evidently noticed her interest, and without asking any questions about her, one day slid open the window above the counter where she was standing, and held out a piece of meat—unwrapped—for her to touch, smell, and examine for as long as she wished. In this silent fashion, over a period of months, he brought out bones, fish, chickens, turkeys, and every kind of meat for her to study and experience. He never asked any questions; he never spoke a word to her. Without knowing anything about her, he simply accepted her on her own terms and gave to her without asking anything in return, not even a greeting. We were all sad when this man stopped working there. We never knew his name. We never thanked him.

The first month, when I saw Genie almost daily, I spent the time trying to get to know her and to establish a relationship with her that would help her develop trust in me and enable me to work with her effectively. At that time she was still not testable, and was so bizarre in her behavior that had I attempted to gain information formally from her, I would not have known how to interpret

---

[1] Since the time of writing, Genie's inappropriate masturbatory behavior has almost entirely disappeared.

her performance. Thus, I spent my time with her simply joining her in activities, taking her to visit places, being with her, and talking to her. Very often Dr. K was with us, and although I refrained from making notes when I was talking with Genie, I did take some notes when Dr. K or someone else was talking with her, so that I would have some record of her language during each of my visits.

Most of the time Genie said nothing. She rarely, almost never, in fact, said anything except in answer to a direct question. Most of the time she merely emitted squeaks and whimpers and nothing more. But every now and then she did speak; she even initiated speech, and I found that as the days wore on I was glad I had brought pen and paper.

For example, on June 14, 1971, when I arrived at the Rehabilitation Center, Genie had thrown the glasses that had just been prescribed for her up onto the roof of the building. When Dr. K came, he noticed that she was not wearing the glasses, so he asked,

> K: *Where are your glasses?*
>   G took him outside and looked at the roof and laughed.
> K: *We'll have to get the ladder.*
> G: *Ladder* [læd].
> K: *The glasses are up there.* (Pointing to the roof.)
> G: *Up. Up. Up.*

After the glasses-on-the-roof episode, the three of us went to a shopping center. Genie seemed thrilled to leave Rehab and could hardly wait until we reached the shopping center. As we drove along, she pointed to every building we passed en route and "asked" *store*? (She said the word with a quizzical look on her face, but without a pitch change.)

We went to Woolworth's and walked around the store together, Genie curiously examining almost everything. There were two sections of the store where Genie spent the most time, the aisle with plastic containers and the section with live animals. We could hardly draw her away from the aisle of plastics. She longingly fondled every item on the shelves—from wastebaskets to freezer storage containers. While she was so totally focused on the array before her, Dr. K pointed out that Genie made a distinction between pails and buckets on the basis of some classification which he had not yet figured out. As there were plenty of plastic pails before us, Dr. K said he'd demonstrate this to me. Pointing to a pail, he asked Genie what it was. She replied, *Pail.* Then pointing to what he assumed was another pail, he asked, *What's this?* Genie answered, *Bucket.* I couldn't see the difference; Dr. K. couldn't see the difference. But Genie could.

We finally moved on to the animals. We talked to her about how different in size the different animals were, and Genie imitated the words "big" and "small" and at one point "small turtle." A little later, we saw a pile of different-sized balls. Genie pointed to a big one and said, *Big.*

Dr. K noticed that Genie had to go to the bathroom. He said to her, *Maybe they have a bathroom.* Genie repeated, *Bathroom.* The store did not have one, and at the next storefront, Genie spontaneously said, *Bathroom.* None of the stores had restrooms, so we returned to the Rehabilitation Center.

We walked into the parking lot, and when she spotted Dr. K's car, Genie spontaneously said, *Car.*

On June 16, 1971, we visited the home of another therapist, Dr. R. Genie was intrigued with houses. On walks, she would often go to the front door of a house, hoping that someone would open the door and let her inside. To this girl who had spent her life on only one side of her bedroom door, every door held the promise of new discoveries, new sights, new smells, a new world. So, on that day, a visit to the R house was a great adventure for her. She eagerly explored every room, running her fingers along the walls and furniture, intently examining each thing she saw.

She was having such a good time, she didn't want to interact with any of us and ignored our attempts to engage her or signal her that it was soon time to leave. Finally, Dr. K got her attention and explained that it was time to go and that she should put on her coat. A search for her coat followed; after a few minutes, Dr. K asked her, *What are we looking for?* Genie answered, *Coat.*

Before leaving, we all gathered in the kitchen. Genie was holding a decorator pillow in her arms. Dr. K said, *Tell Dr. R what that is.* Genie turned to Dr. R and said, *Pillow.* There was a cat in the house and Dr. R asked Genie if she wanted to see it. *No. No. Cat,* Genie replied, shaking her head vehemently.

As my visits with Genie at the Rehabilitation Center continued, I became familiar with some of the "rituals" used with her. She had learned to say certain specific things "on cue." For example, if she wanted something that she couldn't reach, the ritual was:

X: *What do you want?*
G: *Getit.* (One word to her.)

If she sat in a car waiting to go for a ride, the ritual was:

G: *Turnon.* (One word to her.)

Then the driver would start the engine. If Genie wanted a container, a door, or window opened, the ritual was:

X: *What do you want?*
G: *Open.*

Later she would say *open* without prompting.

If she wanted someone to come with her or come to see her, she would say, *Come.*

Many, if not all, of these rituals had been taught to her by the staff with the "what-do-you-say" method, but by the time I met her, the staff interacting with her no longer needed to use the "what-do-you-say" cues. I had to piece together the background for her stereotypic utterances, noticing at first only that her utterances at certain times were very predictable. Another predictable feature of her speech at this point was her repetition of the last word of most utterances addressed to her. Examples occurring on June 22, 1971 are given below:

    a. K: *You're angry.*
        G: *Angry.*
    b. K: *Do you want to touch it?*
        G: *Touch.*
    c. K: *Should I do it?*
        G: *Do it.*
    d. K: *It's stuck.*
        G: *Stuck.*
    e. K: *I have to go home.*
        G: *Home.*
    f. K: *Are you angry?*
        G: *Angry.*

At other times her speech was more purposeful and clearly uncued, and her behavior evidenced growing comprehension of language and of social situations.

For example, on July 1, 1971 Genie had some gumdrops that had been bought for her. She was sitting with some children, eating her gumdrops, when one of them, a little girl, asked to see Genie's gumdrops. Genie quickly drew them toward herself and away from the little girl, slyly looked at her, and continued eating, a little more quickly at this point. Dr. K, noticing the situation, asked if the little girl could look at the gumdrops. Genie avoided his eyes and pretended she didn't hear or understand.

While Genie lived at the Rehabilitation Center, she had her own bed in a room that housed eight children, and her own storage cupboard by her bed. Dr. K often took her on excursions in the area around the Center, and at the Rehabilitation Center, for the most part, she was permitted to do as she wished. She had made known her mania for plastic and had amassed a sizable collection of plastic items, including beads, containers, and wastebaskets. She had twenty-three plastic wastebaskets stacked up by her bed, which Dr. K. had purchased for her when they went out shopping. She had become attached to several of the staff at the Rehabilitation Center, and having become a proficient manipulator of these people, usually had her way with them. She was more than settled in, she was, to some degree, queen of her new environment. But no institutional setting can offer the warmth of a real home; and so it was fortunate that circumstances developed that led to Genie's placement in a foster home. In late June 1971, Genie was exposed to the German measles and had to be isolated from the other children. The staff at the hospital realized that it could prove a major setback in Genie's development if she were to be confined and isolated from the other children. It was therefore felt imperative that Genie be separated from the others by placing her in a foster home.

Following this decision, Genie was moved to a foster setting—a warm, loving household with two teenage boys (Mike and Sam), an adolescent girl (Ann), a dog (Spot), and a cat. In this new home, Genie had her own room and her own bathroom, a large backyard to play in, and a foster family to provide her with companionship, affection, care, guidance, help, and attention. When she moved to this new home she was still largely unsocialized and underdeveloped, but whereas her previous settings had been largely unrestrictive, Genie now found herself in an environment that placed demands and challenges before her, and thus was to offer her new, directed opportunities for growth and change. Her first opportunity came the day she moved in.

Her new family had a dog. Although only a puppy, it was a golden retriever and thus not a small dog. We knew that Genie was afraid of dogs, but at that point no one knew about the father's dog-like behavior, and so no one knew the basis for her fear. It was assumed that Genie's fear was simply irrational and unfounded. The signs that her fear was deep-rooted and strong were there, however.

Genie normally moved extremely slowly, almost in slow motion, but at the sight or sound of the dog approaching, Genie moved quickly—darting across the room, climbing onto a table, running into another room, trying furiously to put some barrier between herself and the dog. The family insisted, nontheless, that she learn to accept the dog as a member of the household. Remarkably, within a few days Genie learned to restrain her desire to escape and learned to stay near the dog; what is more, she learned to pet her, feed her, and to walk her. It was not until many months later, when the foster mother found Genie frozen in panic clutching a picture of a wolf, unable to let go, and Genie's mother was questioned as to why this should have happened, that we learned about Genie's father and his bizarre and pathological dog-like behavior. Genie associated her father's barking, growling, teeth-baring and other dog-like mannerisms with real dogs and transferred her terror of her father to dogs. It was only with this discovery, long after Genie had been required to confront her fear and learn to cope with the dog in her home, that we realized how great a task had been set before her and what remarkable strength she had shown.

5

September 1971–June 1975

Some of Genie's behavior which I witnessed, and some of the moments I shared with her are presented here since they provide a more complete picture of this remarkable girl. Chapters 2–4 dealt primarily with her behavior while at the Rehabilitation Center. What follows covers incidents during her entire development up to this writing.

5.1. DELAYED RESPONSES

As we began to learn more about Genie, we learned that we couldn't always judge by her initial response whether or not she had comprehended something. Typically, there was a latency in her responses that went along with her general slowness to move or react.

If someone asked Genie to answer a question, to turn off a light, or to get something from the kitchen, and so forth, Genie would often act as if she had not been spoken to. Then, 10 or 15 minutes later, she would obey the request. For example, on November 11, 1971, Genie and I had gone to the hospital to run some errands. We saw a friend named Rita. I said to Genie, *Tell Rita who you went to see this morning.* Genie said nothing. After about 5 to 10 minutes and much conversation had intervened, Genie said *grandma*—the answer to my question.

This pattern of delay in response to a stimulus remained part of Genie's behavior for many years. It was not just true for language. For example, on

February 5, 1973, when I went to visit Genie, I rang the bell many, many times before Genie bothered to answer the door. She finally came to the window to peer out to see who was at the door. I waved frantically at her. When she opened the door, she said, *Curtiss waving*, as if I were the one exhibiting strange behavior.

At the time of this writing she continues to delay in her response to questions or requests as is shown in the conversation below. On May 14, 1975 she was talking to her foster mother, M, about a student car wash her school held:

> G: *At school is washing car.*
> M: *Whose car did you wash?*
> G: *People*['s] car.
> M: *How many cars did you wash?*
> G: *Two car*[s]
> M: *Were they big cars or little cars?*
> G: *Big car.*
> M: *What were the colors of the cars?*

G walked out of the room. M and I talked for a few minutes. G then approached M and said, *Blue and orange car*—the answer to M's question.

5.2. LAZY BEHAVIOR

It also became evident that Genie continually chose the path of least effort. She didn't initiate action. She moved slowly and listlessly; she allowed others to do things for her that she was capable of performing herself. Although being taught to and encouraged to chew, she continued to let her saliva break down the food in her mouth, rather than chew it, and she continued to select foods which did not require chewing as often as she could. When being taught to print, she held her pencil loosely, making barely visible marks on the paper. She would follow directions, obey orders, and cooperate in activities, but she did not initiate activity. Similarly, in her use of language, Genie spoke as little as possible and in the shortest utterances she could use and still manage to communicate. Thus, almost all of the time she spoke in one-word utterances. We discovered that she was capable of producing longer sentences only from observing instances when she failed to communicate with one word and had to elaborate and use more language, or from those even rarer moments when she put two or three words together without special prompting or encouragement. From such singular instances we were able to observe that Genie was developing in her ability to use expressive language.

She thus presented a misleading picture; she was capable of producing longer and more complex strings than those she generally used. She masked her capabilities by her behavior. It was only through getting to know her, through being with her often and over a long period of time, that we were able to determine what she knew, what she could do, and what she did do.

5.3. HAPLOLOGIES

For almost 2 years Genie talked primarily in one-word utterances, even though she was capable of producing longer strings. For the next 2 years she talked primarily in two-word strings, even though by then her grammatical capabilities had developed far beyond the two-word stage. Genie became known as the "Great Abbreviator," who managed to get her way and make her thoughts and wishes known without hardly saying anything. At one point she began to collapse words and create one-syllable utterances to represent strings that earlier would have been several words in length. For example, on May 1, 1972, for the sentence *M come back*, she produced [mæk], and for the utterance, *Monday Curtiss come*, she produced [m $\land$ k]. M and I told Genie that we were unable to talk to her in this way. Sensing that she had overstepped the bounds of acceptability, she abandoned such extreme reductions.

5.4. RITUALISTIC SPEECH

As mentioned above, there were typical ritual exchanges between Genie and the people around her. Genie's dependence on ritual expressions continues to this day.

Much of this ritualistic behavior was the result of routines taught to her. Early rituals taught to her were *Give me X*, *I want X*, and *Help me X*.

A typical ev   ange during mealtimes is illustrated by the following dialogue which occur. _ on November 17, 1971.

M: *G, say give me bread and butter.*
G: *Give me bread.*
M: *And butter.*
G: *Butter.*

Genie asked for soup by saying, "Soup."
M: *Say, Give me soup.*
G: *Give me.*
M: *Give me soup.*
G: *Give me soup.*

Each instance of "Give me" was accompanied with the same two-handed gesture, first pointing outward with both hands, then pointing to herself.

Later rituals included *May I have X*. Instead of *Give me X*, Genie learned to use this stereotypic phrase, as shown in the following examples:

May I have circle.
May I have box.
May I have graham cracker.
May I have material.
May I have rug.

She learned to say this phrase more readily and more frequently than earlier rituals, although using the correct ritual did not always get her what she wanted. For example, on November 21, 1973, Genie and I were in the kitchen eating cupcakes. The cupcakes were on a plastic tray, and Genie wanted the tray (probably because it was made of plastic). She asked me, *May I have tray*. I replied, *You have to ask M*. Her foster mother was in the other room. Genie went into the other room to ask her for the tray. By the time she got there she had decided to ask for the paper cupcake wrapper instead. *Ask M. May I have paper.* M, tired of her requests for trash, changed the subject. *Would you like to have some milk with your cupcake?* Genie answered, *Genie mad. Genie mad. Genie mad.*

Genie discovered some power with this ritual phrase. Starting in the summer of 1973, those who worked with her began to pay her for her work in pennies, dimes, and quarters. For setting the table she received ten pennies. It was during this period that Genie was also being taught to count, so as often as possible she was paid in pennies which she was required to count before they became hers. In addition to being paid for performing, Genie was learning to save her money to buy items she wanted, toy plastic cars and boats, plastic containers of all sorts, plastic jewelry, wastebaskets, anything plastic that caught her fancy at the stores she shopped in. Because of this, she soon learned the importance of her reward and never let anyone escape without paying her. For example, on December 5, 1973:

Late in the afternoon, close to dinner, I was playing the piano for Genie. She was uncontrollably drawn to the music and never moved away until I stopped. On that day, I realized the importance that money had assumed for her because even though I was in the midst of playing, Genie heard sounds from the kitchen which indicated to her that someone else was going to set the table. Setting the table was Genie's chore. No one was going to cheat her out of those ten pennies. Leaving me at the piano, something she had never done before, she marched into the kitchen saying, *Set table. M set table.* She pushed M out of the way and finished setting the table herself. After she had finished, she said, *May I have ten penny.*

There were attempts to teach her other rituals, for example, to ask specific questions. This attempt failed. Genie could not memorize a well-formed WH-question. She would respond to *What do you say?* demands with ungrammatical, bizarre phrases that included WH-question words, but she was unable to come up with a phrase she had been trained to say. For example, instead of saying the requested *Where are the graham crackers?* she would say *I where is graham cracker*, or *I where is graham cracker on top shelf.* In addition, under pressure to use WH-question words, she came out with sentences such as:

Where is tomorrow Mrs. L?
Where is stop spitting?
Where is May I have ten pennies?
When is stop spitting?

This illustrates that Genie, like normal children, was unable to imitate or even retain in memory, syntactic structures which were not in keeping with her grammatical development.

Attempts were also made to teach her functional phrases to help her deal with real-life situations. For example, at a special school Genie attended in 1973, one of her classmates (P) was evidently pinching her every day and hurting her. We attempted to teach her something to say to the child to make that child stop pinching her. For example, on October 23, 1973:

Genie talked about P's pinching her arm at school. We went through a mini-sociodrama to aid her in dealing with the real situation when it arose in school.

    C: *What do you say when P pinches you?*
    G: *Go way, P.*

Unfortunately, Genie wasn't able to use this phrase when the real situation confronted her, and suffered many bruises on her arm as a result of all the pinching.

Two points here are worth noting. First, it is interesting that the people around Genie, without systematically analyzing her use of language or determining what was absent from it, sensed her need to learn how to make requests and ask questions and tried to give her a method for doing so. The only questions and requests Genie has formulated to this day have been of the form first modeled for her. This is in striking contrast to the novel and obviously spontaneous linguistic forms that are products of her own grammatical system. Second, these ritual uses of language are not language rituals usually referred to as such, the automatic phrases used in particular social situations, such as "Hello," "How are you?," "Thank you," and "Gezundheit." There have been attempts to teach Genie these as well. These attempts have been largely unsuccessful, and such social rituals are absent from Genie's language. (See Part III, Section 11.5 for elaboration.)

In addition to those rituals taught to her by others, Genie has created her own. When Genie wants to talk about something, she often uses a fixed phrase to mean:

$$I'm \begin{bmatrix} going \\ want \end{bmatrix} to \begin{bmatrix} talk \\ communicate \end{bmatrix} about \quad X.$$

In the early days, she used the word "hurt" in this way.

Doctor hurt.	*Cat hurt.*
Hospital hurt.	*Dog hurt.*
Hurt cat.	*Fireplace hurt.*
Snow hurt.	*Elevator hurt.*
Fish hurt.	*Ocean hurt.*

From the context it is clear that the examples cited above did not refer to the lexical meaning of the word "hurt." More recently, and for an extremely long period in her development, she has used '(I) like' in this way.

Like ball.	*Like old school.*
Like Nancy.	*I like enough money.*
Like Lyn.	*I like two towel.*
Like mirror.	*I like yell.*
Like beach.	*I like excited.*
Like Grandma.	*I like grab.*
Like trip.	*I like doctor.*
Like rug.	*I like shape.*
Like fish.	*I like bag.*
Like floor.	*I like Mama Saturday.*
Like dog.	*I like laughing funny.*
Like pinky.	*I like M fix teeth.*
Like hanger.	*I like grab J.*
Like doll bend.	*I like hurt finger.*
	I like animal have bad cold.
	I like hate school.
	I like hate father.

(It should be noted that she was able to use the expression "I like" appropriately, as in the example, "*I like V['s] man* (7/74).)

This type of stereotypic communication became so predominant in Genie's speech that I can often predict with a great deal of accuracy what sentences she is going to produce. For example, I know that when she greets me she will say,

(I) *like Curtiss*, (her name for me) since from September, 1972 on, I have been greeted at the door with, *I like Curtiss* on every visit, almost without exception. (This use of "I like X" is similar to phatic greetings, such as "Hello.")

Such ritual expressions are a major and frequent source of ungrammaticality in Genie's speech. (See Part II, Section 9.11.1 for a discussion.)

5.5. "TUNING IN" TO LANGUAGE

As early as October of 1971, it became clear that Genie was beginning to be responsive in numerous linguistic situations. That is, prior to this period she appeared to ignore all language use around her unless she herself was addressed. On October 13, 1971 I noted:

> Genie listened to three stories. It was the first time she seemed to be interested in and to comprehend what was being read. Her facial expressions as well as her gestures indicated appropriate emotional responses to the story.

Other indications of her increased awareness of language used around her are shown by the following examples.

As my visits to the foster home increased, I became friends with the foster family, as well as with Genie. Often, I would engage in conversation with one of the family. Usually during such times Genie would ignore us, sometimes even leave the room; other times, if she wanted attention, she would attempt to prevent us from talking to each other by standing between us, or plopping herself down on one of our laps, thereby blocking our view, and she hoped, our ability to keep the conversation going. Every now and then, though, she would surprise us and actually listen to what was being said.

> 12/27/71. During lunch, Genie said, *lot food* and *lot animal* while M was discussing their trip to the snow [a visit to the mountains] and Genie's trip to the zoo. Genie wanted to be part of the conversation. At one point in the conversation, M used the word "hardly" in a sentence. Genie recognized the morpheme "hard" and said, *Hard*. Then M began talking about a couple they had visited that weekend. Genie listened and said, *big house* and *tiny baby* in reference to that visit.

> 2/23/72. Genie had an earache. M and I were talking about the earwax and M told me that she had put medication in Genie's ear to dissolve the wax. Genie was listening and at that point interjected, *Five drop*. M explained that she had put in five drops of medicine.

> 5/8/74. After we returned home from our afternoon excursions, I talked to M for a few minutes. I asked a question about a friend, Nadine's, working with

Genie the next day at school. M answered, *I don't know*. Evidently Genie
wanted M to answer yes to that question, because as soon as M answered *I don't
know* to me, Genie came between us and clearly said, *Yes*.

As shown by these examples, Genie became more sensitive to the social
interaction of conversations and anxious to join in and be a part of the group.
It was often amusing and touching to see what she would do to "join in." For
example, in early 1972, during a family dinner conversation about renting
property, the word "tenant" was frequently used; at one point upon hearing
the word "tenant," Genie joined in by saying *ten* and holding up ten fingers.

At times her interruptions showed not only that she was listening to the
conversation, but also that she was learning to use language in a creative way.
For example, on September 26, 1973:

> M and I were discussing the family's upcoming trip to Yosemite. Genie was
> to go along, and she was apprehensive about going. As she listened to us dis-
> cussing the trip, she interjected, *Little bit trip*, expressing her wish that the trip
> would be short.

Another development in this area of paying attention to the conversations
around her is shown by her ability to remember the import of a conversation
she has heard and to recount it later to someone not present when the conversation took place.

On May 20, 1975 Genie listened as neighbors recounted a story about
going camping with their new baby. The story was not directed to her, nor was
she involved. But she listened, understood, and related it much later to D, her
foster father, who was not present at the original story-telling.

5.6.   NEW USES FOR LANGUAGE

In January, 1972, Genie used language for the first time in reflecting about a
past event.

> 1/5/72.   Two weeks prior to this date Genie had had a disconcerting experience
> at the hospital. When we had walked down the hall, a little boy came up to us
> holding a toy gun and pretended to shoot us repeatedly. Genie was visibly
> frightened. Despite my requests and admonishments, the little boy persisted
> in his pretend shooting, and as he continued, Genie clung to me more and more.
> We walked away as quickly as we could, and we talked at some length about
> guns and pretending. I told Genie that the boy was *a bad little boy for not
> stopping and for making us feel afraid*. . . . She said, *Little bad boy*, and *Bad gun*.
> After we returned home from our afternoon excursions on 1/5/72, I played the

piano for her. While I was playing, Genie began talking to herself and making her gesture for "naughty" over and over again. I asked her to tell me what she was saying, so she came over to me and said, *Little bad boy*, and then, *Bad gun*. She continued repeating these phrases aloud to herself for several minutes while I played along with her gesture for "naughty." It was the first time I had ever seen her recapitulate or recall an event to herself with language. She seemed delighted with herself, and she didn't know it, but I was even more delighted.

From that time on Genie has spoken of her past to us—not often and usually not at any length—but still she has been able to use language to express thoughts and feelings about a time in her life she alone had experienced. Through language, Genie has been able to tell us details of her confinement previously unknown to us. For example, Genie said, *Father hit arm. Big wood. Genie cry*. It was from statements like these that we learned that Genie's father used to beat her with a large wooden stick for making noise. At another time, Genie said, *Not spit. Father. Hit face—spit*. Thus we learned that Genie's father used to wipe Genie's face in her spit when she spit out food or saliva. These events were corroborated by her mother.

As her language ability grew, her descriptions of past events increased in detail and richness. In contrast to Genie's early statements given above, some of her later descriptions of how her father beat her for making noise are:

Father hit big stick. Father is angry.
Father hit Genie big stick.
Father take piece wood hit. Cry.
Father make me cry.
Father is dead.

On a few occasions Genie has produced long passages of memories. See Part II, Section 9.3.6 for examples.

In addition to using language to talk about her past, Genie began to use language to manipulate others—or at least to try to.

1/12/72. Genie wandered into [her foster sister] Ann's room. I followed her and as soon as Genie saw me she said, *Ann pencil*. D [her foster father] heard her and came into the room scolding Genie for being there, explaining to me that Ann had some colored pens that Genie was attracted to and that Genie had previously gone into Ann's room to get them. D then explained to Genie that she could not have Ann's pens—that Ann had her pens and Genie had hers. Genie then said *D errand*. Genie was telling him to go away so that she could do what she wanted.

Another such incident occurred on August 6, 1973.

When we got home, Genie wanted me to come downstairs with her to put on a fresh sanitary napkin. She said, *Come here, Curtiss.* That was one of the first times I heard Genie ask rather than grab hold of someone if she wanted someone to come with her.

Genie was also learning to use language to lie, or embellish the truth:

> 3/13/74.   M reported to me that Genie had come home from school earlier in the week and told M that Ms. C, Genie's teacher, wanted Genie to work, but Genie was not doing so. Ms. C told Genie to work, and that made Genie cry. Genie had made up the part about crying to elicit sympathy from M.

On March 5, 1975, when I asked her what she had in her pockets, she answered, *Material.* That was a lie. She had rocks in her pockets, and she was not supposed to. She was also learning to express her fantasies through language. An example occurred on January 9, 1973, when Genie talked about her sexual fantasies involving her school bus driver, Mr. B.

> G: *Mr. B hand.*
>   *Mr. B have hand.*
>   *Mr. B hand tickle vulva.*
>   *Finger tickle vulva.*
>   *Genie vulva.*
> M: *Mr. B drives the bus, his hands are on the wheel.*
> G: *Mr. B on the bus, masturbate alone.*

5.7. SOUND PRODUCTION

Even after Genie started to speak, she remained very limited in her vocal abilities. She didn't sob when she cried, she couldn't sing, whistle, or imitate environmental noises. Moreover, she never screamed, and was unable to control pitch during speech. These difficulties undoubtedly stemmed from her having learned to suppress phonation as a result of having been beaten for making noise. There have been several developments in this area. On November 10, 1971, the following took place:

> I played nursery songs on the piano and sang them. I attempted to get Genie to sing along with me, and Genie actually changed pitch and produced what could be considered singing tones. She also clapped, danced, and stamped her feet to the music upon request.

On November 17, 1971:

On the way to the hospital, I sang a song about going to the hospital. Genie kept repeating *hospital* and at one point sang the word out quite loudly and strongly.

On February 20, 1972, D had attempted to take some of the wax out of Genie's ear. Genie screamed for the first time. On February 14, 1973:

Genie had a tantrum and had scratched her face. M had been talking to her about her scratched face, that it was bad to hurt herself like that, etc. When I came in, Genie immediately said, *Scratch face. At school scratch face.* I asked her, *Why?* Genie imitated my intonation and gesture (I had shrugged my shoulders) and said, *Why?* It was the first time I heard her imitate intonation so directly.

Genie has never screamed since that day in February 1972. She had begun, however, to show some pitch control during speech, although she still does not utilize pitch to mark syntactic or semantic distinctions in sentences[1] (see Part II, Section 7.3).

5.8. GESTURES

As noted earlier, speech is difficult for Genie. In the early days, before speaking, she would tense up her body and take a deep breath, then produce an extremely high-pitched and breathy utterance. Choosing to remain silent much of the time, Genie often gestured instead of speaking. She invented her own gestures and over time expanded her gesture vocabulary. Usually she simply produced a single gesture, such as "angry" or "excited," but as she began speaking in longer strings, she began using gestures in a new way:

2/12/73. Genie had been riding in the grocery cart like small children do, in the front section of the cart. She kept saying to me, *push cart, go ride cart Mama,* and *give ride cart* (pointing to herself, thus indicating herself as the indirect object—elaborating her string by gesture rather than word).

On March 12, 1972 Genie requested a record which she called "Lady Song" to be played for her by saying, *Listen lady song.* "Listen" was not spoken; it was gestured by pointing her hand to her ear. This is the first utterance I witnessed that combined a gesture and words in this way.

In February, 1974, making use of Genie's natural feel for gesture, as a means of expressing herself in a modality better suited to her than speech, Genie was

---

[1] Genie now uses fairly normal active–declarative intonation, but still does not systematically mark yes/no questions by intonation in her speech.

introduced to sign language. She was taught a system somewhere between Ameslan (American Sign Language) and Siglish (Signed English) and began combining speech and sign, mostly in the fashion of speaking sentences and signing whatever words in the sentence she had learned the sign for. From that point on Genie has used signs as she speaks, but she has also continued to use gestures of her own invention.

5.9. WORKING WITH GENIE

Working with Genie has been a little bit of everything—interesting, trying, funny, unpredictable, rewarding, unpleasant, fun, problematic, and challenging. Basically my work with her has fallen into three categories: (1) language testing, (2) neurolinguistic and other cognitive and perceptual testing, and (3) work with the written word.

Testing her was often extremely problematic and difficult. Especially in the first year of my work with her, getting Genie to attend to the test and respond in a meaningful way was difficult. As time passed, however, both of us became more successful at dealing with one another and I learned better how to work around her moods, to motivate her, and to get her to perform. At the time of writing, Genie is still unpredictable, and there are still times when my attempts to test her fail. But to a great degree I can now plan what I will accomplish on a given day, and be reasonably sure that what I plan will be done.

Work with the written word followed a much less smooth or direct course but this work was very interesting. (See Part II, Section 6.9 for a description of this method.) Often Genie cooperated and worked hard. Every now and then, Genie added her own touch to the sessions:

11/17/71. After each sentence that Genie made, I had her read it to me. Prior to today, she just looked at the words and read them—very slowly. When I read the sentences to her, I always put my index finger directly under the word. On this day Genie read each sentence "Curtiss-style," imitating my pointing method. She initiated this on her own, obviously imitating me, thinking this the correct way to read.

In these sessions she showed the ability to construct her own sentences.

12/16/71. We practiced making negative sentences like, *Spot is a dog, Genie is not a dog, Genie is pretty, Curtiss is not angry*, and so forth. At one point I asked Genie to make the sentence, *Curtiss is not a dog*. Genie ignored me and made a sentence she wanted to make: *Curtiss is naughty*.

Sometimes the sessions were fun and one could tell that the words in written form really had meaning for her, as evidenced on December 1, 1972 when:

> We worked on equational sentences, using the names of people Genie knew well plus adjectives that were part of her own spontaneous speech and which carried a lot of affect for her. We made sentences like: *Curtiss is naughty, Genie is silly.* We acted out the sentences as well as reading and constructing them. "Naughty" and "silly" both have gestures associated with them, so the exercise became a dramatic game. Genie not only made every sentence correctly, she went wild gesturing and carrying on a game of her own, even running from one room to the next so that she could gesture at D when he was involved in a sentence.

Sometimes, however, work sessions were discouraging. Genie was (and still can be) completely uncooperative, very restless, and impossible to work with. When Genie was motivated, we had great fun and success working together. When Genie was not, work sessions were exhaustingly unfruitful. There have been some developments which are not contingent on motivation as much as on Genie's psychological growth, as in her ability to switch roles with me.

The first attempts to get her to pretend she was Curtiss and I her, failed totally. She would either not respond at all, or after a while, play both roles—that is, both say a sentence and construct it. Almost every week, I attempted to get her to switch roles with me; each time I tried, I was unable to get her to do so. On August 27, 1973, after almost 2 years of trying, Genie surprised me and readily switched roles:

> We were working on prepositions. After our session, I tried to get Genie to switch roles with me and tell me what to do. (We had been working with colored boxes which I instructed her to juxtapose in various prepositional relationships.) I asked her to take turns with me—I would tell her what to do, then she would tell me what to do, etc. Genie astonished me by joining in the "game" without hesitation.
>
> > G: *Put orange in the green.*
> > C: *Put the yellow box next to the white box.*
> > G: *Put blue box in the white box.*
> > C: *Put the green box on the yellow box.*
> > G: *Put orange box in the white box.*
> > C: *Put the orange box behind the white box.*
> > G: *Put green box in the blue box.*
> > C: *Put the yellow box in front of the orange box.*
> > G: *Put blue box in the white box.*
> > C: *Put the green box over the orange box.*

After 2 years of working with written language, Genie still did not read, although her memory within a session was excellent and, by and large, she learned to play the "games" I presented to her. She did not retain what had been shown to her from one session to another, however. This lack of retention stood in sharp contrast to her often amazing long-term memory for almost everything else: faces, names, details of geographical location, cars, pictures in magazines, possessions of others, and so forth. Thus her inability to learn to read was not simply a problem of general long-term memory. Since 1973, when I stopped working systematically with written language, a few others have attempted to teach her to read, using established and innovative methods. No one has yet been successful. Genie still cannot read.[2]

5.10. AFFECT AND SOCIAL DEVELOPMENT

As Genie has learned to express herself more fully, she has developed a fuller self-concept and has learned to express and control her feelings, as is shown in the following example:

2/23/72.   Earlier, M had spilled some orange juice at the kitchen table. The incident had caused a tantrum, since Genie had difficulty coping with a spilling situation, possibly because she had been punished so severely by her father for spilling anything. After that, M had talked about spilling, explaining that accidents happen, etc. M's attempts to help Genie deal with such situations were fruitful, as evidenced by an incident 2 weeks later. On 2/23/72 some orange juice was again spilled. Genie did not have a tantrum.

7/24/72.   When I arrived Genie was sitting with M and weeping and sobbing. She was crying because M had told her that she would see the doctor this afternoon about her ear. Genie had been complaining that her ear hurt, and she had had a cold and a terrible cough for a few weeks. Despite the sadness that was evoked by Genie's tears, I noted the striking change in this girl who such a short time previously did not sob or shed tears.

1/8/73.   As I was playing the piano for her, Genie suddenly said, *Too warm*, and went downstairs to her room to change into a thin top and shorts. This represented a major change in Genie, who at the time of her discovery had seemed to be impervious to temperature.

5/7/75.   Until now Genie has never initiated play with others. She cooperates in the attempts by others to engage her in play, and on a few occasions she has spontaneously initiated some activity with toys or materials that might be con-

---

[2] Since this writing, Genie appears to be beginning to retain a small set of words (ten to twenty) and can be said to be able to read them.

sidered a form of play, but has never asked others to join her in a play activity of her creation. Today, she did. Possibly acting out her desire to be with her dentist (with whom she is infatuated), she requested me to play dentist with her. We traded off roles; first I was the dentist and Genie was the patient. After that, Genie was the dentist and I was the patient. Genie did not initiate much speech during the play, but she did tell me to *Open mouth*, and *Spit out* my pretend water.

The following journal entries also attest to her emotional and social development:

6/19/72.   Today I took Genie into the city. We browsed through shops for about an hour. We sang and marched and carried on in our own nutty, special way as we walked. Genie seemed elated and delighted by everything I did. She commented, *Genie happy*. So was I. Our relationship had developed into something special.

9/25/72.   Today was a day filled with good and bad—a day filled with evidence of linguistic growth, social growth, and also the difficult problems of being with Genie sometimes. After work we went to Safeway. At Safeway, we passed a stand with Hostess Twinkies on it. Genie picked a package up and looked at it longingly. I asked her if she wanted me to buy it for her, and she answered, *Yes*. So I put it in the cart. Later, at the toy section, she saw a package of plastic rings that she also wanted. I told her she could have only one thing. She immediately picked up the Twinkies and said, *Take back*. I said, *Okay*, and she quickly went right to the appropriate counter and returned the Twinkies.

A little later, when I was looking for some wrapping paper, a woman tapped me on the shoulder and said, "Your friend dropped something," pointing to the floor. There on the floor was Genie's sanitary napkin which she had decided to remove. I wasn't thrilled. I admonished her for taking off her pad in public and talked with her about when it was all right to remove her pad. The rest of the time in the store Genie kept repeating, *Very angry*. I managed to convince her by the time we got home that I was no longer angry at her.

When we got home, I told Genie to open up her package of rings and to try some of them on. She chose a black one and a purple one to put on. I asked her if I could have a ring, and she quickly said, *No*. I asked her if I could have an orange one, and she immediately took out all the orange rings that she could find and put them in her pocket—to make sure there were none left for me. This didn't surprise me, as Genie has never in my experience willingly shared anything. And I really didn't expect her to share her new, cherished plastic rings. But I asked her next, *Can I have a green one?* Genie replied, *No more have. Off*. Then I pretended to cry. I told her how much I wanted a ring to take home, and how sad I felt, ... Genie loves it when I pretend to cry, and she immediately smiled and enjoyed my act. Then she reached into the package and took out two blue rings, and said, *Cry*, and after I started crying again, handed me the rings and said, *Curtiss home*. She had told me I could take those rings home. I was overjoyed. This is the first time Genie has ever given me anything or shared anything with me.

2/26/73.   Today Genie revealed an adolescent crush on Mr. B, her school bus driver. When I mentioned his name to her, she blushed and held her hands over her face. She also talks about him incessantly, mentioning his name over and over. Today I asked her, *Who is Mr. B?* Genie answered *Mr. B.* She was overcome—blushing, she was unable to verbalize.

2/19/75.   Genie has come a long way in controlling her behavior and dealing with her feelings. Not so long ago, many things would have touched off a tantrum that now can be dealt with through reasoning and verbalization. Nonetheless, in all this time, when Genie is actually having a tantrum, I have never been able to reach her through words to help bring her out of her distress. She has never been able to look me directly in the face or focus directly on something I was saying to her during a tantrum. Today was different.

Snacktime had gone smoothly; Genie did not seem particularly agitated or upset. Yet as soon as we sat down to work, a tantrum began to brew. After a few minutes, Genie was stamping and rocking and exhibiting a great deal of agitation and typical tantrum behavior. Normally I would simply have told her it was time to go outside, where she could not destroy anything, and where she would have room to flail out and run or whatever. This is what the foster mother had shown me to do whenever Genie had a tantrum. Today, however, I just sat there and began to talk to her. I still fully expected to have to take her outside, but I was stalling for time, since getting her outside when she's agitated is such an ordeal. To my amazement, Genie really began to listen to what I was saying and, to my further amazement, began to respond to me and actually to look me directly in the face as we talked. She still exhibited tantrum behavior, but our talking about what was upsetting her seemed to calm her down and ease her anger. She paid close attention to what I said, repeated my statements after me, reflected on them aloud, and let their import help her deal with her feelings. In addition to talking about the situation which had upset her, I told her that when she was unhappy, I felt unhappy for her, and that when she felt good, I felt good. I went on and on about my feelings for her, and how I felt when something upset her terribly and I could see her unhappiness on her face, and so forth. After her tantrum had subsided, she came over to me, very close, and said, *Love Curtiss.* I don't think I've ever felt closer to Genie.

My work with Genie continues, and Genie continues to change, becoming a fuller person, realizing more of her human potential. By the time this work is read, she may have developed far beyond what is described here. That is my hope—that I will not be able to keep up with her, that she will have the last word.

Part II

LINGUISTIC DEVELOPMENT

6

The Data

The data analyzed in this work are of several types and were collected in many different ways.

6.1. INTERVIEWS WITH GENIE'S MOTHER

Reports gathered from weekly interviews with Genie's mother by the clinical social worker on the case have been a primary source of information on Genie's life prior to her emergence. Unfortunately, the mother's reports were not always reliable, since it appeared that she would often say what she felt her questioner[s] wanted to hear, confuse dates, and contradict herself from one interview to the next. In addition, she was reluctant to divulge information, perhaps out of fear that action would be taken against her if the truth were known. It was only through Genie's behavior that we were able to discover some of the terrible details of her past. As a result, information gathered from interviews with the mother was weighed accordingly and relied on only when other sources have been unavailable.

6.2. REPORTS FROM THE DIVISION OF PSYCHIATRY, CHILDREN'S HOSPITAL

Information regarding the case history was obtained from the reports written by members of the staff (Hansen, 1972; Kent, 1972). After her admission to the hospital, detailed daily notes were kept by Dr. K. These provided a rich source of data on the first 8 months after Genie's emergence.

6.3. VIDEOTAPES

Videotapes using a 3600 Sony videotape machine with a Sony AC 3400 and 3210 DX camera were made several times a week for the first year, and frequently thereafter throughout the entire period that this case has been studied. These tapes, which number in the hundreds, provide data on all aspects of Genie's behavior and development, including language. They are catalogued by number, date, and subject matter.

In analyzing the language data, especially for evidence of comprehension, I have been careful to consider the fact that the videotape camera is focused on only a small space in any given room. Consequently, most of the objective and tangible surroundings for any specific conversation are not captured on film, thus preventing the viewer from having knowledge of the environmental information available to those being filmed. Oftentimes gestures, facial expressions, and movement in the room are hidden from view. In determining Genie's linguistic knowledge and abilities as evidenced by the tapes, therefore, I have been careful not to assume that where no cueing was filmed, none existed.

6.4. TAPE RECORDINGS

Tape recordings of Genie's speech were made on a Nagra III N° tape recorder on Scotch $200\frac{1}{4}$ professional tape, on a Uher tape recorder on Scotch 200 $\frac{1}{4}$ inch professional tape, and on a Sony Tc40 cassette recorder on low-noise cassette cartridges. The first recordings were made in the summer of 1971, and periodically thereafter—sometimes as often as once or twice a week. Because of Genie's special problems associated with speech, especially her reluctance to speak unless required to do so, the tape recordings that were made consist largely of either silence or of someone other than Genie talking. Thus, although tape recordings of Genie continue to be made, they have not served as a principal means of collecting speech data.

6.5. OBSERVATIONS OF GENIE'S SPEECH

The primary source of data for Genie's productive language has been detailed notes taken on the spot, during our sessions with Genie. Even when tape recordings or videotapes were made during these sessions, careful, lengthy notes were written as well. These will be referred to and quoted in the text that follows.

6.6. PSYCHOLOGICAL TESTING

The tests which have been administered over the last $5\frac{1}{2}$ years to determine the level of Genie's psychological and cognitive functioning include: Bank Street Readiness Test (5/72); Bender Gestalt (5/73); Columbia Mental Maturity Scale (9/72, 5/72); Differentiation of Affect (11/73); Draw a Man (5/73); Evaluation of Perceptual–Motor Abilities (6/73); Table 2 Facial Apraxia Routine (9/72); French Pictorial Test of Intelligence (10/71, 11/71); Frostig Developmental Test of Visual Perception (1971, 6/72, 6/73); Frostig Visual Perception Program (6/73); Illinois Test of Psycholinguistic Abilities (2/71, 7/71, 1/73, 5/73, 2/74, 1/75); Leiter International Performance Scale (1/71, 3/71, 4/71, 4/72, 5/73, 2/74, 1/75); Motor Inhibition Tasks (11/73); Peabody Picture Vocabulary Test (3/71, 4/71, 4/72, 9/72, 5/73, 2/74, 1/76); Physiognomic Perception (11/73); Preschool Attainment Record (11/70, 7/71, 6/73); Raven Coloured Progressive Matrices (10/71, 1/72); Siegel Object Sort (11/73); Stanford–Binet (2/73, 5/73, 2/74, 1/75); Summary Evaluation of Perceptual–Motor Abilities (1973); Vineland Social Maturity Scale (11/70, 7/71, 1/72, 2/72, 10/72); Wechsler Intelligence Scale for Children (6/72, 5/73, 2/74, 1/75); and the Wechsler Preschool and Primary Scale of Intelligence (3/71, 11/71).

There were many problems involved in testing Genie. Standard psychological and intelligence tests could not be used at first because such tests rely heavily on verbal comprehension and verbal responses. Other instruments, less dependent on language abilities, had to be used in any attempts to assess Genie. Moreover, for a long period of time, there were the additional problems of not being able to administer the tests either in full or in the usual way and not being able to score Genie's performance in the way provided by the normed scoring data to be used in accompaniment with these tests. Thus, in many cases, the resultant numbers represent merely the examiner's best attempt at quantifying Genie's performance in a way compatible with both the test itself and normal scoring procedures.

6.7. LANGUAGE TESTS

To determine the extent of Genie's receptive knowledge of language, we developed a series of syntactic and semantic comprehension tests which are described in detail in Appendix I. We had hoped to use a language test that was already normed and available as an effective instrument for measuring language comprehension, but at the time (1971) there were no tests which were adequate or suitable, in general, either because they required (and thus tested) speech responses or knowledge of the world that this child did not yet possess, or because they did not effectively test the range of linguistic structures and elements we felt should be tested in order to come to any sort of valid conclusion regarding the true nature and extent of linguistic knowledge she possessed.

Specifically, in our search for a language instrument, we considered the following tests: the Imitation Comprehension and Production Test (ICP) (Fraser, Bellugi, & Brown, 1963); the Berry Exploratory Test of Grammar (Berry & Talbott, 1969); the Preschool Language Scale (Zimmerman, Steiner, & Evatt, 1969); the Northwest Syntax Screening Test (Lee, 1969); the Carrow Test for Auditory Comprehension of Language (Carrow, 1969); and the Utah Test of Language Development (Mecham, Jex, & Jones, 1967). We found them unsuitable and inadequate for our needs for the following reasons. The ICP has a very limited range of language features that it tests, and no phonology section at all. The Berry Exploratory Test of Grammar does not test receptive ability at all, only expressive language. Moreover, it tests no phonology, no syntax, no semantics; it tests only expressive morphology. The Preschool Language Scale fails to test either morphology or syntax. The Northwest Syntax Screening Test tests only syntax and morphology and is limited in the range of elements included in these areas. It relies totally on pictures, pictures which are at times confusing or rely on very subtle cues for differentiation. The pictures, moreover, are frequently not direct representations of test sentences, and test validity is, therefore, open to question. The Carrow Test for Auditory Comprehension of Language contains no phonology items, relies totally on picture identification, tests many language features outside the context of a grammatical sentence, fails to repeat items to determine performance consistency, and does not control for chance by including enough test choices. The Utah Test of Language Development tests only semantic concepts—no phonological, morphological, or syntactic elements. It utilizes pictures that are very small and presents concepts outside of a grammatical context. In addition to the above inadequacies, because of the special problems in testing Genie, no available tests were suitable for the kinds of limited and flexible testing sessions required.

For these reasons, we developed our own set of language tests and continued to modify and add to these tests as Genie's abilities allowed or required us to do. Thus, whereas at first we could use only very short individual tests and had to rely on frequent retesting to determine consistency in performance and thereby knowledge or lack of knowledge of the particular feature of language tested, we were later able to use lengthier tests that could in one administration tell us whether or not a particular aspect of English was part of Genie's receptive knowledge of the grammar.

In designing the language comprehension tests, wherever possible and applicable, each of the tests incorporated the following features in its design:

(1)   The objects or pictured situations were known to be familiar to Genie. This was to ensure that knowledge of the world or words involved was not being tested instead of the structure or syntactic element.

(2)   There were enough choices to keep the possibility of selecting the right answer by chance down to a minimum.

(3)   There was at least one incorrect choice containing all of the elements of the test sentence, but in a different relationship to each other from that of the correct choice. This was to ensure that knowledge of the words in the test sentence was not sufficient to indicate the correct choice, since comprehension of the words in a sentence is not equivalent to comprehension of the grammatical and semantic relationships contained therein.

(4)   There were enough test items for response consistency to reflect degree of comprehension. This feature was not incorporated until Genie was able to attend to tests for longer than a few minutes at a time, long after language testing was begun in 1971.

(5)   All extralinguistic cues which might signal the correct response were eliminated.

There are twenty-six tests; these include tests of negation, both in simple and complex sentences; modification; prepositions *in, on, under, over, behind, beside, next to, in front, in back, between*; singular/plural; conjunction/disjunction; possessive pronouns; personal pronouns; comparative; superlative; tense/aspect; *before* and *after*; *some, one, all*; active voice; WH-questioning of subject versus object; complex sentences; complex negation; relative adjectives; *come/go*; *more/less*; *most, many, few, fewest*. All these tests are described in detail in Appendix I.

In addition to the language comprehension tests, I developed semantic classification tests to assess Genie's ability to classify objects according to specific features. These tests, described in full in Appendix I, test those semantic features overtly marked in the linguistic system of English as well as other features. There are five classification tasks: Animate/Inanimate, Human/Nonhuman, Male/Female, Edible/Inedible, and Part/Whole.

Genie has also been given the Assessment of Children's Language Comprehension (ACLC) (5/73), and the Slope test (10/75).

6.8. NEUROLINGUISTIC TESTS

(1)   Dichotic listening tests designed and administered by Stephen

Krashen and prepared by Sara Spitz and Stephen Krashen were prepared at the UCLA Phonetics Laboratory on a PDP-12 Computer, using computer programs developed by Lloyd Rice. Verbal and environmental sounds tests were administered over a period of a year and a half. These will be discussed in detail in Part III and are described in Appendix II.

(2)   Tachistoscopic tests including Dot Location and Rhyming were designed by Susan Curtiss, David Rigler, and Victoria Fromkin, and were administered on a Scientific Prototype Two–Field Tachistoscope. Descriptions of all the tachistoscopic tests can also be found in Appendix II.

(3)   Several other tests tapping specific cognitive functions have been administered: The Street Gestalt Test (6/72), the Mooney Faces Test (2/75), the Harshman Figures Test (2/75), the Thurstone Figures Test (3/75), the Nebes Arc–Circle Test (5/75), the Knox Cube Test (1/73, 3/73, 10/73, 12/73), Southern California Figure–Ground Visual Perception Test (3/73), the Benton Visual Retention Test (9/75), (10/75), the Graham and Kendall Memory for Designs (10/75), and the Test of Facial Recognition (12/75).

6.9.   WORK WITH WRITTEN LANGUAGE

Because Genie rarely spoke, during my sessions with her less formal methods of tapping her linguistic abilities were used in addition to the formal tests. Attempts were made to use language presented in a visual mode (words printed on index cards), both to ascertain her knowledge of English structures and to intensify the input in areas of syntax that were absent or problematic in her speech or comprehension. These "reading" sessions are referred to in the text to follow and were generally of the following nature: We began the reading sessions by going over the words to be used in that particular session. The words were printed on 3 × 5 index cards. Genie was asked to identify each word; if she was unable to do so, the word was identified for her and she was asked to repeat it. When each of the words had been identified once in this fashion, they were placed in a pocket board. If a new word or words was introduced to her, the word was printed on a card in front of her for her to watch. The word was identified, then repeated aloud by Genie. Typically, when a new word was introduced, Genie would repeat it several times and hold onto the card, even try to play with it for a while. When all of the words were in the pocket board, we began our particular work for the day, including explanation, presentation of examples, and Genie's own productions. She was instructed to make specific strings. After each string that Genie formed, she was required to read it aloud and, if necessary, to correct what she had formed to conform to the instructions she had been given. After this part of the work, Genie was often asked to make sentences of her own choosing; or, later in her development, to switch roles back and forth and both give and follow directions. The sessions lasted from 20 minutes to 45 minutes, depending on Genie's mood and motivation.

6.10. SIGN LANGUAGE

In the spring of 1974, Genie began instruction in sign language. She was taught a system of signing somewhere between American Sign Language and signed English in its grammatical system (for example, including pronouns but excluding articles). I have not been involved in the instruction, but have included references to Genie's use of sign language where it has played a role in her linguistic development.

7

Phonology: Comprehension and Production

7.0

In this chapter I will discuss aspects of Genie's phonological knowledge and abilities. Section 7.1 will deal with phonological perception, i.e., receptive phonological abilities, Section 7.2 will deal with spontaneous phonetic and phonological production, Section 7.3 will deal with suprasegmental phenomena, followed by Section 7.4 which gives a short summary of her abilities.

7.1. RECEPTIVE PHONOLOGY

It was apparent within a few weeks after Genie was discovered that she could differentiate the sounds constituting speech from other sounds around her, and could, furthermore, scan that stream of sound for familiar patterns constituting words she recognized ("Mama," "Genie," "red"). To some extent, therefore, she was capable of some phonological perception from the onset of her exposure to language. From that point until the time I began to examine this aspect of her linguistic abilities, much time had passed and Genie's knowledge of English had grown considerably. Observationally, it appeared that Genie could recognize and differentiate the sounds of English. As before, however, to determine the actual extent of her abilities it was necessary to formally test her phonological perception—a task once again constrained by the problems of testing her and of finding suitable test items.

53

7.1.1.

In the fall, of 1973 I first administered the Receptive Phonology Test (Test Number 27 in Appendix I) which tested Genie's ability to discriminate many of the phonological distinctions of English phonology.

The test consisted of thirty picture pairs, each member of which differed by only one distinctive feature from the other member (e.g., *hill/heel, pie/tie*). In addition to the thirty pairs that differed only by one distinctive feature, there were seven pairs that differed by the absence or presence of an added consonant (e.g., *train/rain, lamb/lamp*), one pair that differed by the order of phones only, and one pair which differed by an additional consonant plus a feature difference in the stop.

The picture pairs were presented, one pair at a time, and Genie's task was to point to the picture corresponding to the word I spoke. Words from the A column (see Appendix I) were presented in one session. Column B words were presented in a following session. The items tested are given in Table 7.1.

TABLE 7.1
Phonological Minimal Pairs Test

Distinctive feature	Sample items	
for consonants	Syllable-initial	Syllable-final
±voice	pea – *bee*	
	*f*ace – *v*ase	
	*c*oat – *g*oat	ba*ck* – ba*g*
	*p*ear – *b*ear	
±nasal	*b*ud – *m*ud	hea*d* – he*n*
	*b*eat – *m*eat	bu*d* – bu*n*
		clou*d* – clow*n*
±coronal	*p*ie – *t*ie	ca*p* – ca*t*
(labial/alveolar)	*f*ox – *s*ocks	com*b* – co*n*e
	*s*pool – *s*tool	
	*m*ail – *n*ail	
±back		
(labial/velar)	*b*oat – *g*oat	

TABLE 7.1 (*Continued*)

Distinctive feature	Sample items	
for consonants	Syllable-initial	Syllable-final
±continuant	$t$ub – $s$ub	
±lateral	g$r$ass – g$l$ass	bea$r$ – bell
	$r$ake – $l$ake	

Distinctive feature	Sample items	Phonetic distinctions
for vowels		
±tense	h$i$ll – heel	$[I] - [i^j]$
	sh$i$p – sheep	$[I] - [i^j]$
	b$a$ll – bowl	$[ɔ] - [o^w]$
±high	pen – pin	$[ɛ] - [I]$
	toe – two	$[o^w] - [u^w]$
	bird – beard	$[ɚ] - [ir]$
±back	cap – cup	$[æ] - [ʌ]$
	map – mop	$[æ] - [a]$
±low	men – man	$[ɛ] - [æ]$
	bowl – b$a$ll	$[o^w] - [ɔ]$

Other oppositions	Sample items
CCVC versus ∅CVC	clock – lock
	train – rain
	swing – wing
	broom – room
	stop – top

TABLE 7.1 (*Continued*)

Other oppositions	Sample items
CCVC versus $\emptyset$CVC	clock – lock
	train – rain
	swing – wing
	broom – room
	stop – top
CV versus C$\tilde{\text{V}}$C	key – king
CVC versus CVCC	lamb – lamp
C_1VC_2 versus C_2VC_1	top – pot
CCVC versus CVC	stair – chair[a]

[a]This item was included even though it could be said to include a phonetic cluster [tš]. However it functions in English as a single consonant.

This test did not cover all of the relevant features in English phonology, but I was limited by the vocabulary which Genie knew and which could be illustrated.

From September 1973 to June 1975, the test was administered twelve times. In all the tests Genie made only two errors, one on *key* versus *king*, one on *lamp* versus *lamb*. Thus it is clear that Genie can discriminate at least those phonological features tested.

7.1.2. Rhyming

A second body of data relating to Genie's receptive phonological abilities comes from rhyming tests. After introducing and working on the concept of rhyming with her, her ability to make rhyming judgments was tested. Specifically, Genie had to select from a set of pictured objects, the one(s) whose name(s) rhymed. In each case a model picture(s) (the word[s] to be rhymed) was placed to the left of the set of pictures from which a selection was to be made. The choices were placed in a row, vertically arranged from top to bottom in the order corresponding to the horizontal order presented in the charts below. From the row of pictures, Genie had to select the one(s) that rhymed with the target picture to the left. Genie's answers in the rhyming tests are given in Tables 7.2–7.4. Table 7.5 lists the results for all tests.

TABLE 7.2
Rhyming Test, February 5, 1974

Target words	Choices available (in order of presentation)	Genie's choice
1. chair, stair, pear	hat, bear	bear
2. mail, nail	jar, tail	tail
3. tail, mail, nail	pail, key	pail
4. lake, rake	rake[a], nose	rake
5. lake, rake	soap, tree, cake	cake
6. goat, coat	gun, hat, boat	boat
7. pea, bee	key, car, house	key
8. key, pea, bee	bat, soap, flower (rose), tree	tree
9. rose	jar, mouse, cat, nose, soap	nose
10. hat	bee, chair, tail, gun, cat	cat
11. car	coat, pear, jar, cap, soap	jar
12. house	mouse, hat, nose, pail, cake	mouse
13. bat	mouse, hat, boat, tree, bear	(1) mouse (2) hat
14. gun	soap, house, car, sun, cap	sun
15. soap	rose, boat, mouse, rake, rope	rope
16. cat	nose, jar, mouse, bat, tree	(1) jar (2) mouse (3) nose (4) bat[b]
17. cat, bat	rose, boat, mouse, chair, hat, key	hat
18. jar	car, bee, coat, cap, tail	car
19. pear	boat, house, bear, pail, rope	bear

TABLE 7.2 (*Continued*)

Target words	Choices available (in order of presentation)	Genie's choice
20. key	hat, tree, pail, rake, cat	(1) rake
		(2) cat
		(3) pail
		(4) hat
		(5) tree[b]
21. pail	chair, bear, nose, sun, tail	tail
22. rose	nose, soap, bat, boat, cake	nose
23. cake	sun, key, tail, cap, rake	(1) sun
		(2) rake
24. sun	jar, mouse, soap, gun, hat	gun
25. tree	cat, key, rose, rake, tail	key
26. bear	pail, pear, rope, tail, house	pear
27. mouse	rose, chair, hat, house, nose	house
28. rake	cap, sun, car, gun, cake	cake
29. rope	soap, sun, bee, nose, boat	soap
30. bat	cake, boat, cat, hat[c], mouse	(1) cat
		(2) cake
		(3) boat
		(4) hat

[a]By accident, *rake* was made a choice. (There were two different pictures of *rake*.)

[b]On the occasions when she made an incorrect choice and I indicated to her that it was not correct, she seemed upset and frustrated and selected choices at random, not even looking at what she was pointing to.

[c]Genie's instructions were to select two.

TABLE 7.3
Rhyming Test, May 8, 1974

Target word	Choices available (in order of presentation)	Genie's choice
31. jar	boat, sun, car	car
32. gun	chair, sun, soap	sun
33. rose	nose, house, boat, pail	(1) boat
		(2) house
		(3) nose
34. pail	rake, tail, cake	tail
35. hat	car, coat, cat	cat
36. pear	boat, jar, bear	bear
37. tree	cap, key, house	key
38. rat	boat, bat, coat	bat
39. soap	rose, rope, rake	rope
40. rose	house, mouse, nose	house, nose

It is possible that after the first session Genie was merely matching pictures on the basis of prior association, but her performance in the first session necessarily involved her ability to learn and use the notion of rhyming and the phonological manipulation and matching that rhyming involves. Her success with the task implies that Genie had a mental representation (at some level) of the "normal" adult phonetic forms that she was able to use. There is no other way she would have been able to make the kind of comparisons and matches against my pronunciation with such consistency, especially in light of her own highly variable pronunciation of the vowels and consonants involved (see Section 7.2).

The ability to determine whether or not words rhyme involves several kinds of phonological knowledge and abilities. First, rhyming necessitates being able to separate the segment or segments preceding the vowel from the rest of the phonological content of the word (in this case, syllable). This operation (Operation 1) involves knowledge of whether a segment is a vowel or a consonant, and knowledge of where the segments occur in relationship to the syllable as a whole. That operation also involves ignoring the phonetic form of the initial consonant or cluster. Second, rhyming necessitates storing the portion of the target syllable from the vowel to the end of the syllable as a model for

TABLE 7.4
Rhyming Test, September 25, 1974

| | Choices available | Genie's |
Target word	(in order of presentation)	choice
41. tree	soap, chair, key	chair, key
42. boat	car, rose, coat	(1) rose
		(2) coat[a]
43. mouse	house, cap, bear	house
44. hat	cake, bat, pear	bat
45. pail	rope, cat, tail	tail
46. sun	gun, nose, jar	gun
47. rake	bee, mouse, cake	cake
48. soap	cat, rose, rope	rope[b]
49. chair	pear, key, tail	pear
50. car	coat, house, jar	jar
51. rose	mouse, rake, nose	nose
52. bear	gun, pail, chair	chair
53. bee	tree, hat, cat	(1) cat
		(2) hat
		(3) tree

[a]When Genie chose *coat*, she said and signed, *boat* **and** *coat* (signing **and**). (I had said, *boat and...*, waiting for her answer.)

[b]In data collected in 1971 by V. Fromkin, Genie regularly aspirated initial stops and deaspirated stops that were part of an underlying initial [s] + stop cluster, thereby differentiating the two on the surface. My own data do not reveal this regularity. It is possible that a rule "re-ordering" occurred.

comparison. Third, the kind of rhyming involved in these sessions necessitates performing Operation 1 on each of the choices and then performing a comparison procedure of the forms to determine if they match. Comparison of the vowels is insufficient, e.g., test items 9, 15, 22, 23, 29, 34, 42; comparison of the final consonant is insufficient, e.g., test items, 6, 11, 13, 17, 30, 35, 36, 38. Only

TABLE 7.5
Results of the Rhyming Tests, All Sessions

Date	Session	Number		Percentage correct
		Correct	Incorrect	
2/5/74	I	25	6	84
5/8/74	II	8	2	80
9/25/74	III	10	3	77
Total all sessions		43	11	80

comparison of the entire syllable minus the initial consonant or cluster will yield the correct match.

Genie was able to do all of this consistently and correctly. She did not inappropriately compare initial consonants (e.g., 6, 11, 13, 19, 23, 50); she did not inappropriately compare semantic representation (e.g., 6, 16, 35); she did not compare vowels alone and ignore final consonants (except in one instance); and she did not compare final consonants, ignoring what came before. There were items testing all of these possibilities, but, except for a few errors, Genie persisted in considering the necessary and appropriate information only.

7.1.3. Homonyms

A third source of data on Genie's phonological knowledge comes from her own spontaneous response to homonyms. Genie has created gestures in many different situations, usually to correspond to a single word. A few times Genie created a single gesture to correspond to more than one word—words with phonetically identical portions in almost every instance. She created a single gesture for *here* and *hear*; for *two* and *too*, and the [tu] of *Tuesday*; for *ten* and the [tɛn] of *tenant*; for *sick* and *sit*, for *knock* and *not*, and for *disappear* and *disappointed*.

Her use of a single gesture for both words indicates that she perceived at least portions of the pair as being phonologically identical. She did not use a single gesture for words that were alike in any other respect (such as semantically). Since her acquisition of sign language (see Chapter 9), through which she has learned the signs for several of these words, she no longer gestures homonyms with the same gesture. This is probably because through sign language she has learned to associate gesture with semantic content rather than with phonological form.

7.2. PHONOLOGICAL PRODUCTION

7.2.1.

A few general comments about Genie's spontaneous speech are in order. Genie's voice quality is abnormal. Although her vocal control is improving and normalizing, untrained people often remark that she sounds like a deaf or a cerebral-palsied individual. Comments from trained speech pathologists suggest that she sounds like a child with cerebral palsy and not like a person who is deaf. Regardless, there are abnormal aspects to her speech that color almost all of her spontaneous output, segmental and nonsegmental, and make the use of traditional IPA symbols inexact. Her vowels are generally laxed and centralized; her off-glides, too, are laxed and centralized. During the first year (1971) her speech was highly glottalized—probably due to her inability to control laryngeal mechanisms. Her average fundamental frequency is still abnormally high, her output very breathy, so breathy that she often speaks in something like a whisper. In contrast, every once in a while she utters a word "creaky-voiced." All of these distortions make transcriptions only approximations to her speech.

These distortions and abnormalities in Genie's spontaneous speech disappear almost completely when she imitates a model. In imitation, her articulation is far clearer and devoid of most of the substitutions and deletions of her spontaneous speech. She imitates the model as it was pronounced for her, almost exactly except for volume and pitch.

Her imitations, i.e., her phonetic ability (articulatory and perceptive), stand in marked contrast to her spontaneous speech. Thus there is a great disparity between Genie's phonetic ability and her phonological system. A variety of factors may contribute to this difference, but her distorted phonological system of rules (presented below) seems to be the major cause.

Tables 7.6 and 7.7 list an inventory of sounds present with enough consistency to represent "phonemes" in Genie's speech. The inventory covers the period from July 1971 to June 1975 and basically did not change during that time.

There are some gaps in the occurrence of these sounds. For the most part, the occurrence restrictions of consonants correspond to those in adult English phonology, e.g., [h] does not occur finally, [j] and [w] do not occur finally except as off-glides. There are other gaps, however, which may represent occurrence restrictions in Genie's phonology. For example, [θ], [f], and [b] do not occur in final position. There is so much substitution and deletion in Genie's speech, however, that these gaps might merely be a function of the high variability in the phonetic realization of phonological forms in her speech. There is no way

TABLE 7.6
Consonant Phoneme Inventory

	p	b	f	v	m	t	d	Θ	ð	n	s	z	č	ǰ	š	k	g	h	r	l	w	j
vocalic	-	-	-	-	-	-	-	-	-	-	-	-	-	-	-	-	-	-	+	+	-	-
consonantal	+	+	+	+	+	+	+	+	+	+	+	+	+	+	+	+	+	-	+	+	-	-
high	-	-	-	-	-	-	-	-	-	-	-	-	+	+	+	+	+	-	-	-	+	+
back	-	-	-	-	-	-	-	-	-	-	-	-	-	-	-	+	+	-	-	-	+	-
anterior	+	+	+	+	+	+	+	+	+	+	+	+	-	-	-	-	-	-	-	+	-	-
coronal	-	-	-	-	-	+	+	+	+	+	+	+	+	+	+	-	-	-	+	+	-	-
voice	-	+	-	+	+	-	+	-	+	+	-	+	-	+	-	-	+	-	+	+	+	+
continuant	-	-	+	+	-	-	-	+	+	-	+	+	-	-	+	-	-	+	+	+		
nasal	-	-	-	-	+	-	-	-	-	+	-	-	-	-	-	-	-	-	-	-		

TABLE 7.7
Vowel Phoneme Inventory

	i	ɪ	u	ʊ	e	ɛ	o	ɔ	æ	ʌ	a	ə
high	+	+	+	+	−	−	−	−	−	−	−	−
back	−	−	+	+	−	−	+	+	−	+	+	−
round	−	−	+	+	−	−	+	+	−	−	−	−
low	−	−	−	−	−	−	−	−	+	+	+	−
tense	+	−	+	−	+	−	+	−	+	−	+	−

to be sure with the data we have whether these reflect systematic constraints or random errors.

The segments [ð], [č], and [ǰ] did not appear until 1973 in our data. None of these sounds appears to be stable in Genie's speech, but they involve little more variability in their realization than most of the other segments and so were included in the phoneme chart.

The decision as to what were phonemes in Genie's phonology was difficult to make. Unlike a normal child's phonological development, Genie's phonology has not followed a course of highly systematic and restricted substitution succeeded by stabilization of forms. To be sure, Genie's substitutions are not totally random. Vowels are never substituted for true consonants; consonants are not substituted for vowels. Many substitutions preserve much of the distinctive feature composition of the underlying phone (e.g., Rules 9–14) but not always. Some substitutions are highly unlike the underlying segment in feature composition (see Rule 16). Moreover, a variety of substitutions exist for a number of phones and in total produce a very unstable pattern of surface realization of underlying forms.

I have chosen to describe and account for the substitutions and phonological alternations and processes that appear with regularity in Genie's speech by putting them in rule form. The variability in these occurrences is partly captured by their optionality. So many of these "rules" occur unpredictably with regard to grammatical context, I make no claims about their psychological reality. I present them to exemplify the state of phonological affairs in Genie's speech.

7.2.2. Syllable Structure

Most of the following rules account for Genie's CV syllables. All but one simplify consonant clusters—word-initial, across syllable boundaries, and word-finally.

Rule 1: $C \rightarrow \emptyset/\_\#$ (optional).

This rule operates to produce words such as those in Table 7.8.

TABLE 7.8
Examples of Rule 1

	Pronunciation	
Normal	Genie's	Gloss
[ɔl]	[ɔ]	'all'
[tʰʌč]	[tʌ]	'touch'
[wɛt]	[wɛ]	'wet'
[sup]	[su]	'soup'
[faʲv]	[faʲ]	'five'
[tʰãʲm]	[taʲ]	'time'
[blaʷs]	[bæʷ]	'blouse'

This rule does not usually operate on final [r]s. Retroflexion (or a surface reflex) usually remains in her utterances—whether in final position or next to the final consonant, as exemplified in Table 7.9 (see p. 66).

There is reason to believe that Genie treats [r] after vowels as a feature of the vowel and not as a consonant (see Rules 23 and 24) because it was exempt from an otherwise very pervasive rule even in 1971, when all other final consonants were deleted in almost every case.

Rule 1 is optional even for a simple $\#(C)CVC\#$ syllable. In 1971 and 1972, it was used far more often than not; since 1973, final consonants have appeared more and more frequently. But at no time has Rule 1 applied obliga-

TABLE 7.9
Examples of Final-[r] Retention

Pronunciation		Gloss
Normal	Genie's	
[bord]	[bɔr]	'board'
[mark]	[mar]	'Mark'
[skɚt]	[kɝ]	'skirt'
[kʰar]	[kar]	'car'
[mor]	[mɔr]	'more'

torily. We find words with surface-final consonants all along, as shown in Table 7.10.

TABLE 7.10
Examples of Word Final Consonants

Genie's Pronunciation	Gloss	Date
[wan]	'one'	August 1971
[fɪnɪš]	'finish'	July 1971
[pʰʊl]	'pull'	July 1971
[pʰam]	'palm'	December 1971
[sup]	'soup'	January 1972
[rʌv]	'rough'	January 1972

Rule 1 is not only optional, there is no apparent factor, phonological or otherwise, that determines whether the rule applies or not. All types of consonants have at times been deleted, at times retained; length of word or other aspects of the syllable structure have played no apparent part. The same word, on the same day, can at one time contain its final consonant and at another, not (e.g., [sup] 'soup'; [su] 'soup' both occurred on January 19, 1972). The optionality of this rule is not a variable rule in the sense of Labov (1972), either (see also Cedergren & Sankoff, 1974), since to the best of our knowledge it is not dependent on sociological or phonological factors. We cannot, of course, be certain of this since we have no corpus of running text to analyze, due to Genie's reluctance to speak.

Additional evidence that this rule has been optional is the fact that through-out this period Genie could at will produce a final consonant she had just deleted if an adult imitated her (Genie's) pronunciation of the word. Typically Genie would laugh and say, *Silly*, (with a gesture) at someone's imitation of her dis-torted pronunciation of a word, and immediately would repronounce the word *with* the final consonant (as well as other phonological content she had pre-viously deleted). It was often as if she simply did not monitor her own output; and when someone monitored it for her (by imitating her), she could modify and "correct" it. In any case, the optionality of this rule clearly shows that the stored words were phonologically represented with the final consonants, ex-emplifying the difference between phonological representation and phonetic output or performance.

Rule 2: $\begin{bmatrix} C \\ +\text{liquid} \end{bmatrix} \rightarrow \emptyset /\,\#\,C\_V$ (optional).

This rule functioned to simplify initial consonant plus liquid ([r] or [l]) clusters. Its application produced forms such as those in Table 7.11. This rule

TABLE 7.11
Examples of Rule 2

	Pronunciation	
Normal	Genie's	Gloss
$[\text{bla}^w\text{s}]$	$[\text{bæ}^w]$	'blouse'
$[\text{p}^h\text{le}^j]$	$[\text{pe}^j]$	'play'
$[\text{gri}^j\text{n}]$	$[\text{gɪ}]$	'green'

became an optional rule after a period of about 6 months, when it functioned obligatorily. First, a sort of archi-liquid entered her speech—something pho-netically between an [l] and an [r]—and lexical representations of words with initial consonant + liquid clusters may have specified the liquid only as [+ liquid]. After another period of perhaps 6 months, when the only liquid to appear in clusters was this archi-liquid, [r] stabilized and more often than not, surfaced in initial clusters, whereas [l] was usually deleted (see Table 7.12, p. 68). Nonetheless, Rule 2 became optional for both [r] and [l] and, as before, within 1 day a single word could be pronounced with or without the liquid.

In 1973 Rule 2 seemed to have become inoperative or lost. Genie began to break up C + liquid clusters by inserting an epenthetic [ə] between them

TABLE 7.12

Pronunciation		Gloss
Normal	Genie's	
[grĩʲn]	[grɪ]	'green'
[drĩʲk]	[drĩ]	'drink'
[pʰleʲ]	[peʲ]	'play'
[bleʲd]	[beʲ]	'blade'

(see Table 7.13). This environment was one of several for the application of

TABLE 7.13
Examples of Epenthetic [ə]-Insertion

Genie's pronunciation	Gloss
[bəlú]	'blue'
[pəráʷ]	'proud'
[fəló·r]	'floor'

Rule 5, which seemingly functions to preserve all of the phonological information by breaking up the cluster with a vowel rather than deleting one of the
segments. After this rule was introduced, pronunciation of C + liquid clusters
varied between (1) a full, unsimplified cluster ([traʲ] 'triangle'; [kloz] 'close'),
and (2) a C + liquid cluster broken up by a [ə]: (pəráʷ] 'proud'; [fəlúʷ] 'flu')
The variability in the surface form of this cluster-type persists at this writing,
and as before, no phonological or other controlling factor can be identified.
Nonetheless, again it is clear that even when her system "preferred" simple
consonants to clusters, the cluster was phonologically stored.

Prior to 1973, Genie deleted all final clusters.

Rule 3: $\begin{bmatrix} C \\ + \text{ consonantal} \end{bmatrix} \rightarrow \emptyset \; /\_\_ \; C\$.$

Rule 3 entered in 1973 and functions to simplify final clusters by deleting the
consonant preceding the final consonant (as shown in Table 7.14). Genie has no
surface final clusters in her speech at all except liquid + consonant clusters, so

TABLE 7.14
Examples of Rule 3

Pronunciation		Gloss
Normal	Genie's	
[vɛst]	[vɛ·t]	'vest'
[gərl]	[dɪl]	'girl'
[šarp]	[šap]	'sharp'

this rule is, perhaps, obligatory for all clusters not involving liquids, and optional for these: [hælp] 'help'; [arm] 'arm'. If one considers retroflexion a feature on the vowel, the optional domain of this rule decreases even more.

If [r] is considered a consonant, one cannot predict when Rule 3 will apply in the optional cases, and the relationship between Rules 1 and 3 is confounded. Rules 1 and 3 are in a bleeding relationship when Rule 1 applies first, for Rule 1 removes the environment under which Rule 3 applies. No ordering relationship can be assumed, however, because there are surface forms reflecting both possible orders (i.e., reflective of either rule having applied, since forms where both rules have applied do not reveal which has applied first): [sɪk] 'six', where Rule 1 has applied, eliminating the environment for Rule 3 to apply, and [vɛ·t] 'vest', where Rule 3 has applied and Rule 1 has not.[1]

Considering forms with [r], the situation appears even more variable, since the surface form of a word with a final cluster involving an [r] may contain a full final cluster (e.g., [šarp] 'sharp'), may contain only the final consonant of a cluster ([šap] 'sharp'), may contain only the first member of a cluster ([šar] 'sharp'), or may contain no final consonants at all ([sʲaᵒ] 'sharp'). The variability of rule application, even for the same word, precludes a fixed ordering relationship between these two rules.

Rule 4: [s] → ∅ / #__C.

This rule simplifies [s]C clusters by deleting the [s]. This rule was obligatory until early 1973, when it became optional for [s] + nasal clusters: [s·nɛ] 'snake', [smɔ·] 'small'. At that time Rule 5 began to apply to these clusters, optionally: [səmó] 'smoke', so [s] + nasal clusters were realized as (1) an unbroken cluster, (2) a cluster simplified by [ə], or (3) a single nasal, the [s]

---

[1] Such examples indicate that the rules in Genie's phonological system are unordered. Whether this is phonologically normal or nonnormal is equivocal because the issue of rule order in phonological theory has not been decided. Other possibilities are discussed on page 83.

having been deleted. This variability in [s] + nasal clusters persists and no determining factor can be isolated.

Rule 4 remained obligatory for [s] + stop clusters until 1974, when Rule 5 began to operate on these clusters. Deletion of the initial [s] occurred far more frequently than insertion of the [ə] and persists as the most frequent realization of [s] + stop clusters: [pɪt] 'spit', [tap] 'stop', [kræč] 'scratch'. When Genie deletes the [s] the stop is often unaspirated, but not always; here as elsewhere (cf. Rule 7) aspiration is not predictable.

Rule 5: $\emptyset \rightarrow [ə] \left/ \begin{bmatrix} C \\ +\text{consonantal} \end{bmatrix} - \begin{bmatrix} C \\ +\text{consonantal} \end{bmatrix} \right.$

This rule breaks up consonant clusters by inserting a [ə] (or [ə]-like vowel) between the consonants. It applies to obstruent + resonant, obstruent + liquid, and obstruent + obstruent clusters in initial position (Table 7.15), and to clusters across syllable and word boundaries (Table 7.16). The vowel-insertion

TABLE 7.15
Examples of Rule 5

Pronunciation		Gloss
Normal	Genie's	
[bluʷ]	[bəlú]	'blue'
[smáʲlĩŋ]	[sɨmáʲlĩ]	'smiling'
[stoʷv]	[sətó·]	'stove'

TABLE 7.16
Further Examples of Rule 5

Pronunciation		Gloss
Normal	Genie's	
[wɘkhárd]	[wɘkəhá·r]	'work hard'
[stæ̀pspídĩŋ]	[tápəpítɪ]	'stop spitting'
[ʌpsét]	[ʌpəsɛ́ʔ]	'upset'
[pʰíkčɘ]	[pítəšə]	'picture'

does not apply to clusters where one of the segments is a glide, and it does not apply to final clusters (Table 7.17).

TABLE 7.17
Examples of Environments Where Rule 5 Does not Apply

Pronunciation		Gloss
Normal	Genie's	
[séʲfweʲ]	[séʲfweʲ]	'Safeway'
[nʌ̀ʲswúmn̩]	[nʌɪtwúbə̃]	'nice woman'
[hɛlp]	[hælp]	'help'

Before the end of 1972, Genie deleted almost all final consonants and final consonant clusters, and had only obstruent + liquid initial clusters. Thus, the phonological contexts in which this rule was to apply rarely occurred. It was not until early 1973, when more of the relevant phonological contexts appeared on the surface, that Rule 5 was adopted. Rule 5 was optional until early 1974, when it appeared to become obligatory for clusters across syllable and word boundaries. Later that same year, the rule was clearly optional again in this environment as well (e.g., [wə˄təhár] 'work hard', [wə˄khár] 'work hard' [11/74]), and as before, no factor determining whether or not this rule applied is apparent.

A sixth rule, not dealing with specific segment structure, is the following:

Rule 6: $\begin{bmatrix} \text{syllable} \\ \text{-stress} \end{bmatrix} \rightarrow \begin{Bmatrix} \emptyset \\ \text{ə} \end{Bmatrix}$ (optional).

In 1971 and at least the first half of 1972, Rule 6 applied far more frequently than not, and most of Genie's words were monosyllables throughout this period. There were some exceptions, however, as shown in Table 7.18, and, conse-

TABLE 7.18
Exceptions to Rule 6

Pronunciation		Gloss	Date
Normal	Genie's		
[jélóʷ]	[jélo]	'yellow'	7/71
[bəlún]	[balú]	'balloon'	7/71
[dáktə̀]	[dátə]	'doctor'	11/71
[fʌ́niʲ]	[fʌ́tʌ]	'funny'	1/72

quently, it appears to have been optional even during this time.

Rule 6 functions to delete or reduce nonstressed syllables. Syllables are more frequently deleted than reduced (e.g., [frɪ] 'refrigerator', [jɔ] 'yogurt', [kəˆ] 'Curtiss') but at times a surface phonological place-holder of sorts—a [ə] (or [ə]-like vowel)—surfaces to mark an underlying syllable (Table 7.19).

TABLE 7.19
Examples of Rule 6

	Pronunciation	
Normal	Genie's	Gloss
[tʰíkl̩]	[tíə]	'tickle'
[bíznəs]	[bítə]	'business'
[lídl̩]	[líə]	'little'
[láʲbrɛ̀riʲ]	[láɪbrə]	'library'

7.2.3. Segment Structure Rules

Genie's phonological system also includes several rules which apply specifically to single consonants. We posit them as rules since they are optional. If this were not so, the feature representation would be different from the adult sounds. First there are three rules which apply to classes of consonants.

Rule 7: $\begin{bmatrix} +\text{stop} \\ -\text{voice} \end{bmatrix} \rightarrow [-\text{aspirated}] \; /\$— $ (optional).

This rule deaspirates syllable-initial voiceless stops (see Table 7.20.) These substitutions have occurred optionally in Genie's speech from 1971 on, as shown in Table 7.21.

Because of Rule 7, Genie does not mark a surface distinction in the stop between the stop of a [s] + stop cluster where the [s] has been deleted and an initial stop. Either one can be aspirated or deaspirated (e.g., [kʰul] 'school', [tʌ́bə] 'stomach').[2]

---

[2] In data collected in 1971 by V. Fromkin, Genie regularly aspirated initial stops and deaspirated stops that were part of any underlying initial [s] + stop cluster, thereby differentiating the two on the surface. My own data do not reveal this regularity. It is possible that a rule "reordering" occurred.

TABLE 7.20
Examples of Rule 7

Pronunciation		Gloss
Normal	Genie's	
[kʰar]	[kar]	'car'
[tʰɛ̃n]	[tæ̃]	'ten'
[pʰlejpʰjǽnoʷ]	[pejpǽto]	'play piano'

TABLE 7.21
Examples of Optionality of Rule 7

Genie's pronunciation	Gloss	Year
[pʰam]	'palm'	1971
[pʊ]	'pool'	1971
[pa]	'palm'	1972
[pʰa⁀ʊtə]	'park'	1972
[pʰʊ·r]	'poor'	1973
[pʌt]	'push'	1973
[pʰɪr]	'period'	1974
[pĩ]	'pink'	1974

Rule 8: $\begin{bmatrix} +\text{stop} \\ -\text{voice} \end{bmatrix} \rightarrow [+\text{aspirate}] / — \begin{Bmatrix} \$ \\ \# \end{Bmatrix}$ (optional).

Rule 8 aspirates syllable (or word) final voiceless stops, sometimes even those which are surface substitutions for voiced sounds (see Table 7.22, p. 74). The operation of Rule 8 first occurred in 1973 and is infrequently applied.

TABLE 7.22
Examples of Rule 8

	Pronunciation	
Normal	Genie's	Gloss
[ʌpsét]	[ʌpʰəsɛ́ʔ]	'upset'
[rʌg]	[rʌkʰ]	'rug'

Rule 9: $\begin{bmatrix} C \\ +\text{obstruent} \end{bmatrix} \rightarrow [-\text{voice}] \ / \text{—} \ \# \ \text{(optional)}.$

Rule 9 devoices final consonants as illustrated in Table 7.23 (p. 74). Rule 9 is rarely applied and entered sometime in 1974. Because it is rare, it may actually be more of a segment-specific rule rather than a process of final devoicing, but because there is so much variability in the surface form of underlying segments it is hard to tell.

There are, in addition, a large number of rules that deal with specific consonant substitutions. All of these rules are optional. Their optionality, taken together with the range of sounds covered by these rules, contributes in large measure to the great variability of Genie's surface pronunciation.

Rule 10: $\begin{bmatrix} C \\ +\text{back} \\ -\text{coronal} \end{bmatrix} \rightarrow \begin{bmatrix} -\text{back} \\ +\text{coronal} \end{bmatrix} \text{(optional)}.$

$\qquad\qquad\quad$ g, k $\qquad\qquad$ d, t

TABLE 7.23
Examples of Rule 9

	Pronunciation	
Normal	Genie's	Gloss
[rʌg]	[rʌkʰ]	'rug'
[wæʲgṇ]	[wæk]	'wagon'

Rule 10 (which is optional in all positions) substitutes [d] for [g] and [t] for [k] (see Tables 7.24 and 7.25). But, as shown in Table 7.25, on the same day, the rule may or may not apply (see Table 7.26). However, random substitutions for [g] and [k] do not occur. It is for this reason that a rule is suggested.

Rule 11 (optional):
$$\begin{bmatrix} C \\ +\text{coronal} \\ +\text{continuant} \end{bmatrix} \rightarrow [-\text{continuant}] / V\_\_.$$
$$ \text{s, z} \text{t, d}$$

TABLE 7.24
Examples of Rule 10

	Pronunciation	
Normal	Genie's	Gloss
[gɚl]	[dɚ]	'girl'
[goʷ]	[doʷ]	'go'
[grĩ ʲn]	[drĩ]	'green'
[trá ʲæ̃ŋl̩]	[tráæ̃dl̩]	'triangle'
[kʰæt]	[tʰæ]	'cat'
[kʰæ̃p]	[tæ̃p]	'camp'
[park]	[pá tə]	'park'
[wɚ́kɚ]	[wɚ́tɚ]	'worker'

TABLE 7.25
Examples of Rule 10's not Applying

	Pronunciation	
Normal	Genie's	Gloss
[grĩn]	[grĩn]	'green'
[gʊd]	[gʊ]	'good'
[rʌgz]	[rʌgd]	'rugs'
[kʰʌ̃m]	[kʌ]	'come'
[tʰeʲk]	[tæk]	'take'
[wɚkhard]	[wɚkhar]	'work hard'
[sĩŋk]	[sĩk]	'sink'

TABLE 7.26
Examples of Rule 10's Optionality

Pronunciation			
Normal	Genie's	Gloss	Date
[grĩ^jn]	[drĩ]	'green'	6/25/74
[grĩjn]	[grĩn]	'green'	6/25/74
[wɘ́khard]	[wɘ́təhár]	'work hard'	10/30/74
[wɘ́khard]	[wɘ́khar]	'work hard'	10/30/74

Rule 11 substitutes [d] for [z] and [t] for [s] medially and finally (see Table 7.27). It is also optional.

TABLE 7.27
Examples of Rule 11

Pronunciation		
Normal	Genie's	Gloss
[rʌgz]	[rʌgd]	'rugs'
[ɪz]	[id]	'is'
[klázət]	[ḷad]	'closet'
[bla^ws]	[bəla͂^wt]	'blouse'
[glǽsəz]	[gəlǽtə]	'glasses'
[jɛs]	[jɛt]	'yes'
[no^wz]	[no^wz]	'nose'
[pí^jsu^wp]	[písu]	'pea soup'
[ʌpsέt]	[ʌp^həsέʔ]	'upset'

Although [θ] and [ð] occur very infrequently, Rule 11 also applies to these phones. It substitutes [d] for [ð] and [t] for [θ], although as with [s] and [z] these substitutions are optional as shown in Table 7.28.

Rule 12 (optional): $\begin{bmatrix} C \\ +\text{nasal} \end{bmatrix} \rightarrow \begin{bmatrix} -\text{nasal} \\ \alpha \text{ voice} \end{bmatrix}$.

TABLE 7.28
Examples of Rule 11's Applying to [θ] and [ð]

Pronunciation		
Normal	Genie's	Gloss
[θĩ˜ʲŋz]	[teʲ]	'things'
[ðə]	[dʌ]	'the'
[kʰǽθiʲ]	[kǽtɪ]	'Kathy'
[θriʲ]	[θri]	'three'
[ðə]	[ðə]	'the'
[ənʌ́ðə]	[nʌð]	'another'

Rule 12 substitutes [t] or [d] for [n] and [p] or [b] for [m]. According to the data it has two parts:

Rule 12.1 (optional):

$$\begin{bmatrix} N \\ +\text{anterior} \\ -\text{coronal} \\ m \end{bmatrix} \rightarrow \begin{bmatrix} -\text{nasal} \\ \langle -\text{voice} \rangle \\ b, p \end{bmatrix} / \begin{Bmatrix} \# \\ \langle V \rangle \end{Bmatrix} \_\_\_ .$$

Rule 12.2 (optional):

$$\begin{bmatrix} N \\ +\text{coronal} \\ n \end{bmatrix} \rightarrow \begin{bmatrix} -\text{nasal} \\ \langle -\text{voice} \rangle \\ d, t \end{bmatrix} / \begin{Bmatrix} \langle V\_\_\_ \rangle \\ \_\_\_ \# \end{Bmatrix} .$$

Rule 12.1 substitutes either [p] or [b] for [m] in initial or medial position. Rule 12.2 substitutes [t] or [d] for [n] medially or word-finally. The position restriction may represent a gap in the data or it may reflect an actual difference in the denasalization of [n] as opposed to [m]. Examples of these substitutions are listed in Table 7.29 (p. 78). Like the others, this rule is optional, as shown in Table 7.30 (p. 78).

Rule 13 (optional):

$$\begin{bmatrix} C \\ +\text{delayed release} \\ č, ǰ \end{bmatrix} \rightarrow \begin{bmatrix} -\text{delayed release} \\ (+\text{palatal release}) \\ \begin{Bmatrix} t, d \\ t^j, d^j \end{Bmatrix} \end{bmatrix} .$$

TABLE 7.29
Examples of Rule 12

	Pronunciation	
Normal	Genie's	Gloss
[mʌ́niʲ]	[mʌ́deʲ]	'money'
[ĩn]	[ĩd]	'in'
[wʌ̃n]	[wʌ̃d]	'one'
[mɔr]	[bɔr]	'more'
[kʌ́mĩŋ]	[kʌ́pɪ]	'coming'
[stʌ́mək]	[tˢʌ́bə]	'stomach'

TABLE 7.30
Examples of Optionality of Rule 12

	Pronunciation	
Normal	Genie's	Gloss
[pʰʲǽnoʷ]	(1) [pǽto]	'piano'
	(2) [pǽno]	
[mor]	(1) [mɔr]	'more'
	(2) [bɔr]	
[fʌ́niʲ]	(1) [fʌ́niʲ]	'funny'
	(2) [fʌ́tiʲ]	
[wʌ̃n]	(1) [wan]	'one'
	(2) [wʌ̃d]	

Rule 13 optionally substitutes [t] or [tʲ] for [č] and [d] or [dʲ] for [ǰ] (see Table 7.31).

These affricates did not occur in Genie's speech until 1972, and not with any frequency until 1973. Other substitutions for [ǰ] have appeared in the data, but each only once: [dzʲ] for [ǰ], [č] for [ǰ], [dz] for [ǰ]. [č] has only occurred once initially ([čɪr] 'cheers'), and rarely otherwise. Perhaps that is why there are fewer different substitutions for it than for [ǰ].

TABLE 7.31
Examples of Rule 13

Pronunciation		Gloss
Normal	Genie's	
[ǰiʲp]	[diʲp]	'jeep'
[čɪ̃n]	[tɪ]	'chin'
[čiʲk]	[tʰi]	'cheek'
[rɪfriǰərèʲtə]	[frɪd]	'refrigerator'
[ǰóəl]	(1) [dʲóɛl]	'Joel'
	(2) [ǰóɛl]	
[ǰɪ̃m]	(1) [dʲɪ̃]	'gym'
	(2) [ǰɪ̃]	
[čɛr]	[tʲɛᵛ]	'chair'
[skræč]	[kræč]	'scratch'

Rule 14 (optional):

$$\begin{bmatrix} C \\ +\text{continuant} \\ +\text{high} \\ -\text{coronal} \\ -\text{voice} \\ \check{s} \end{bmatrix} \rightarrow \begin{bmatrix} +\text{coronal} \\ +\text{palatal release} \\ s^j \end{bmatrix}.$$

Rule 14 optionally substitutes [sʲ] for [š] (see Table 7.32, p. 80). The only substitution for initial [š] is [sʲ]. Before 1973, except for one occurrence, [š] did not occure in word-final position; it was always deleted. Later, it was still often deleted; but when it appeared on the surface it was never as [sʲ], but always as [š] (e.g. [fínɪš] 'finish') or [t] (e.g., [pʌt] 'push').

Rule 15 (optional):

$$\begin{bmatrix} C \\ +\text{obstruent} \end{bmatrix} \begin{bmatrix} +\text{consonantal} \\ +\text{vocalic} \end{bmatrix} \rightarrow [\underset{0}{l}].$$

Rule 15 optionally substitutes a [l]—a voiceless lateral with other peculiar characteristics besides its voiceless quality—for initial obstruental + liquid

TABLE 7.32
Examples of Rule 14

	Pronunciation	
Normal	Genie's	Gloss
[šɛ́rən]	[sʲɛ́rɪ]	'Sharon'
[šæ̃mpúʷ]	(1) [šæpú]	'shampoo'
	(2) [sʲæ̃pú]	
[šeʲk]	[šœk]	'shake'
[šarp]	(1) [ša·ᵁ]	'sharp'
	(2) [sʲaᵁ]	

clusters. Examples of this rule and its optionality are shown in Table 7.33. Unlike other rules, this rule stands out as one of the few that substitutes a non-English segment into the phonetic output of Genie's speech. Like the other rules there is no apparent context determining when this rule applies.

TABLE 7.33
Examples of Rule 15

	Pronunciation	
Normal	Genie's	Gloss
[klázət]	[l̥ad]	'closet'
[klɔ]	(1) [l̥ɔ]	'claw'
	(2) [klɔ]	
[flápiʲ]	[l̥ápɪ]	'floppy'
[drɔ]	[l̥ɔ]	'draw'
[dráʲvĩŋ]	[dráʲvi]	'driving'
[floʷr]	[fəló·r]	'floor'
[kloz]	[kloz]	'close'

Rule 15, which entered toward the end of 1973, added an additional possible surface realization of C + liquid clusters. Such clusters could surface as [l̥], as a cluster interrupted by a [ə] (from Rule 5), or as an uninterrupted cluster.

Stop + [r] clusters tend to be realized in intact form (e.g., [drajⁱ] 'dried'), voiced stops, or fricative + liquid clusters tend to surface with a (ə) vowel inserted (e.g., [bəlú] 'blue', [fəlɔ́ʲ] 'Floyd'), and voiceless stops + [l] clusters tend to be realized as [l̥]. But these tendencies were not rules; each occurred at some time as any of the three possibilities.

7.2.4 Consonant Substitutions

Many other substitutions occur in Genie's speech but not with sufficient frequency to warrant rules; they occur only once or twice in the data. Some examples are listed in Table 7.34.

TABLE 7.34
Consonant Substitutions

Substitution	Example	Gloss
[f] → [v]	[rʌv]	'rough'
[h] → [ʔ]	[ʔæ̃]	'hand'
[s] → [š]	[šátɪ]	'Saturday'
[g] → [dʲ]	[dʲɚ]	'girl'
[s] → [k]	[klǽpĩ]	'slapping'
[ð̃] → [g]	[nʌ́gə]	'another'
[s] → [z]	[zĩ]	'swim'
[gr] → [čʷ]	[ǽⁱčʷɪ]	'angry'

7.2.5 Vowel Substitutions

The preceding rules and substitutions deal only with consonants. There is an even larger number of substitutions and surface alterations of vowels. First, there are a few rules affecting vowels in general.

Rule 16: $\begin{bmatrix} V \\ +\text{stress} \end{bmatrix} \rightarrow$ [overlong].

Rule 16 lengthens stressed vowels. Length is not phonemic in Genie's phonology, but she frequently produces vowels whose duration far exceeds normal adult vowel length. This tendency to lengthen stressed vowels may be a result of the lack of pitch control in Genie's speech. Because she does not indicate stress through a rise in pitch, she relies on the other parameters to indicate stress: volume and duration. And because her speech is typically below normal volume, she emphasizes the remaining feature—length—to mark stress (see Section 7.3). This lengthening process has been part of Genie's speech since the beginning of my research in 1971, but it has been optional throughout. As she has gained some control over pitch, Rule 16 has been applied less frequently, but it is still part of her phonological system.

Since stress in English is phonetically realized by pitch change, increased duration, and increased amplitude, with pitch being the main cue according to the published literature (Lehiste, 1970), it is interesting that Genie's production problems have not prevented her from encoding stress and using the one parameter to express it in her speech.

Rule 17 (optional) (as in normal grammar):
$$V \rightarrow \tilde{V} /\underline{\quad} N.$$

Rule 17 is obligatory before a nasal that appears on the surface. It is optional before nasals that are deleted on the surface, and optional before underlying nasals that surface as a [t] or [d] (see Rule 12). Examples are given in Table 7.35. Because nasals may be deleted, substituted, or realized on the surface and because there is no phonological environment determining which of these possibilities will be actualized, Rule 17 cannot be ordered with respect to Rule 12. Since the nasal segment does at times cause nasalization of the vowel, however, it must obligatorily be present in underlying form. The rules may apply in linear order, but the ordering between any two rules appears to be random. This is interesting in light of some of Anderson's (1974) suggestions regarding local ordering of rules.

Rule 18 has two alternate forms, both of which are optional.

Rule 18.1 (optional): $V \; G \rightarrow 1 \;\; \emptyset.$
$$ 1 \; 2$$

Rule 18.2 (optional): $V \; G \rightarrow \begin{bmatrix} 1 \\ -\text{tense} \end{bmatrix} \emptyset.$
$$ 1 \; 2$$

Rule 18 thus serves as both a monopthongization rule and a laxing rule. Its effect and optionality are exemplified in Table 7.36 below. Both alternatives are unpredictably applied.

TABLE 7.35
Examples of Rule 17

Pronunciation		Gloss
Normal	Genie's	
[gõn]	[gɔ]	'gone'
[ɔ́ldʌ̃n]	[ɔ́dɔ̀]	'all done'
[tɛ̃n]	(1) [tɛ]	'ten'
	(2) [tɛ̃]	
[hæ̃d]	(1) [hæ]	'hand'
	(2) [hæ]	
[wʌ̃n]	(1) [wʌ̃]	'one'
	(2) [wa]	
	(3) [wʌ́d]	
[fʌ́niʲ]	(1) [fʌt]	'funny'
	(2) [fʌ́di]	
[kʌ́miŋ]	[kʌ́pɪ]	'coming'
[æ̃d]	[æd]	'and'
[ĩn]	[ĩd]	'in'
[stʌ́mək]	[tsʌ́bə]	'stomach'

TABLE 7.36
Examples of Rule 18

Pronunciation		Gloss
Normal	Genie's	
[tʰuʷ]	(1) [tʊ]	'two'
	(2) [tu]	
[óʷpən]	(1) [ɔ́pɛ]	'open'
	(2) [ópɛ̃]	
[pʰẽʲt]	(1) [pʰɛ̃tʰ]	'paint'
	(2) [pʰeʲ]	

TABLE 7.36 (*Continued*)

Pronunciation		Gloss
Normal	Genie's	
[grĩ^jn]	(1) [grɪ]	'green'
	(2) [grĩ^j]	
[mi^j]	[mɪ]	'me'
[jó^wgɘt]	[jɔ]	'yogurt'
[še^jk]	[še]	'shake'
[ra^jd]	[rɔ]	'ride'
[t^ho^w]	[to]	'toe'
[we^j]	[we]	'way'
[jo^wk]	[jo^w]	'joke'

Rule 19 (optional): $\begin{bmatrix} G \\ -\text{back} \\ j \end{bmatrix} \rightarrow [-\text{tense}]/V\underline{\quad}\,.$

In contrast to Rule 18, Rule 19 applies only to [j] and optionally laxes it as illustrated in Table 7.37.

TABLE 7.37
Examples of Rule 19

Pronunciation		Gloss
Normal	Genie's	
[nʌ́^jtga^wn]	[na·ᴵ]	'nightgown'
[sɘ́praj^jz]	[pra·ᴵz]	'surprise'
[nʌ^js]	[nʌᴵt]	'nice'
[bé^jbi^j]	(1) [bɛᴵ]	'baby'
	(2) [bé^jbi]	
[fa^jv]	[fa^j]	'five'
[pli^jz]	[pi^j]	'please'

Rule 20 (optional): $V \rightarrow [-\text{voice}]/\begin{bmatrix} C \\ -\text{voice} \end{bmatrix}.$

Rule 20 optionally devoices vowels ([kr̥i̥ʲm̥i̥ʲ] 'Christmas,' [kʰʌ̥] 'come'). At times a whole phrase can be devoiced, but more frequently, single syllables are voiceless if the initial consonant is voiceless. The application of this rule, unfortunately, adds to the already abnormally breathy quality of Genie's speech.

There are other rules which apply to specific vowels or specific groups of vowels.

$$\textbf{Rule 21 (optional):}\quad \begin{bmatrix} V \\ \alpha\,\text{back} \\ \beta\,\text{tense} \end{bmatrix} \rightarrow \begin{bmatrix} -\alpha\,\text{back} \\ -\beta\,\text{tense} \end{bmatrix}.$$

TABLE 7.38
Examples of Rule 21

		Pronunciation		
		Normal	Genie's	Gloss
(a)		[aʲ]	[æʲ]	'I'
		[blaʷs]	[bæʷ]	'blouse'
		[tʰãʲm]	[tã·ᴵ]	'time'
		[hard]	[ha·]	'hard'
(b)		[pʰʊ́dĩŋ]	(1) [piʲ]	'pudding'
			(2) [pʊt]	
		[gʊd]	[gʊ]	'good'
(c)		[bæk]	(1) [bak]	'back'
			(2) [bæ]	
		[hæv]	(1) [hav]	'have'
			(2) [hæv]	
		[sǽtədèʲ]	[šátɪ]	'Saturday'
		[kʰr̥ǽkə]	[træ]	'cracker'
(d)		[brʌš]	[breʲ]	'brush'
		[bʌs]	[bʌ·]	'bus'
		[kʰʌt]	[kʌ]	'cut'

Rule 21 handles the following substitutions in Genie's speech.

(a) [a] → [æ]
(b) [ʊ] → [iʲ]
(c) [æ] → [a]
(d) [ʌ] → [eʲ]

Examples of this rule's application and optionality are presented in Table 7.38 (p. 85). This rule, like many others, appears to be randomly applied. Data indicate Rule 21 to have been part of Genie's phonological system from 1972 on.

Rule 21 operates on a group of vowels that have little in common acoustically or articulatorily. This rule is especially noteworthy, therefore, because it demonstrates that Genie may have failed to organize the vowels in her productive phonology into natural classes. Unlike her feature-based consonant substitutions, Genie does not appear to make use of distinctive features or natural classes in systematizing vowels or vowel substitutions. See also Table 7.41 (p. 88).

TABLE 7.39
Examples of Rule 22

	Pronunciation		
Normal		Genie's	Gloss
[flor]		(1) [flɔ·]	'floor'
		(2) [fɛló·r]	
[gɚl]		(1) [dɪl]	'girl'
		(2) [dɚ]	
[kʰar]		(1) [ka]	'car'
		(2) [kar]	
[hard]		(1) [ha·]	'hard'
		(2) [har]	
[mor]		(1) [mɔ]	'more'
		(2) [mɔr]	

Rule 22 (optional):

$$\begin{bmatrix} V \\ +\text{retroflex} \end{bmatrix} \rightarrow [-\text{retroflex}] \, / \underline{\quad} \#$$

Condition: V ≠ [ɛr].

Rule 22 deretroflexes vowels word-finally. It does not apply to [ɛr] and is optional for the other retroflexed vowels. Examples are shown in Table 7.39. It is possible to consider these instances of V + [r] sequences; in that case the rule would be:

Rule 22: [r] → ∅ / __ #

Condition: V ≠ [ɛ].

In either form, Rule 22 does not apply when the vowel nucleus is [ɛ]. These vowels undergo an additional rule:

Rule 23 (optional): $\begin{bmatrix} V \\ +\text{retroflex} \end{bmatrix} \rightarrow [V^{\upsilon}] \, / \underline{\quad} \#$

or

[r] → [ʊ] /V__ #.

Rule 23 applies to [ar] and [ɛr] only and is optional in both cases (see Table 7.40).

TABLE 7.40
Examples of Rule 23

	Pronunciation		Gloss
Normal		Genie's	
[skʷɛr]	(1)	[gwɛ$^{\upsilon}$]	'square'
	(2)	[gwɛr]	
[čɛr]		[tʲɛ$^{\upsilon}$]	'chair'
[ɛ́rɜnd]		[ɛ·$^{\upsilon}$]	'errand'
[šarp]	(1)	[sʲa$^{\upsilon}$]	'sharp'
	(2)	[sʲar]	

The relationship between Rules 22 and 23 is not a problem. Except in the case of [ar], no other retroflex segment (or sequence) can undergo both rules. In order to ensure that that is the case, Rule 23 must be made more specific.

$$\textbf{Rule 23}': \begin{bmatrix} V \\ -\text{high} \\ -\text{round} \\ \alpha\,\text{low} \\ \alpha\,\text{back} \\ +\text{retroflex} \end{bmatrix} \rightarrow [V^{u}] \,/\_\_\#\,.$$

Even [ar] poses no problem, however. It can optionally undergo Rule 22 (which would then prevent its applicability to Rule 23), Rule 23 (which would prevent Rule 22 from applying), or neither. In no case would any retroflexed forms undergo more than one rule per pronunciation.

There are many other vowel substitutions in Genie's speech, but since they are not changes applying systematically to any class of vowels (e.g., back vowels, high vowels, etc.) I merely list them, in Table 7.41. All are optional. These substitutions, together with all of the other stated rules and substitutions, create a situation of highly variable and unpredictable phonological production.

TABLE 7.41
Vowel Substitutions

Substitution		Example	Gloss
[ʌ]	[ɔ]	[ɝdɔ́]	'all done'
[ʌ]	[a]	[nãmwãn]	'number one'
[ʌ]	[iʲ]	[krí͡ʲmí͡ʲ]	'Christmas'
[aʲ]	[ɔ]	[rɔ]	'ride'
[aʲ]	[iʲ]	[fɜ́i͡ʲdɪ]	'Friday'
[iʲ]	[e]	[tev]	'Steve'
[ɛ]	[æ]	[jǽloʷ]	'yellow'
[ɪ]	[iʲ]	[krɪ́ʲmiʲ]	'Christmas'
[ʊ]	[ʌ]	[pʌt]	'push'
[eʲ]	[œ]	[šœk]	'shake'
[u]	[ɷ]	[nɷ]	'new'

7.3. SUPRASEGMENTALS

7.3.1. Stress

One aspect of Genie's speech production that stood out as unusual for early speech was the variety of consonants and vowels that appeared even in monosyllables and disyllables. This variety, although subject to rules resulting in great unpredictability of surface forms, reflected the range and variety of sounds in adult English phonology. This, therefore, was an unusually adult aspect of Genie's phonology. Stress assignment was another.

The first disyllables I have on record had correct (adult) stress. They are listed in Table 7.42. Every polysyllabic word I have on record since then (except, interestingly, her name) has also had correct word stress assignment.

TABLE 7.42
Early Disyllabic Stress

Pronunciation			
Normal	Genie's	Gloss	Date
[stápət]	[tápɪ]	'stopit'	1/71
[máma]	[máma]	'mama'	1/71
[bəlũn]	[bəlú]	'balloon'	5/71
[dáktɚ]	[dátə]	'doctor'	5/71
[fínɨš]	[fɪnɪš]	'finish'	7/71

As Genie acquires a lexical item, she acquires its stress pattern; if it contains more than one syllable, the stressed syllable always surfaces despite what else gets deleted (see Table 7.43, p. 90).

As stated earlier, stress in Genie's speech is signaled mainly by increased vowel duration. In the first 2 years, vowel duration was really the only parameter signaling stress; in 1973, Genie began to mark stress with changes in volume as well, and in the next year, she had gained enough control over pitch to vary pitch to some small degree as well. Vowel duration remains the most prevalent feature signaling stress, but the differences in vowel length between stressed and unstressed vowels in a word are not as exaggerated as they were when volume and pitch remained unchanged.

TABLE 7.43
Polysyllabic Stress

Pronunciation		
Normal	Genie's	Gloss
[rəfrɪ́jərèᴶtɚ]	[frɪd]	'refrigerator'
[bɪ́znəs]	[bɪt]	'business'
[tɛ́ləfõʷn]	[tɛl]	'telephone'
[hɑ́spədl̩]	[hɑ́pɪl]	'hospital'

7.3.2. Intonation

While word stress has been marked consistently and appropriately according to the adult model, phrasal stress has not been present in Genie's
utterances. Phrasal stress involves intonation, and until 1974, Genie did not
evidence any ability to control pitch in her speech. Until 1973, Genie's fundamental pitch was abnormally high, much higher than that of a very young
normal child. Then her pitch began to lower—very gradually and almost im-
perceptibly to those of us who saw her frequently. As of this writing her pitch
has normalized considerably. More importantly, she has gained enough control
to systematically vary pitch in the marking of stress, and at times to vary pitch
across an utterance of several words in a manner resembling sentence intonation, although she still does not use systematic or predictable intonation patterns, either in declarative or interrogative sentences.[3]

Although no formal testing of her ability to differentiate stress or intonation patterns has been carried out, there are many instances on record—in
every year from 1971 to 1975—where Genie recognized yes/no questions marked
only by intonation, as questions calling for a yes/no response. With this observational evidence of recognition of intonation patterns and her growing control
and exercise of pitch variation in her speech, we are hopeful that the future will
see the development of phrasal stress and intonation in Genie's speech.

7.4. SUMMARY

Genie's phonological system appears abnormally variable and unpredictable. Almost all of the rules are optional, and many of the substitutions and

---

[3] Genie now uses fairly normal active–declarative intonation, but still does not systematically
mark yes/no questions by intonation in her speech.

deletions distort the phonological structure to a degree which at times makes Genie's speech almost impossible to understand.

Her substitutions, however, are not random and utilize classes of sounds. Vowels are not substituted for consonants, nor consonants for vowels. Furthermore, it is not the case that any consonant may be substituted for any other. Only stops are substituted for other stops. In all substitutions where voicing and nasality vary, place of articulation remains stable. Where place of articulation varies, voicing remains stable. Such restrictions on how many features may vary reflect the reality of features and feature-based phonological classes of sounds in Genie's phonology. Her distinct treatment of these classes implies knowledge of the natural classes of consonants in language in general, and the subset found in English in particular.

Her vowel substitutions are far more variable, and as such, alter the distinctive feature representation of the underlying segment to a greater degree. More importantly, the rules and substitutions do not reflect an organization of vowels into the natural classes found in language (front versus back, low versus high). But again, the variability is not random. If an underlying vowel is [+ high, + tense], either its tenseness or its height is preserved on the surface. If a vowel's roundness is changed, its height and tenseness are preserved. Moreover, in keeping with the neutral or "minimal" vowel of English (Hooper, 1973), it is a [ə]-like vowel which is the reduced vowel and the vowel inserted to break up clusters in Genie's speech. She could have randomly chosen any other vowel or vowels to use for this purpose. Her consistent and predictable use of [ə] in such instances indicates a knowledge of the function of [ə] in English phonology.

Another area of phonological organization that Genie demonstrates an awareness of, and one which her speech preserves, is the order of phonological segments within a word. Phonological content may be deleted or altered, but it is not rearranged. The order of phones in the underlying form of a word is the order one finds on the surface.

Not only does Genie preserve the position of phones within syllables and words, but nowhere in Genie's speech does one find a violation of the morpheme structure restrictions of English phonology. If a phoneme does not occur in a particular position within a syllable in adult English, it is not found in that position in Genie's phonology.

Although beset by problems of pitch, breath, and volume control, Genie also shows a knowledge of suprasegmental phenomena and demonstrates an awareness that speech is marked by such phenomena. Stress, in particular, because one of its parameters has been within her control all along, has been marked on every word Genie has spoken. Thus, her own speech behavior and her response to the speech of others evidences an awareness of suprasegmental information and a knowledge of English stress and intonation in particular.

   Genie's performance on the rhyming tests and the optionality of her rules deleting final consonants and segments in clusters demonstrate that her own phonetic output differs from its phonological representation. She does not simply memorize the phonetic form of words spoken to her and mimic that pronunciation in her speech, sans analysis, sans phonological organization. Genie's language, like that of normals, includes a set of phonological rules, rules that organize and classify the sounds and sound sequences of her language, rules which are often motivated by universal phonological principles, e.g., simplification of segment, cluster, and syllable.

   What is most important is that Genie's speech is the output of a system of rules that are extracted from her input data. There is a system underlying her phonetic output, although this system is less reflective of the phonology of normal English than of some idiosyncratic and/or universal processes at work. Her phonological competence is not transparent. It underlies the system of rules that produces her phonetic performance, and is distinct from it.

8

Syntax, Morphology, Semantics: Comprehension

8.0.

This chapter will deal with attempts to determine the extent of Genie's comprehension of English, from the time she entered the hospital in November 1970, through the following $4\frac{1}{2}$ years. Section 8.1 deals with evidence from videotapes on Genie's comprehension during the first weeks after her emergence. Section 8.2 deals with the data resulting from the comprehension tests which I have given her and includes a discussion of the tests themselves. Section 8.3 discusses anecdotal evidence, in the context of a more general discussion of the nature of comprehension.

8.1. VIDEOTAPES

As stated in Part I, when Genie emerged from isolation she did not speak, but it was not known at that time how much receptive linguistic knowledge she had. The major source for determining something about how much language she knew and what kinds of structures she could process, under what conditions, was the set of thirty videotapes. These were made several times a week over the first 2 months while Genie was at the hospital. Although tapes were made frequently, sometimes almost daily, only eleven contain information on her language abilities during this period.

A detailed analysis of these tapes follows.

November, 1970
1. 11/23/70 (earliest videotape).   Dr. K held Genie's interest by playing
with puppets, one of which was a rabbit. At one point during the play, K gave
Genie a rattle to hold, and instructed her, *Don't let bunny get that rattle!*
    Genie kept the rattle in her hand and didn't allow the puppet to get it,
despite K's attempts to do so.

Genie appeared to comprehend the sentence, *Don't let bunny get that rattle!* Dr. K did not know whether he had played that game with her before this particular taping session. The game play, itself, therefore, may have produced the response rather than the comprehension of the sentence. In addition, notes from Dr. K dated December 7, 1970 indicate that Genie understood negative commands or warnings. It is possible, therefore, that Genie behaved appropriately by merely understanding negative warning + *bunny* + *rattle*.

2. 11/24/70.   K asked Genie, *Genie, would you like to go back?*
    Genie went to his kit and took out a toy, giving no indication
    that she knew she was being spoken to.

Genie's behavior in response to K could be construed as a ploy not to return to the Rehabilitation Center, thus implying comprehension of K's sentence. But such a sophisticated response was not, at that time, characteristic of Genie, who typically either made manifest her feelings of powerlessness or more directly displayed her unhappiness with a situation. Thus, it appears more likely that Genie did not understand what K asked.

3. 11/24/70.   Genie took out a ruler and hit K with it.
    K: *Was I a bad boy? I'm sorry.*
    G: *Sorry.* [sa]

Genie was obviously tuned in to K when he said, *I'm sorry,* and this familiar phrase (or word) evoked a moderately acceptable imitation, which indicated that Genie was at times motivated to speak, but did not indicate any comprehension.

4. 11/70 (composite tape of the first few months at the hospital).   K
motioned Genie to a chair. He asked her to sit down, clearly gesturing to her
at the same time.
    Genie sat down.

Her sitting response did not indicate comprehension of anything other than the gesture.

> 5. 11/70 (composite tape).   Dr. H talked with Genie's mother who sat next to Genie.

Genie appeared completely oblivious to the conversation about her mother and herself, and after a few minutes began tactilely exploring the room. Genie's lack of visible interest in the conversation may be reviewed as evidence only that the tangible new world around her held more attraction for her than the conversation. It may also reflect her inability to make sense of what was being said.

> 6. 11/70 (composite tape).   Genie was asked to return to her seat. She did so when the request was gestured and her hand was taken.

The fact that she did not sit down on a purely verbal request, but only when visual signs and cues were added, seems to indicate that the verbal request alone was not sufficient to cause her to respond appropriately, especially since she offered no resistance to being returned to her seat.

> 7. 11/30/70 (in the schoolroom at the Rehabilitation Center, with J, the teacher, and other children).
> J: *Why don't you sit here, Genie?* J gestured and held out the chair for Genie.
> Genie sat down.

As in the comments above, Genie's appropriate sitting response is not evidence for comprehension of more than the visual cueing she received.

> 8. 11/30/70.   J talked to Genie. Genie did not pay any visible attention to her.

The reason for Genie's lack of attention could have been disinterest, inattentiveness, or preoccupation with her own thoughts as much as lack of comprehension.

> 9. 11/30/70.   J: *Want to point?*
> Genie did not respond, although she looked at J as she spoke.

> 10. 11/30/70.   J talked to Genie and the other children.

Genie appeared oblivious to the conversation around her and indicated no comprehension of it.

> 11. 11/30/70.   J: *Genie, look at what Donald did.*
>   Genie turned her head toward J and Donald.

This indicates that Genie responded to J's talking to her and possibly that she recognized the name "Donald."

> 12. 11/30/70.   J wrote Genie's name on a picture she'd drawn.   J: *That says "Genie "* (pointing to the word). Genie looked at what J had pointed to.

Again this indicates nothing more than Genie's response to gestures.

> 13. 11/30/70.   Genie did a five-piece puzzle, easily fitting each piece into its hold. She did it one-handed (using her right hand), barely looking as she did it. J took the pieces out again. Genie just sat there.
>   J: *Can you put them in?*
>   Genie just sat there.
>   J: *See if you can put them in again.*
>   Genie just sat there.
>   J: *Genie, try this puzzle.* (J picked up a piece.)
>   Genie took the piece from J and worked the puzzle.
>   J: *Want to do that one again?* (J turned it over and placed it back in front of Genie.)
>   J: *You can do it again, if you like.*
>   Genie did it again.
>   J: *Fine, very good.*

Genie's behavior represents her ability to respond to gesture and example, and in no way indicates comprehension of language.

> 14. 11/30/70.   Genie got a book.
>   J: "You want me to help you read it to you, Genie?"
>   Genie appeared oblivious.
>   J: *You want me to read this to you?* (J is holding the book and leaning over to her.)
>   Genie also takes hold of the book and moves closer.
>   J: *It says "our puppy." Can you find the ball? Where's the ball?*
>   Genie closed the book.
>   J: *Don't you want . . . .*
>   Genie shook her head "no."
>   J (to another adult in the room): *It's the first time she's ever shaken her head at me.*

This dialogue exemplifies the fact that sentences without added cues meant nothing to her. It also shows the direct way Genie made her desires known (simply by closing the book), and her possible comprehension of *don't* + intonation and facial cues to prompt an appropriate response.

15. 11/30/70.   Genie had a deflated balloon.
    J: *Can I have it?*
    Genie got up and wandered around, not leaving the balloon with J.

December, 1970
16. 12/3/70 (at the Rehabilitation Center classroom).
    J: *You wanna sit down?*
    Genie did nothing.

17. 12/3/70.
    J: *Show me the red crayon.* (The crayons were in front of J.)
    Genie did nothing.
    J: *Show me the red crayon.*
    Genie did nothing.
    J: *Show me the red crayon.*
    Genie did nothing.
    J: *Where is the red one?*
    Genie did nothing.
    J gave the crayons to Genie and indicated that Genie was to point to the color that was named.
    J: *Red.*
    Genie showed the red one.
    J: *Green.*
    Genie pointed to the green one.
    J: *Blue.*
    Genie pointed to the blue one.
    J: *Brown.*
    Genie pointed to the brown one.

This not only exemplifies Genie's inability to comprehend instructions which were totally verbal, but demonstrates her ability to understand and follow a nonverbal example and shows her comprehension of four color words.

18. 12/4/70 and 12/7/70 (at the Rehabilitation Center where Genie's mother was visiting.)   Genie nodded her head "no" several times, but it may have been in imitation of a boy who was talking to her.

19. 12/4/70 and 12/7/70.   Genie began to vocalize, but her vocalizations were unintelligible on tape. She may have said, *No more,* but it was extremely difficult to tell.

20.   12/4/70 (in the Rehabilitation Center classroom).
      J: *Is that fun?*
      G: *Fun.* [fʌ]
      J: *Do you want to look again?*
      Genie looked.
      J: *Look at Mrs. M, now; do you see her?*
      G: [sípɪ.] (She went up to her and touched her.)
      J: *Can you see Candy?*
      G: [kɪsæ] . . . . (Her vocalization seemed to be several syllables, but was
      unintelligible except for the first sounds.)

This tape reveals Genie's readiness to imitate speech, her comprehension
of the name Mrs. M, and her ability to vocalize spontaneously more than
one syllable.

21.   12/8/70 (R is the occupational therapist.)
      R: *Wanna take your chair over there?* (Points.)
      Genie does nothing.

Either Genie does not wish to respond (on film she appeared tuned in
and attentive), or she is unable to respond with certainty because she cannot
fully understand the question.

22.   12/8/70.
      R: *Stand up.*
      Genie just sat there.
      R: *Stand up.*
      Genie just sat there.
      R: *Stand up.*
      Genie stood up.

It is difficult to determine why, unless some additional cue not captured
on film plays a role (such as pointing), Genie does not respond until the third
command. It could be a question of motivation or attention, or it could be a
situation where Genie knew she was being asked to do something, was unsure
of what that was, and sat there until situational cues suggested that she stand
up. The process of figuring out a response with a good chance of success may
well have caused the lack of response to the first two requests.

23.   12/8/70.
      R: *Can you help me put the tops back on the jars?*
      Genie didn't make a move.

R: *Can you put that top on that jar for me?* (Motioning in the direction of both the jar and top.)
Genie put the top on.
R: *Put the top in the red one.* (Cannot see if R is gesturing or not.)
Genie did so.

This seems to suggest that Genie either understood enough of the question to make sense of it, or, more probably, that the gesture plus the situational cues (e.g., lids, jars, and their normal relationship and juxtaposition) were sufficient to permit Genie's correct response. Her comprehension of the word "red" added to her evident success at solving the previous request may have been sufficient for her second appropriate response.

24. 12/11/70.
Someone: *Pick up that one for me and we'll put it on here.*
G: *Up. Up.*
Genie made several more vocalizations, but we could not make them out because the tape was very unclear.

Genie here again reveals her ability to spontaneously vocalize and to imitate words spoken to her.

25. 12/17/70.
J: *Say "ow!"*
Genie mouthed the word together with J. She later said the word aloud again, *Ow.* [ʔaʷ]

26. 12/25/70.   J tried to get Genie to imitate the word "fun." Finally, Genie said [fʌ] after the third request, with a slight nudging of Genie's arm.

27. 12/25/70.
J: *Give that one to your mother.*
Genie did so. (One couldn't tell if J was pointing or not.)
J: *May I have one? May I have _____?*
Genie gave her three.
Someone else asked Genie for one. Genie gave her one.

With or without additional gestures on J's part, the situation, coupled with Genie's knowledge of the word "mother," could have been sufficient to account for her appropriate response. The situational game, plus the pattern of giving to the speaker (especially when no other name is mentioned in the request) can account for Genie's additional responses, although why Genie gave three to J is not clear. It may be that she did not understand the word "one."

In the above examples of language activity as recorded on the videotapes, seven (2, 8, 9, 11, 15, 16, 21) are responses having nothing to do with what was said to her. In two of these (9 and 21), Genie appeared visibly interested and attentive to the speaker and situation. Six (3, 19, 20, 24, 25, 26) are responses of Genie, herself, vocalizing or speaking; none of these, however, indicates comprehension of the words themselves; five (4, 6, 7, 12, 13) are responses where gesture alone is sufficient to explain or account for her ability to respond appropriately. In one (23), comprehension of a single word plus comprehension of gesture accounts for her behavior. Seven (1, 11, 14, 17, 20, 23, 27) are responses where knowledge of individual words plus the situational context and information can account for her successful behavior; eight (2, 8, 9, 10, 11, 14, 15, 21) are instances where she failed to obey commands or to respond to sentences, all of them instances where gesture or other apparent nonlinguistic information did not exist.

In summary, then, there is evidence that Genie comprehended some individual words. It would be difficult to account for her behavior if she had not understood *rattle*, *bunny*, *red*, *blue*, *green*, and *brown*, or known who "Mother" and "Mrs. M" were. There are also data which evidence Genie's ability to extract the information NEG and WARNING from negative commands, and possibly the information QUESTION from yes/no question intonation.

Since there are no instances on record where Genie responded appropriately without gesturing or contextual support, there is no evidence that Genie had any knowledge of the syntax of English. Similar conclusions regarding the nature of Genie's linguistic abilities can be made from the tapes and from Dr. K's notes. In both sets of data, she was unable to respond without extralinguistic cueing, showing that her comprehension of English was negligible.

8.2. COMPREHENSION TESTS

The extent of Genie's linguistic knowledge began to change rapidly at the Rehabilitation Center. Her receptive vocabulary steadily increased, and it became evident to all who worked with her that the language spoken to and around her was becoming more meaningful to her! What, specifically, she understood we did not know (for no language testing had been done) and again, as before, her sensitivity to nonverbal cues made it difficult to get even an accurate general impression with regard to how much comprehension was present.

On March 3, 1971, Genie was visited by Dr. Ursula Bellugi and Dr. Edward Klima. Their report of this visit states: "[Genie] *seems* to understand a good deal more than she says of language, but it is not always clear what cues she is using to respond to sentences." They recommended "the use of tests and games [to establish] *how much* and *what aspects* of spoken language she understands and responds to . . . [which would be] a far better index of her knowledge of language than the handful of words she uses spontaneously." Furthermore, to distinguish between her understanding, which depended on "tone of voice, gestures, hints, guidance, facial and bodily expressions" and her understanding based on linguistic knowledge, they suggested that "In the situations reserved for testing and evaluating her understanding of spoken language alone, all these [extralinguistic cues] must be eliminated."

Determination of Genie's linguistic comprehension had to await careful testing, which was not feasible during this period. Moreover, because of the problems in working with Genie and in trying to assess her behavior, careful assessment of Genie's language required tests that were especially suited to Genie's special problems and which would consider her lack of knowledge of the world and her inexperience with most life situations.

As stated in Chapter 6, we were unable to use any of the available language tests, and therefore decided to develop our own tests, designed specifically for Genie.

The question of what constitutes comprehension of language is not a simple one. Moreover, it is not at all clear when a normal child can be said to comprehend language as adults do, that is, on the basis of the linguistic information alone. Certainly when any normal person uses language, he or she is aware and makes use of extralinguistic information, perceptual cues, situational factors, conversational information, gestures, and facial and affective embellishments. Children also make use of extralinguistic information. The critical difference, here, however, is that adults do not require the extralinguistic information to comprehend most language spoken to them. It has not, however, been determined whether children (younger than 4 years) require such information for comprehension (Bloom, 1974). It may be that children cannot comprehend sentences on the basis of their linguistic information alone. Thus, it might be considered unreasonable to require that Genie manifest the ability to understand language from linguistic information alone before crediting her with comprehension of language. But since measures for determining comprehension in children have not been established, and since we had to determine as fully as possible the nature and extent of linguistic knowledge Genie possessed in order to study her language development and determine how much language Genie had, we felt compelled to test her understanding of language in the absence of extralinguistic cues.

Initially, the tests were very short, in part to keep Genie's attention, and in part because we were forced to limit the number and range of test objects and pictures to those we were sure that Genie knew. Because of their brevity, it was possible to assess linguistic knowledge only through performance consistency, over many administrations of the same test. Thus these tests were administered regularly, approximately once a month.

As Genie became more testable, as we became more familiar with testing her, and as her language developed, new tests were constructed and old ones were modified, thereby increasing the range of linguistic elements and structures tested, and making each test a more reliable instrument for assessing Genie's knowledge of a particular linguistic feature or structure at any given time.

The set of receptive language tests we have designed and used with Genie is described in full in Appendix I. Below I will consider each linguistic element or structure tested and present Genie's comprehension of it as measured by her test performance.

8.2.1. Simple Negation

Description: Four pairs of pictures were presented. Each pair was identical except for the presence or absence of a specific feature. Genie had to point to the picture being described by the test sentence. The test sentences included the contracted and uncontracted form of the negative particle.

> *Examples:*   Show me the bunny that has a carrot.
> Show me the bunny that does not have a carrot.
> Show me the bunny that doesn't have a carrot.

Results (11/71–6/73):   Correct: 96, Incorrect: 0, Percentage Correct: 100[1]

This test presents affirmative/negative sentence pairs, and consequently tests both the ability to decode affirmative and negative declarative sentences as well as the ability to differentiate one from the other. Although to choose the correct picture in response to an affirmative test sentence, one perhaps may need only to comprehend the mentioned nouns (i.e., for "The bunny has a carrot" one could choose the right picture just by knowing "bunny" and "carrot"), the fact that Genie never pointed to both nouns, but always to the whole picture suggests that she processed the sentence as a whole, rather than just the nouns. Her statistically significant 100% correct performance ($p < .001$ using χ^2)[2] on this test was consistent and clear evidence that she understood the function and meaning of *not* and its contracted form *n't*.

---

[1] Each item occurred once in a session, so the chance of a response in one session influencing a response in another session is remote. Therefore, we can consider responses to be independent across sessions. Each sentence–picture, sentence–action, or sentence–object combination was a novel stimulus, unique within a session; thus unless Genie was test-wise, we can assume within session as well as across-session independence.

[2] Comparing expected and observed frequencies by χ^2, the probability that Genie's performance could have occurred by chance (taking into account the number of response possibilities available to her) is less than 0.001. This is a statistically significant result.

8.2.2. Simple Modification (One Adjective + Noun)

Description: Red plastic circles, squares, and triangles, each of three different sizes were arranged in rows in scrambled order. Genie had to point to the object named in the test sentence. (The test sentences included two adjectives plus a noun, but since all the objects were red, only the first adjective plus the noun had to be attended to.)

Examples:

$$\text{Point to the } \begin{Bmatrix} \text{big} \\ \text{little} \end{Bmatrix} \begin{Bmatrix} \text{circle} \\ \text{triangle} \\ \text{square} \end{Bmatrix}.$$

Results: The results of these tests are given in Tables 8.1 and 8.2 [3] (p. 104).

TABLE 8.1
Responses on Simple Modification Test, November 1971–May 1972

	Circle	Square	Triangle	Big	Little	Medium
Circle	33	0	0			
Square	0	33	0			
Triangle	0	0	34			
Big				50	0	0
Little					26	25

Genie's performance on this test was interesting. At first I thought she was making numerous errors. When I reviewed my notes, I noticed that many of what I had considered to be errors turned out to be consistent responses in which Genie interpreted "little" as a term indicating some absolute size rather than a relative size, and the absolute referent was correspondent to the size of the middle-sized objects in the array before her. I reassessed her performance, and the results given above reflect the reassessed performance. By spring of 1972, I began to substitute the word *tiny* for *little*; for Genie, *tiny* corresponded to the smallest object in the array.

From spring 1972 on, Genie made no errors on this test, clearly demon-

---

[3] Each item occurred once in a session, so the chance of a response in one session influencing a response in another session is remote. Therefore, we can consider responses to be independent across sessions. Each sentence–picture, sentence–action, or sentence–object combination was a novel stimulus, unique within a session; thus unless Genie was test-wise, we can assume within session as well as across-session independence.

TABLE 8.2
Responses on Simple Modification Test[a], June 1972–July 1973

	Circle	Square	Triangle	Big	Little	Medium
Circle	24	0	0			
Square	0	24	0			
Triangle	0	0	24			
Big				36	0	0
Little				0	36	0

[a] $p < .001$ by the sign test, hypothesizing that only one parameter is being guessed. If more than one parameter is being guessed, the probability is far smaller.

strating the ability to process adjective + noun strings correctly. At that point a more complex modification task was introduced.

8.2.3. Complex Modification (Two Adjectives + Noun)[4]

Description: This test had the same format as the earlier version, but added yellow circles, triangles and squares, three different sizes of each, to the array. The entire array consisted of rows of red objects interspersed with rows of yellow objects, with each row randomly placed as before with respect to object size. Genie, again, had to point to the object named.

Examples:

$$\text{Point to the } \begin{Bmatrix} \text{little} \\ \text{big} \end{Bmatrix} \begin{Bmatrix} \text{red} \\ \text{yellow} \end{Bmatrix} \begin{Bmatrix} \text{circle} \\ \text{triangle} \\ \text{square} \end{Bmatrix}.$$

Results: Results are given in Table 8.3.

8.2.4. Prepositions in, on, under

Description: Using a dish, a button, a pencil, and two glasses (one turned upside down), Genie had to manipulate the objects according to the directions in the test sentences.

---

[4] Each item occurred once in a session, so the chance of a response in one session influencing a response in another session is remote. Therefore, we can consider responses to be independent across sessions. Each sentence–picture, sentence–action, or sentence–object combination was a novel stimulus, unique within a session; thus unless Genie was test-wise, we can assume within session as well as across-session independence.

TABLE 8.3

Responses on Complex Modification Test, August 1973–June 1974[a]

	Circle	Square	Triangle	Big	Little	Red	Yellow
Circle	35	0	1				
Square	1	35	0				
Triangle	0	2	34				
Big				54	0		
Little				0	54		
Red						54	0
Yellow						0	54

[a] $p < .01$ by the sign test, hypothesizing that only one of our three parameters is being guessed. If more than one is being guessed, p = far less.

Examples: Put the button on the glass.
Put the button under the dish.
Put the pencil in the glass.

Results:[5] Results are given in Table 8.4.

TABLE 8.4

Responses on in, on, under Test; November 1971–March 1973

	In	On	Under	Unclassifiable[a]
In	40	7	4	1
On	9	25	11	8
Under	0	12	33	7

[a] Unclassifiable response:
Tester: *Put the button under the dish.*
Genie placed the dish on the glass.

The objects used on this test, upon later consideration, proved to present certain difficulties: (1) Their inherent physical features limited the range of possible relationships they could bear to other objects (a glass cannot go *in* a button, etc.); (2) Their real-life functions suggested certain responses, e.g., a glass, which is normally a container, would cue Genie to place things *in* it.

---

[5] Since response possibilities cannot be defined, and since there appears to be an early developmental bias toward *in* responses, no statistical tests were run.

Such factors may have affected Genie's performance on this test. For example, with the upside-down glass, Genie either put something *on* it or placed the glass over something, in neither case turning the glass over. It appears, therefore, that once Genie selected certain objects on this test, her range of responses was biased by the strategies she selected. In addition, the physical properties and normal functions of the objects may have been the principal factors as to why she never gave *next to*, *in front of*, or *behind* responses to any of these prepositions.

This test was discontinued and a new preposition test overcoming the shortcomings of this one was substituted (see Section 8.2.6).

8.2.5.   Prepositions Behind, In Front of, Beside, Next to[6]

Description: A set of three pictures in which a house and a tree appeared in different relationships to each other was presented. Genie had to point to the appropriate picture.

Examples: Show me the house that is *next to* the tree.
              Show me the house that is *behind* the tree.

Results: Results are shown in Table 8.5.

TABLE 8.5
Responses on behind, in front of, beside, next to Test[a], November 1971–August 1973

	Behind	In front of	Next to	Beside
Behind	15	19	0	0
In front of	22	14	0	0
Next to	0	0	4	0
Beside	0	0	0	31

[a]Comparing expected and observed frequencies by χ^2, her performance on the prepositions involved is as follows:
behind, not significant, $p > .05$;   *next to*, significant, $p < .005$;
in front, not significant, $p > .05$;   *beside*, significant, $p < .001$.

On the *behind, in front of* test we made the mistake of using pictures with

---

[6] Each item occurred once in a session, so the chance of a response in one session influencing a response in another session is remote. Therefore, we can consider responses to be independent across sessions. Each sentence–picture, sentence–action, or sentence–object combination was a novel stimulus, unique within a session; thus unless Genie was test-wise, we can assume within session as well as across-session independence.

a house—an object which has an obvious side, front, and back, thus providing nonlinguistic cues in the test. It is interesting, however, that Genie did not appear to make use of these cues in responding to the test items (note her poor performance on *behind* and *in front*.on this test). Despite the presence of the house in the pictures she confused *behind* and *in front*, although it is possible that her confusion reflected subject–verb–object (SVO) word order reversals (see discussion of word-order comprehension, Section 8.2.18) rather than confusion of the prepositions. In any case, we realized that we needed a preposition test free of extralinguistic cues and discontinued the use of this test.

8.2.6. General Preposition Test[7]

Description: Five plastic nesting cubes, each a different color, were placed on a table—some with the open side up, some with the opening facing the table, some with the opening to the side. Genie had to manipulate the cubes according to the test sentences.

Examples:

$$\text{Put the blue box} \left\{ \begin{array}{l} \text{in} \\ \text{on} \\ \text{next to} \\ \text{behind} \\ \text{in front of} \\ \text{under} \end{array} \right\} \text{the white box.}$$

Results: The results are listed in Tables 8.6 and 8.7 (see p. 108).

This preposition test, administered for the first time in September 1973, used objects entirely neutral with regard to front, back, side, even top or bottom. All of the prepositions tested on the original two tests plus *over* and *in back of* were tested in this new test, in random order. Because the cubes themselves failed to cue one particular response over any other, Genie's responses could reflect her knowledge of the prepositional terms involved. In summary, Genie's comprehension of English locative prepositions appears to be as follows:

(1) *In:* Genie's performance shows consistent, clear comprehension of *in* starting with September 1973.

(2) *On:* Before September 1973, her test performance suggested doubtful comprehension of this term (only 48%), with most incorrect interpretations consisting of *in* or *under* responses. Since after August 1973 there was such a striking change in test performance in response to *on* test items (from 48% to

---

[7] Each item occurred once in a session, so the chance of a response in one session influencing a response in another session is remote. Therefore, we can consider responses to be independent across sessions. Each sentence–picture, sentence–action, or sentence–object combination was a novel stimulus, unique within a session; thus unless Genie was test-wise, we can assume within session as well as across-session independence.

TABLE 8.6
Responses on General Prepositions Test, September 1973–June 1975[a]

	In	On	Under	Over	Front	Back	Next to
In	88	2	0	0	0	0	0
On	5	50	0	0	0	0	0
Under	0	0	26	38	0	0	0
Over	0	0	11	29	0	0	0
In front of	0	0	0	0	26	9	0
In back of	0	0	0	0	12	33	0
Behind	0	0	0	0	15	31	0
Next to	0	0	0	0	0	0	15
Beside	0	0	0	0	0	0	40

[a] Assuming eight possible responses, all equal in probability, by χ^2: *in*, $p < .001$; *on*, $p < .001$; *under*, $p < .01$; *under*, $p < .001$; *over*, $p < .001$; *front*, $p < .01$; *back*, $p < .01$; *behind*, $p < .01$; *next to*, $p < .001$; *beside*, $p < .001$. All results were significant.

TABLE 8.7
Percentage Correct for Each Preposition, September 1973–June 1975

Preposition	Percentage correct
In	97.7
On	90.0
Next to	100.0
Beside	100.0
Under	40.6
In front of	74.2
Between	100.0
Over (9/73 – 1/74)	55.0
Over (2/74 – 6/75)	90.0
In back of (9/73 – 2/74)	69.2
In back of (3/74 – 6/75)	79.4
Behind (9/73 – 2/74)	55.0
Behind (3/74 – 6/75)	76.9

90% correct) her earlier performance may have reflected a problem with the test being used, rather than a lack of comprehension. In any case, since September 1973 there has been complete comprehension of *on* as measured by this test.

(3) *Next to* and *beside:* Since the beginning of testing, there has been 100% comprehension of both of these terms.

(4) *Under:* Analysis of her errors shows that before September 1973, *under* was misinterpreted as *on* and *over*, and often elicited a confused response; whereas after September 1973, *under* was misinterpreted only as *over* (in the sense of *cover*). Such a change in interpretation indicates a possible growth in comprehension of the word *under* despite the test results; for this new consistent misinterpretation reveals that Genie now knows that *under* includes some sense of 'adjacent on a vertical plane' just as *over* does, and thus she now comprehends a relationship between the two terms based on their spatial meaning. Another way of stating this is that since September 1973 Genie has learned that *under* and *over* are related terms (on the same continuum of verticality), but has not yet differentiated *under* from *over*. We might say that at present *under* is under-differentiated in its semantic feature representation.

(5) *Over:* Unlike *under*, test performance with *over* shows clear growth in comprehension.[8] Interestingly, *over* was not tested until September 1973, and incorrect responses consisted entirely of *under* responses. We see again that from September 1973 on Genie had begun to relate these two terms.

(6) *In front of:* Here, too, there has been clear growth in comprehension (44.1% to 74.2%). Perhaps as a by-product of the way *in front of* had been tested on the early preposition test, the only incorrect response-type has been a *behind* response. Whether the relationship between *in front of* and *behind* is one that Genie picked up on her own or one that resulted from early testing, we cannot determine. But her test behavior shows clearly that Genie relates these terms semantically now. Her incorrect responses reflect a tendency to respond using her own body as a reference, a normal developmental strategy.

(7) *In back of* and *behind:* Test performance with both of these terms shows a decided increase in correct interpretation. It is interesting to compare performance with these two terms. *In back of* is semantically more transparent; i.e., the form of the word itself gives a clue to its meaning. *Behind*, although it means the same thing, gives no such cue. This extra bit of semantic information seemed to make a difference in Genie's comprehension of the two terms: from September 1973 through February 1974 she responded correctly to *behind* only 55% of the time; during that same period, correct responses to *in back of* totaled 69.2%. Since that time, Genie appears to have learned that these two terms are semantically identical. She makes the same response errors with both at about the same frequency (20.6% errors for *in back of*, 23.1% errors with

---

[8] By "growth in comprehension" I mean increasingly correct interpretation.

behind). In summary, although both *behind* and *in back of* have always elicited only one form of misinterpretation (as *in front of*), the term *behind* has seen the most growth in comprehension (from 38.8% to 76.9%) while the term *in back of* has seen the most consistent differentiation from *in front of*.

Looking at Genie's comprehension of *in front of* and *behind* together, we find that Genie did not learn one term first and then consistently interpret both as that term, as Clark's Semantic Feature Hypothesis (1973) would predict. Still in the process of acquiring these terms, Genie appears to be learning them simultaneously and, furthermore, knows that they are opposites on an axis. Although in conflict with Clark's predictions, this comprehension pattern is consistent with normal development of at least some children (Parisi & Antinucci, 1970; Kuczaj & Maratsos, 1975). Regardless of which developmental strategy a child exemplifies, all appear to pass through an earlier stage in the acquisition of *front* and *back* in which they are not able to respond correctly with non-fronted objects, but are able to correctly identify the fronts and backs of fronted objects. Genie can do this, as well, as evidenced by her performance on the Relational Terms Test (see Test Number 22, this chapter).

(8) *Between:*   At the time of this writing, I have just started to test comprehension of *between*. To date, it appears that Genie fully comprehends this preposition.[9]

8.2.7. Singular/Plural[10]

Description: Pairs of pictures—a single object on one member of the pair, three of the same objects on the other—were placed before Genie. Genie was asked to point to the appropriate picture. The test sentences differed only by the presence or absence of the plural marker. All three regular morphophonemic plural markers were tested.

Examples:

$$\text{Point to the} \begin{Bmatrix} \text{balloon} \\ \text{balloons} \end{Bmatrix}.$$

$$\text{Point to the} \begin{Bmatrix} \text{carrot} \\ \text{carrots} \end{Bmatrix}.$$

---

[9] Since the time of writing, Genie's comprehension of *between* has been tested on several occasions. On each of these, Genie has demonstrated full comprehension of this term.

[10] Each item occurred once in a session, so the chance of a response in one session influencing a response in another session is remote. Therefore, we can consider responses to be independent across sessions. Each sentence–picture, sentence–action, or sentence–object combination was a novel stimulus, unique within a session; thus unless Genie was test-wise, we can assume within session as well as across-session independence.

$$\text{Point to the } \begin{Bmatrix} \text{dish} \\ \text{dishes} \end{Bmatrix}.$$

Results: Results are listed in Tables 8.8 and 8.9.

TABLE 8.8
Responses on Singular/Plural Test, October 1971–July 1972

	Plural	Singular
Plural	40	37
Singular	37	40

TABLE 8.9
Responses on Singular/Plural Test[a], August 1972–November 1974

	Plural	Singular
Plural	184	0
Singular	0	185

[a]Comparing expected and observed frequencies by χ^2, the probability that Genie's performance could have occurred by chance (taking into account the number of response possibilities available to her) is less than .001. This is a statistically significant result.

It was obvious after 9 months of testing that Genie did not know the meaning of the plural marker on nouns. Stepping out of my normal role of linguistic observer, I decided to intervene and attempted to teach her this particular element of English morphology. Using the pictures from the test, their written counterparts printed on index cards, a big red "S," and the numbers 1, 2, and 3, I set about in July 1972 to teach Genie the English plural rule (in crude form to be sure). By matching the test pictures to strings of cards (such as: *1 dish*; *2 dish + S*; etc.) at first using numbers, later omitting the numbers, I taught Genie the rule: "If there's more than one, you need an S." With each example, I pronounced the plural form, demonstrating the different morphophonemic forms. (See Curtiss, Fromkin, Krashen, Rigler & Rigler 1974 for a more elaborate description of this event.) She clearly learned the rule, and since that time has comprehended the singular/plural distinction as marked on nouns, regardless of morphophonemic variation. (After August 1973 the test I had been using was lengthened substantially. Genie's performance did not change, however.)

8.2.8. Conjunction/Disjunction

Description: Five objects were set in a row before her. Genie was to follow the directions as stated in the test sentences.

Examples: Point to the spoon and the pencil.
Point to the spoon or the pencil.
Point to either the spoon or the watch.

Results: Results are listed in Table 8.10.

TABLE 8.10
Responses on Conjunction/Disjunction Test, October 1971–June 1975

	Correct	Incorrect	Percentage correct
and	145	0	100.0
or	7	71	8.9

This tests only tests disjunction. In order to respond correctly to the conjunction items, one need only know the nouns mentioned. Regarding disjunction, Genie's performance demonstrates a lack of comprehension of *or* and *either/or*. Genie does not know what *or* means, yet she appears to know that it does not mean the same thing as *and*. In response to a test sentence with *or*, Genie hesitates, looks at me for a cue and demonstrates by facial expression as well, that she knows that *or* doesn't mean *and*, but she doesn't know what to do in response. She has tried some rather ingenious but unanalyzable responses—responses that are not *and* or *or* responses—perhaps in attempts to express her frustration at not knowing what *or* means. This pattern of uncertainty, hesitation, and frustration has been present almost since this test was first administered.

8.2.9.   Possessive Pronouns

Description: A picture of a boy and a girl was shown to Genie. She had to point in response to the test sentences, sometimes to items on the picture, sometimes to herself or the tester or both.

Examples: Point to his hand.
Point to your mouth.
Point to our mouths.

Results: Results are given in Table 8.11.

TABLE 8.11
Responses to Possessive Pronouns Test, October 1973–June 1975

	Correct	Incorrect	Percentage correct
his	13	11	54.1
her	25	13	65.8
their	0	36	0.0
our	0	22	0.0
my	17	11	60.0
your	11	14	44.0
Total	66	117	32.4

The only possessive pronouns that Genie appears to comprehend at all on this test are *my* and *her*, but she continues to make a sufficient number of errors to indicate that she has not yet completely mastered the meaning of these pronouns. Moreover, it appears that the percentage of correct responses to *her* is at least partly attributable to her focus on the picture before her (where she had a 50% chance of guessing correctly). When the test began with a sentence containing *my* or *your*, and her attention was from the first focused away from the picture, she made more errors on *her* items, and tended to interpret *her* as *my* or *your*, rather than *he*, which was her usual substitution otherwise. Her lack of comprehension of the object pronoun *her* is revealed in the pronoun test (see Test Number 17, this chapter).

8.2.10. Comparative[11]

Description: Two white buttons, only slightly different in size, and two strips of paper with only a small difference in length were presented. Genie had to point to the appropriate item.

Examples:

$$\text{Which button is} \begin{Bmatrix} \text{smaller} \\ \text{bigger} \end{Bmatrix} ?$$

$$\text{Which paper is} \begin{Bmatrix} \text{longer} \\ \text{shorter} \end{Bmatrix} ?$$

Results (January 1972—March 1973):   Correct, 20; Incorrect, 0; Percentage Correct, 100%.[12]

8.2.11. Superlative I

Description: Five white buttons, all small and similar in size, and three strips of paper, all the same width, each varying approximately one-half inch in length from the next in size, were presented. Genie had to point to the appropriate object.

Examples:

$$\text{Point to the} \begin{Bmatrix} \text{smallest} \\ \text{biggest} \end{Bmatrix} \text{button.}$$

$$\text{Point to the} \begin{Bmatrix} \text{shortest} \\ \text{longest} \end{Bmatrix} \text{paper.}$$

Results: Results are shown in Table 8.12.

In contrast to the comparative marker, the superlative marker appears to have been a linguistic feature that Genie still did not completely understand by the end of the second year.

[11] Each item occurred once in a session, so the chance of a response in one session influencing a response in another session is remote. Therefore, we can consider responses to be independent across sessions. Each sentence–picture, sentence–action, or sentence–object combination was a novel stimulus, unique within a session; thus unless Genie was test-wise, we can assume within session as well as across-session independence.

[12] Comparing expected and observed frequencies by χ^2, the probability that Genie's performance could have occurred by chance is less than .005.

TABLE 8.12
Responses on Superlative Test

Date	Correct	Incorrect	Percentage correct
11/71 – 1/72	14	6	70.0
8/72 – 12/72	11	2	84.6

8.2.12. Superlative II[13]

Description: The same array of objects as used in the Modification Test above was presented. Genie had to point to the appropriate object.

Examples:

$$\text{Point to the} \begin{Bmatrix} \text{littlest} \\ \text{biggest} \end{Bmatrix} \text{red} \begin{Bmatrix} \text{circle} \\ \text{triangle} \\ \text{square} \end{Bmatrix}.$$

Results (December 1972—December 1973):   Correct, 84; Incorrect, 0; Percentage Correct, 100%.[14]

Because Genie consistently chose the medium-sized objects in response to the word *little* in the Simple Modification Test, I decided to use the same test arrangement and test the difference between her responses to *little* and *littlest*. The results seemed to show that Genie knew the meaning of *-est*, but these results must be compared with the test which is discussed below.

8.2.13. Comparative and Superlative[13]

Description: Seven circles, each a different size, were lined up in unseriated order on a piece of colored paper. I pointed to a circle (never

[13] Each item occurred once in a session, so the chance of a response in one session influencing a response in another session is remote. Therefore, we can consider responses to be independent across sessions. Each sentence–picture, sentence–action, or sentence–object combination was a novel stimulus, unique within a session; thus unless Genie was test-wise, we can assume within session as well as across-session independence.

[14] Comparing expected and observed frequencies by χ^2, the probability that Genie's performance could have occurred by chance (taking into account the number of response possibilities available to her) is less than 0.001. This is a statistically significant result.

the largest or the smallest). I told Genie: *Point to one that is bigger/littler.* In the case of the superlative, Genie was asked, *Point to the biggest/littlest circle.*

Results: See Table 8.13.

TABLE 8.13
Responses on the Comparative and Superlative Test October 1973–June 1975

	Correct	Incorrect	Percentage correct
Comparative	33	0	100^a
Superlative	10	2	85

^{a}Comparing expected and observed frequencies by χ^2, the probability that Genie's performance could have occurred by chance (taking into account the number of response possibilities available to her) is less than .001. This is a statistically significant result.

It is clear that Genie comprehends the comparative marker, but as with earlier testing of the superlative, it appears that Genie had not fully mastered the meaning and function of the morpheme *-est*. Perhaps the previous test array helped her to avoid errors, since the biggest circle, square, or triangle, was the size she would have pointed to even without the superlative ending in response to *big*, thus eliminating half of the possible errors.

8.2.14.   Tense/Aspect

Description: Six picture sets, three pictures in a set, were presented to Genie. Each picture set depicted an action sequence familiar to Genie. The task was to point to the picture described by the test sentence. The test sentences varied only in the tense and/or aspect marked on the verb phrase. Comprehension of the following was tested: past irregular, past regular, present progressive (*be + ing*), future with *will*, Future with *going to/gonna, finish + VP.*[15]

Examples: The girl will open the umbrella (future).

[15] Noting that children learning American Sign Language acquired completive aspect far earlier than children who were learning English marked past tense (Fisher, 1973), and noting that Genie did not appear to comprehend past tense, I added items which marked the verb phrases with the verb "finish" to determine if Genie comprehended the semantics of past completive action.

The girl opened the umbrella (past).
The girl is opening the umbrella (present progressive).
The girl is going to open the umbrella (future).
The girl finished opening the umbrella. (past completive).

Results: Results are listed in Tables 8.14 and 8.15.

TABLE 8.14
Responses on Tense/Aspect Test, October 1973–January 1974

	Correct	Incorrect	Percentage correct
Future with *will*	4	5	44.0
Future with *going to*	17	1	94.4
Progressive	10	8	55.5
Past regular	3	8	27.0
Past irregular	6	1	85.7

TABLE 8.15
Responses on Tense/Aspect Test[a], February 1974–June 1975

	Correct	Incorrect	Percentage correct
Future with *will*	26	31	45.6
Future with *going to*	26	32	44.8
Progressive	30	30	50.0
Past regular	24	29	45.0
Past irregular	12	4	75.0
finish + VP	59	1	98.3[b]

[a]Each item occurred once in a session, so the chance of a response in one session influencing a response in another session is remote. Therefore, we can consider responses to be independent across sessions. Each sentence–picture, sentence–action, or sentence–object combination was a novel stimulus, unique within a session; thus unless Genie was test-wise, we can assume within session as well as across-session independence.

[b]Comparing expected and observed frequencies by χ^2, the probability that Genie's performance could have occurred by chance (taking into account the number of response possibilities available to her) is less than .001. This is a statistically significant result.

There are a few surprising results. First, in early testing it appeared that Genie understood *going to/gonna* (94% correct responses), but later testing showed little, if any, comprehension of this aspect marker. It seems unlikely that Genie would at one time have understood *going on* and then lost her comprehension of it. Yet the possibility that she could have performed so well on *going to* items (in three different test sessions) without comprehension is remote. The striking change in performance is but one example of the "waxing and waning" ability that has marked Genie's linguistic behavior throughout the $4\frac{1}{2}$ years of observation. Second, her far superior performance on irregular past tense items (*blew*, *lit*) compared to regular past tense items (*opened*, *tied*, *poured*, *brushed*) is somewhat unexpected, since the regular past tense verbs used here are more common and also since regular past tense appears to be comprehended earlier in normals than irregular past (Carrow, 1968b; Curtiss, fieldtesting). Perhaps the clear phonological contrast between the present and past forms of the irregular verbs ([blo^w] versus [blu^w], [lʌ^{j}t] versus [lɪt]) provides a sufficiently more salient cue to promote comprehension of these irregular forms.

The third interesting result is Genie's comprehension of past marked by *finish* in contrast to her noncomprehension of the regular past tense marker. Genie clearly has the semantic notion of past; she just does not know its morphological reflex. This is in keeping with Fisher's (1973) finding and with my own finding from work in progress in collecting normative data on this test. Many normal children who do not yet comprehend either regular or irregular past tense morphology, perform perfectly on the *finish* items on this test. Moreover, comprehension of *finish* + VP appears to be the earliest tense/aspect "marker" to develop receptively (Curtiss, fieldtesting; Fisher, 1973). When children fail in all of the other test items, they still often succeed on the *finish* items. This is shown to be the case with Genie.

The results show no other understanding of tense or aspect.

8.2.15. Before/After

Description: The test consists of ten two-part commands to touch parts of her body.

Examples: Touch your nose *before* you touch your ear.
Before you touch your pinky, touch your ear.
After you touch your eye, touch your chin.
Touch your nose *after* you touch your cheek.

Results:[16]   Table 8.16 shows the results of this test.

----

[16] Each item occurred once in a session, so the chance of a response in one session influencing a response in another session is remote. Therefore, we can consider responses to be independent across sessions. Each sentence–picture, sentence–action, or sentence–object combination was a novel stimulus, unique within a session; thus unless Genie was test-wise, we can assume within session as well as across-session independence.

Before$_1$ = Touch your X *before* you touch Y.
Before$_2$ = *Before* you touch X, touch Y.
After$_1$ = *After* you touch X, touch Y.
After$_2$ = Touch X *after* you touch Y.

TABLE 8.16
Responses on Before/After Test[a], October 1973–June 1975

	Correct	Incorrect	Percentage correct
Before$_1$	44	4	91.6
Before$_2$	3	32	8.5
After$_1$	30	1	96.8
After$_2$	39	9	81.0

[a]Comparing expected and observed frequencies by χ^2, the probability that Genie's performance could have occurred by chance (taking into account the number of response possibilities available to her) is less than .001. This is a statistically significant result.

As Bever (1970) and Clark (1971) have found with normal individuals, Genie comprehends sentences in which the clauses follow the temporal order of events more easily than sentences where the clauses occur in an order opposite to the order of events. Inconsistent with Clark's hypothesis regarding the order of acquisition of these two terms, however, Genie has learned the full range of meaning for *after* prior to *before*. This is not inconsistent with all normative data, however, as Coker (1975) found that normal children may learn either first. Unlike normal children, Genie understood these terms and structures (except for Before$_2$) before she learned future or past-tense markings. This uneven linguistic knowledge is characteristic of much of Genie's language, rich semantic comprehension and/or production as opposed to impoverished syntactic and morphological comprehension and/or production.

8.2.16. Some, One, All

Description: Plastic circles (five), triangles (eight), and squares (five) were placed on a table; also on the table were a box and a dish. Genie had to follow the instructions in the test sentences.

Examples:

$$\text{Put} \begin{Bmatrix} \text{some} \\ \text{all} \\ \text{one} \end{Bmatrix} \text{of the} \begin{Bmatrix} \text{triangles} \\ \text{circles} \\ \text{squares} \end{Bmatrix} \begin{Bmatrix} \text{in the dish} \\ \text{in the box} \\ \text{on the table} \end{Bmatrix}.$$

Results:[17]   Results are shown in Table 8.17.

TABLE 8.17
Responses on Some, One, All Test, October 1973–June 1975

	Some	One	All
Some	5	6	9
One[a]	1	19	0
All[a]	0	0	20

[a]Comparing expected and observed frequencies by χ^2, the probability that Genie's performance could have occurred by chance (taking into account the number of response possibilities available to her) is less than .001. This is a statistically significant result.

Genie clearly comprehends *all* and *one*. Her comprehension of *some* is changing. At first, her incorrect response to *some* was to interpret it to mean *all*. After a few months of testing (around January 1974), Genie began to interpret *some* as *one* which in some sense is a more correct interpretation than is *all*. (*Some* can be said to include the features [−none, +more than one, +part of the total]. *All* contains only one of these features, whereas *one* includes two of the three.) This new interpretation has only recently become the consistent response to *some* items. It appears then that Genie is still in the process of learning the meaning of the quantifier *some*, and is progressing closer to its adult interpretation.

8.2.17. Pronouns

Description: Pictures of children eating or being fed by other children

---

[17] Each item occurred once in a session, so the chance of a response in one session influencing a response in another session is remote. Therefore, we can consider responses to be independent across sessions. Each sentence–picture, sentence–action, or sentence–object combination was a novel stimulus, unique within a session; thus unless Genie was test-wise, we can assume within session as well as across-session independence.

were presented. Genie had to point to the appropriate picture in response to the test sentence.

Examples: Show me, "He is feeding him."
Show me, "He is feeding himself."
Show me, "He is feeding her."
Show me, "The boy is feeding him."

Results: From July 1972 to Steptember 1973, Genie would often not respond at all, except to the sentences containing only nouns. The data shown in Tables 8.18–8.21 (pp. 121–124) represent only those instances when she responded, about 50% of the time, until September, 1973.

TABLE 8.18
Percentage Correct on Pronoun Test, September 1972–January 1974

Pronoun	Percentage correct
he	62.80
she	44.40
they	90.00
him	45.80
her	41.67
each other	100.00
himself	37.50
herself	50.00
themselves	100.00
self in general	75.00

Genie had great difficulty with this test, more so than with any other. At first, she refused to take it, and for almost a year after the test was first administered, the test caused her great frustration. Many times she simply did not respond at all to the test items. When she did respond, it was clear by her behavior that she was guessing. Later test results (from 1973 on) indicated that Genie clearly comprehends *each other* and *self/selves*. She does not, however, comprehend pronoun gender or number. Thus, her frequent errors with reflexive pronouns are actually errors in interpreting the subject and/or object pronouns involved (i.e., to interpret *she is feeding herself* correctly, both *she* and *her* of *herself* must be understood.) In addition, her apparent comprehension of *they* is probably a reflection of the fact that *they* always appeared with a reflexive or

TABLE 8.19

Percentage Correct on Pronouns Test, March 1974–June 1975

	He	She	They	Him	Her	Himself	Herself	Themselves	Each other
he	22	11	2	0	0	0	0	0	0
she	8	8	2	0	0	0	0	0	0
they	0	1	9	0	0	0	0	0	0
him	0	0	0	11	8	3	1	0	0
her	0	0	0	7	5	0	0	0	0
himself	0	0	0	3	1	3	1	0	0
herself	0	0	0	0	0	0	1	1	0
themselves	0	0	0	0	0	0	0	6	0
each other	0	0	0	0	0	0	0	0	9

TABLE 8.20
Responses on Pronouns Test, September 1972–January 1974

Pronoun	Percentage correct
he	72.5
she	34.6
they	84.0
him	52.9
her	18.0
himself	64.7
herself	64.7
themselves	62.5
each other	100.0
self in general	92.0

reciprocal object, and therefore only the plurality of the object need be attended to.

8.2.18. Active Voice Word Order

8.2.18.1. Active versus Passive

Description: A set of pictures was presented.

$$\left\{ \begin{array}{l} \text{boy} \\ \text{girl} \\ \text{both} \end{array} \right\} \text{pulling} \left\{ \begin{array}{l} \text{girl} \\ \text{boy} \\ \text{wagon} \end{array} \right\}$$

Genie had to point to the appropriate picture. Both simple present and present progressive verb phrases were used.

Examples: Point to: "The boy pulls the girl."
Point to, "The boy is pulled by the girl."

Results: See Table 8.22 (p. 124).

TABLE 8.21
Responses on Pronouns Test, March 1974–June 1975

	He	She	They	Him	Her	Himself	Herself	Themselves
he	29	11	0	0	0	0	0	0
she	17	9	0	0	0	0	0	0
they	3	0	16	0	0	0	0	0
him	0	0	0	9	3	3	2	0
her	0	0	0	5	2	2	2	0
himself	0	0	0	1	2	11	3	0
herself	0	0	0	0	0	6	11	0
themselves	0	0	0	1	0	4	1	10

TABLE 8.22
Results of the Active/Passive Word Order Test October 1971–October 1972

Voice	Correct	Incorrect	Percentage correct	Reversals
Active	18	24	42.9	19
Passive	20	22	47.6	11

As can be seen in Table 8.22, Genie was not responding correctly to either active or passive word order. The major difference between her performance on active sentences as opposed to passive sentences, was that the majority of incorrect responses to active sentences were subject/object reversals (79%) whereas only half the errors on passive sentences were reversals of the noun phrases. The other errors were responses in which NP_1 and NP_2 were interpreted as a compound noun phrase subject. Since the passive construction is used infrequently (especially around Genie, with whom people tend to simplify their speech), and since Genie showed no consistency in processing the more frequent S–V–O active voice word order, I stopped administering the passive test items and presented an elaborated version of the test, testing active voice word order only.

8.2.18.2. Active Word Order

Description: A second picture set was added.

$$\left\{ \begin{array}{l} \text{a girl} \\ \text{a boy} \\ \text{both} \end{array} \right\} \text{pulling} \left\{ \begin{array}{l} \text{girl's hair} \\ \text{boy's hair} \\ \text{own hair} \end{array} \right\}$$

Again, Genie had to point to the appropriate picture.

Examples: Point to, "The boy is pulling the boy's hair."
Point to, "The boy is pulling the girl's hair."
Point to, "The boy and girl are pulling their own hair."

Results: See Tables 8.23 and 8.24.

TABLE 8.23
Results on the Active Voice Word Order Test, October 1972–December 1973

Type	Correct	Incorrect	Percentage correct	Reversals
Reversible Actives	18	16	52.9	9
Nonreversibles				
(compound subject)	8	7	53.3	

TABLE 8.24
Results on the Active voice Word Order Test, January 1974–June 1975

Type	Correct	Incorrect	Percentage correct	Reversals
Reversible actives	29	10	74.3	4

As before, Genie did not clearly process S–V–O word order correctly. There was change in her performance with these sentences, however. Prior to January 1974, she missed about half the test items; and the majority of incorrect responses were subject/object reversals. After January 1974, an even greater improvement in test performance was shown: In 74% of the cases, Genie processed S–V–O word order correctly.

Her performance on this test, although improved over time, remains a puzzling phenomenon. First of all, it stands in marked contrast to her use of consistent word order to mark grammatical/semantic NP function in her own production (throughout the entire period that this test has been administered). (See Chapter 9 for a discussion of her use of word order.) Second, it stands in marked contrast to her performance on the Pronouns Test which includes sentences using only nouns, which are, then, reversible actives. (These sentences served as a check to ensure that the test pictures did not serve as the source of error and were also included to "monitor" her attention, as well as to provide a standard of comparison for noun versus pronoun performance.) On such sentences, e.g., "The boy is feeding the girl" and "The girl is feeding the boy," from September 1972, to June 1975, there was only one reversal response (one out of forty-six), and S–V–O word order was apparently processed correctly on all the others. Third, her performance on this test would predict that she would be largely unable to deal with complex sentences with potentially reversible noun phrases, and such is not the case (see Section 8.2.20).

Another test which requires strict word-order processing of reversible NPs is the preposition test (e.g., Put the yellow box in the white box.). It is possible that word-order confusion has contributed to her errors on this test. In other words, it is possible that the reason she fails at times to put X behind Y and instead puts Y behind X is because she has incorrectly interpreted the order relation between X and Y as opposed to the prepositional relationship between the two. However, it seems unlikely that she would confuse order only on sentences with certain prepositions and never on sentences with other prepositions. Since she never makes errors with *in, next to, beside, between,* and *over,* and almost never with *on,* it is highly unlikely that her performance with locative prepositions reflects anything other than her knowledge of these terms. There is one other test which requires S–V–O word-order processing involving reverssible NPs: WH-questioning of subject versus object.

8.2.19. WH-Questioning of Subject Versus Object

Description: Four boxes, two of the same color were placed as follows:

yellow	blue
blue	green

Genie had to answer the questions asked of her.

Examples: What is on blue?
                        What is blue on?

Results: See Table 8.25.

TABLE 8.25
Results of the WH-Questioning of Subject versus Object Test, May 1973–May 1975

	Correct	Incorrect	Percentage correct
Subject questioned	13	5	72.2
Object questioned	9	9	50.0
Total	22	14	61.0

(All of the incorrect responses here are, of course, reversals.) The differential performance between questioning of the subject as opposed to questioning of the object indicates that Genie's performance on this test may not simply reflect her ability to deal with word order. Her performance may also reflect the fact that sentences involving no transformation of constituent word order in decoding are easier for her to comprehend than sentences involving word-order transformations. This is in keeping with the results of tests with normals, yet one which conflicts both with Genie's performance on the Active Voice Word Order Test and with her ability to comprehend and answer any Wh-question she is asked in real-life (if she knows the answer), regardless of whether the subject or object is being questioned (see Section 8.3).

These data taken together with the data from the Pronouns, Preposition, and Complex Sentence tests suggest that there may be a problem with the Active Voice Word Order Test which causes Genie special problems with that test alone, and, which, therefore, does not reflect her comprehension of word order constraints in English.

8.2.20. Complex Sentence Processing

Description: Two sets of pictures were used:

$$A \begin{Bmatrix} \text{girl} \\ \text{boy} \end{Bmatrix} \text{sitting,} \begin{Bmatrix} \text{facing} \\ \text{not facing} \end{Bmatrix} a \begin{Bmatrix} \text{boy} \\ \text{girl} \end{Bmatrix}.$$

$$A \begin{Bmatrix} \text{girl} \\ \text{boy} \end{Bmatrix} \begin{Bmatrix} \text{smiling} \\ \text{frowning} \end{Bmatrix} \begin{Bmatrix} \text{facing} \\ \text{not facing} \end{Bmatrix} a \begin{Bmatrix} \text{boy} \\ \text{girl} \end{Bmatrix}.$$

Genie had to point to the picture which corresponded to the test sentence.

Examples: The boy is looking at the girl who is frowning.
The girl who is sitting is looking at the boy.
The girl who is looking at the boy is sitting.

Results: (Some test items were repeated during administration.) See Tables 8.26 and 8.27.

TABLE 8.26
Results of the Complex Sentence Test, November 1973–April 1974

	Correct	Incorrect	Percentage correct
Subject relativized	23	8	74.0
Object relativized	18	11	62.0
Embedded clause ending in a noun directly followed by the VP of the matrix clause	8	3	72.7

The test sentences involve complex grammatical structures, and the test pictures involve a great deal of conceptual complexity. For example, the task involved in responding correctly to the sentence *The boy is looking at the girl who is frowning* involves making a choice from four pictures: (1) a similing boy looking at a frowning girl turned away from him, (2) a similing girl looking at a frowning boy who is looking back at her, (3) a frowning girl looking at a smiling boy turned away from her, and (4) a frowning boy and a smiling girl turned away from each other. Each child pictured is in the act of kicking a ball. Genie must not only decode the sentence, figuring out the relationship of the stated VPs to all of the stated NPs, etc., but must then store the complex structure and map the linguistic interrelationships in that structure to a correct pictorial representation of those relationships. Taking all of this into account, Genie's performance is remarkably good.

The only structure she cannot decode successfully is one in which the embedded clause ends in a noun followed directly by the VP of the main clause yielding a noun–verb sequence, which Genie consistently interprets as subject–verb. For example, the sentence: *The boy who is looking at the girl is sitting*, ends in the sequence *the girl is sitting*. Genie interprets this sentence to mean: *The*

TABLE 8.27
Results of the Complex Sentence Test[a], May 1974–July 1975

	Correct	Incorrect	Percentage correct
Subject relativized	37	6	86.0[b]
Object relativized	37	7	84.0[b]
Embedded clause ending in a noun directly followed by the VP of the matrix clause	1	21	4.5

[a]Each item occurred once in a session, so the chance of a response in one session influencing a response in another session is remote. Therefore, we can consider responses to be independent across sessions. Each sentence–picture, sentence–action, or sentence–object combination was a novel stimulus, unique within a session; thus unless Genie was test-wise, we can assume within session as well as across-session independence.

[b]Comparing expected and observed frequencies by χ^2, the probability that Genie's performance could have occurred by chance (taking into account the number of response possibilities available to her) is less than .05. This is a statistically significant result.

boy is looking at the girl and the girl is sitting (or, *The boy is looking at the girl who is sitting*).

This misinterpretation of such complex strings is one that is also found in normal language development (Bever, 1970; de Villiers & de Villiers, 1973). Children in the course of language acquisition appear to make use of a noun–verb strategy that influences them to interpret a noun–verb string (with no major intervening elements) as actor–action. This strategy in normals is presumably the source of the consistent misinterpretation of passives and of complex sentences of the type mentioned above. It is interesting then, and somewhat confusing, that Genie did not appear to use this strategy with passives. More confusing, however, is the fact that she does not appear to consistently use this strategy on simple active sentences. Since everywhere on the complex sentence test Genie makes use of the "noun–verb-as-actor–action" strategy, it would appear again that there are special problems with the simple Active Voice

Order Test which prevent her performance on that test from revealing her true comprehension.

8.2.21. Complex Negation

Description: Four pictures were presented to Genie: (1) a red book on a black table, (2) a red book on a black chair, (3) a blue book on a black table, and (4) a blue book on a black chair. Genie had to point to the picture corresponding to the test sentence.

Examples: The book that is red is not on the table.
The book that is not red is on the table.

Results: It was shown in Genie's performance on the simple negation test that she comprehended negation in simple sentences (see Table 8.28). Her performance on this test reveals comprehension of negation in complex sentences where one clause is negated and thus comprehension of the scope of negation. We have not yet tested her comprehension of negation in both clauses.

TABLE **8.28**
Results of the Complex Negation Test[a], October 1973–June 1975

	Correct	Incorrect	Percentage correct
Matrix clause negation	35	1	97.2[b]
Embedded clause negation	33	3	91.6[b]
Affirmative complex sentences	36	0	100.0[b]

[a]Each item occurred once in a session, so the chance of a response in one session influencing a response in another session is remote. Therefore we can consider responses to be independent across sessions. Each sentence–picture, sentence–action, or sentence–object combination was a novel stimulus, unique within a session; thus unless Genie was test-wise, we can assume within session as well as across-session independence.
[b]Comparing expected and observed frequencies by χ^2, the probability that Genie's performance could have occurred by chance (taking into account the number of response possibilities available to her) is less than .001. This is a statistically significant result.

8.2.22. Relative Terms

Description: Milton Bradley Space Relationship Cards were presented one at a time. Genie had to point to the appropriate figure on the card. Each card contained two figures representing opposites of a relationship.

Examples: Point to "high."
        Point to "wide."

Results: Results are listed in Table 8.29 (p. 132).

There are only two choices on each card, so with each item Genie had a 50% chance of responding correctly. In addition, some of the pictures are confusing and difficult to interpret. I therefore present these results with the consideration that they may not accurately reflect Genie's knowledge of these terms.

Taking these items in pairs we find that Genie understands both terms of most of them. There are no instances where she consistently interprets both members of a pair in the same way, i.e., as the "unmarked" or "positive" member as Clark (1973) hypothesized is the case in normal development. Others (Eilers, Oller, & Ellington, 1974; Parisi & Antinucci, 1970; Kuczaj & Maratsos, 1975) have found, however, that many children appear to learn both members of some relational pairs (locatives like *front* and *back*) simultaneously, and learn the "marked" or "negative" member of some pairs (such as *narrow, few,* and *short*) before their positive counterparts. Genie appears to fit this latter picture. On many of these pairs—*back/front, top/bottom, in/out, off/on, left/ right, big/little, tall/short, under/over, high/low, near/far, come/go*—she comprehends both members equally well. Genie's responses to pairs like *left/right* and *come/go*, where her performance has not reached 100% accuracy yet where she has performed identically on both terms, are especially convincing as evidence that she is learning these terms simultaneously. Her performance with other pairs (*high/low, thick/thin, far/near*) further coincides with normal acquisition patterns. On still other pairs, however, (*wide/narrow, on/off, here/there*) her performance is in the direction that Clark predicts, although on two of these pairs her performance was so low the differences may not be meaningful.

The cards with the most difficult pictures to interpret are those for *to/from, here/there, around/through,* and *come/go.* Her performance on these pairs, especially, may not reflect how well she actually understands these terms. See the Come Here–Go There Tests for comparison.

8.2.23. Come Here–Go There

(A.) *Description:* Two circles, both large enough for two people to stand in were drawn on the ground. An adult stood in one circle and told Genie to *Come here* or *Go there.*

TABLE 8.29
Results of the Relative Terms Test, December 1973–July 1975

Item	Correct	Incorrect	Percentage correct
1. back	12	0	100.00
front	12	0	100.00
2. top	12	0	100.00
bottom	12	0	100.00
3. wide	3	9	25.00
narrow	2	10	16.66
4. up	12	0	100.00
down	12	0	100.00
5. in	9	3	75.00
out	10	10	83.33
6. off	11	1	92.50
on	12	0	100.00
7. around	3	9	25.00
through	6	6	50.00
8. left	8	4	66.66
right	8	4	66.66
9. big	12	0	100.00
little	12	0	100.00
10. tall	12	0	100.00
short	12	0	100.00
11. under	7	5	58.33
over	8	4	66.66
12. high	11	1	92.50
low	12	0	100.00
13. near	10	2	83.33
far	11	1	92.50
14. thick	9	3	75.00
thin	12	0	100.00
15. to	11	1	92.50
from	7	5	58.33
16. come	9	3	75.00
go	9	3	75.00
17. here	7	5	58.33
there	4	8	33.33

Results: The results of the first Come Here–Go There Test from October 1973 to January 1975 are included in Table 8.30. In all but one instance, Genie went to the empty circle.

TABLE 8.30
Results of the First Come Here–Go There Test

Item	Correct	Incorrect
Come here	1	4
Go there	5	0

(B.)   *Description:*   Two circles were drawn in a row, several feet apart. An adult stood in each circle. Genie stood in the middle between the two circles. The adults in turn instructed Genie to *Come here* or *Go there*.

Results: Results of the second Come Here–Go There Test from October 1973 to January 1975 are included in Table 8.31 below. In each case, Genie joined the adult who had issued the instruction.

TABLE 8.31
Results of the Second Come Here–Go There Test

Item	Correct	Incorrect
Come here	14	0
Go there	0	16

(C.)   *Description:*   The same circles were drawn as in Test B. Genie was not in line with the circles. An adult stood in one circle; the remaining circle was empty. The adult in the circle told Genie to *Come here* or *Go there*.

Results: The results of the third Come Here–Go There Test, from October 1973 to January 1975, are included in Table 8.32. Genie came to the speaker each time.

TABLE 8.32
Results of the Third Come Here–Go There Test

Item	Correct	Incorrect
Come here	5	0
Go there	0	5

(D.)   *Description:*   The same circles as in Test B were drawn. No one was in the circles. An adult stood closer to one circle than the other. Genie stood several feet away, equidistant from the two circles. The adult said, "Come here" or "Go there."

Results: The results of the fourth Come Here–Go There Test, from October 1973 to January 1975, are included in Table 8.33. Genie went to the circle farthest from the speaker every time.

In each of these subtests, Genie seems to have adopted a strategy for responding, a strategy having little or nothing to do with her comprehension of

TABLE 8.33
Results of the Fourth Come Here–Go There Test

Item	Correct	Incorrect
Come here	0	5
Go there	5	0

"Come here" or "Go there." Her performance might, however, indicate real confusion of the two and a resultant lack of comprehension.

8.2.24.   More and Less

Description: Using plastic triangles, squares, and circles of different sizes, colors, and thicknesses, different combinations of sizes and numbers were put into each hand. Triangles were always matched against triangles, etc. Genie had to point to the hand containing "more" or "less," ignoring every dimension except number. For example, Genie was presented with six mixed triangles in the left hand versus three mixed triangles in the right hand and asked *Which hand has more? Which hand has less?*

Results: Results are given in Table 8.34.

8.2.25.   Many, Most, Few, Fewest

Description: Four pictures of apple trees were presented: (1) a tree with one apple, (2) a tree with two apples, (3) a tree with five apples, and (4) a tree with eight apples. Genie had to point to a picture corresponding to the test sentence.

Examples: Which tree has few apples?
                     Which tree has the most apples?

TABLE 8.34
Results from the More/Less Test[a], August 1973–March 1974

Item	Correct	Incorrect
More[b]	48	0
Less[b]	48	0

[a]Each item occurred once in a session, so the chance of a response in one session influencing a response in another session is remote. Therefore, we can consider responses to be independent across sessions. Each sentence-picture, sentence-action, or sentence-object combination was a novel stimulus, unique within a session; thus unless Genie was test-wise, we can assume within session as well as across-session independence.

[b]Comparing expected and observed frequencies by χ^2, the probability that Genie's performance could have occurred by chance (taking into account the number of response possibilities available to her) is less than .001. This is a statistically significant result.

Results: Results are given in Table 8.35.

TABLE 8.35
Responses on Many, Most, Few, Fewest Test, February 1974–July 1975

Item	Many	Most	Few	Fewest
Many	9	0	0	0
Most	3	1	0	5
Few	5	4	0	0
Fewest	1	2	2	4

Genie's performance suggests that she does not understand any of these quantifiers.

8.3.   REAL-LIFE COMPREHENSION

What constitutes language comprehension? If in response to verbal message A an individual behaves appropriately—answers the question, follows the
command, responds to the statement with further information—this certainly
constitutes real comprehension of that message. Yet if the same individual cannot consistently perform appropriately in response to similar sentences on a
formal test—where real-life cues have been eliminated—what claims can be
made regarding his or her understanding of those grammatical structures?
There may be special problems inherent in formal testing, especially with
children and retarded and disturbed individuals, that make it difficult to assess
actual ability or knowledge through such techniques.

These are questions of concern in the field of language acquisition and
language assessment. Examining the language acquisition literature in detail,
one finds a large gap in time between the point at which a child produces a
structure or element and appears to comprehend that element or structure, and
the point at which he can show mastery of that same structure or element on a
formal comprehension test (Clark, 1973; Brown, 1973; Carrow, 1969; Waryas
& Ruder, 1974).

Real-life use of language is accompanied by a variety of contextual support
features: gestures, facial expressions, tone of voice, restricted possibilities for
response based on the physical situation and objects involved, knowledge about
the function of objects, expected behavior in relation to specific situations,
shared knowledge of the speaker and hearer, conversational context, etc. Very
little is spoken in real-life, especially to a child or to a retarded or severely
disturbed individual, that is not accompanied by many extralinguistic cues.
A language user is rarely if ever required to make full use of or make use only
of his or her knowledge of the linguistic system in order to understand a sentence, except in a formal comprehension test.

In testing Genie on our comprehension tests we have obtained one type
of information about her receptive knowledge of English. But because of the
problems in testing her—the problems of formal testing, in general, and of the
disparity between Genie's language behavior in real-life and on tests—her test
performance does not reveal the whole picture. Genie responds to language
every day, in a large variety of situations; and her responses provide another,
somewhat different picture of her language comprehension. I will call this her
"real-life" comprehension and will present areas where her "real-life" comprehension differs from her test performance.

Considering the difficulties of formal tests, Genie's test performance is
quite impressive. It shows clear comprehension of negation; most relativization;
at least two term modification; possessive; noun pluralization; comparative and
superlative; the prepositions *in, on, over, next to, beside, between*; temporal
terms *before* and *after*; many relational terms (e.g., *more* and *less, up* and *down,
off* and *on, big* and *little, tall* and *short, high* and *low*); quantifiers *one* and *all*;

the reciprocal pronoun *each other*; and the reflexive morphemes *self/selves*. In addition, she understands all of the vocabulary used on these tests.

The tests also indicate that there are many linguistic elements and structures she does not understand: disjunction; subject and object pronouns; possessive pronouns; future tense, regular past tense, present progressive, the quantifiers *some*, *most*, *few*, *fewest*; relational terms *wide/narrow*, *around/through*, *here/there*; relational verbs *come here–go there*; the prepositions *under* and to some extent *front*, *back*, and *behind*; and WH-questioning of an object.

Several of the elements and structures that Genie fails to comprehend in formal testing, however, she does appear to understand in real-life situations: disjunction, *few(er)*, the prepositions *under*, *front*, and *back*, and all WH-question types. However, in real life, Genie at times demonstrates less comprehension of the possessive forms *my* and *your* than she does in formal testing situations. These disparities are discussed in the sections that follow.

8.3.1. Disjunction

In real life, one is rarely asked to "Give me the *X* or the *Y*." Disjunction usually is heard in the form of questions, such as, "Do you want *X* or *Y*?" or "What do you want, *X* or *Y*?"

Genie responds to such questions consistently, always evidencing full comprehension of the question, always making a choice. The following are examples of Genie's comprehensions of questions involving disjunction.

1. July 1972.   C: *Do you want to listen to records or read stories?*
        G: *Read story*
2. January 1973.   C: *Do you want to sit in front or back?*
        G: *Front.*
3. March 1973.   C: *Which day? Monday, Friday, Saturday?*
        G: *Wednesday.*
4. November 1973. C: *Did you feel mad on the bus or at school, or did you feel mad after you came home?*
        G: *At school.*
5. December 1973. C: *You want to take your jacket off or you want to leave it on?*
        G: *Leave on.*
6. January 1974.   C: *A locomotive or a jeep?*
        G: *Locomotive.*
7. April 1974.   C: *Which one do you like, the yellow one or the green one?*
        G: *Yellow.*
8. July 1974.   C: *You do exercises all day, or do you do anything else?*
        G: *Swimming pool.*

There are twenty-five *or* questions in my data, and in all cases Genie made a deliberate choice, thus responding appropriately.

One way of analyzing *or* questions is to relate them to yes/no questions, and to consider yes/no questions as a special case of *or* questions. There are several recorded examples where Genie has treated yes/no questions as *or* questions, in that she responds with an unstated alternative. The following are some examples:

1. May 1973.   C: *Is yours empty?*
                                    G: *No. Full.*
2. July 1973.   C: *Do you want to leave it in the car?*
                                    G: *Stay* [with] *Genie.*
3. May 1974.   C: *Is D a black man?*
                                    G: *No. White man.*
4. April 1974.   C: *Do you want me to play the piano for you a little bit?*
                                    G: *Long time.*

Unfortunately, there are no documented yes/no questions involving conjoined structures to compare real-life *and* versus *or* comprehension. It is clear, nonetheless, that Genie does comprehend the linguistic expression of disjunction, at least in some form, in language spoken to her in real life.

8.3.2. Few(er)

The one recorded case of something being said to Genie involving the word *few* (actually *fewer*) strongly suggests comprehension of the term. The following example took place on May 29 1974:

G: *I want graham cracker.*
    [+sign]
M: *How many do you want?*
G: *Five.*
M: *How about fewer?*
G: *Four.*
M: *How about fewer than that?*
G: *Three.* (She got three.)

8.3.3. Under, Front, Back, Behind

Genie always, without exception (if she responds at all), behaves appropriately in response to directions to:

$$\text{Put } X \begin{cases} \text{under} \\ \text{in front of} \\ \text{behind} \end{cases} Y,$$

or to

$$
\begin{matrix}
\text{Look} \\
\text{Stand} \\
\text{Get}
\end{matrix}
\left\{
\begin{matrix}
\text{under} \\
\text{in front of} \\
\text{in back of}
\end{matrix}
\right\} X.
$$

Of course, Y in real-life situations is almost always something like a chair or table in the case of *under*, and always something with a definable front, in the case of *in front of*, *behind*, and *back*. It is not surprising that Genie can respond to these prepositions under these conditions (Clark, 1974; Kuczaj & Maratsos, 1975). Chairs and tables greatly limit response possibilities, and normal children demonstrate comprehension of *front* and *back* with fronted objects before they can do so with nonfronted objects. The only surprising element here is that Genie should perform more poorly on formal tests with *under* than with *front* and *back*, since normal children seem to acquire *under* long before they acquire *front* and *back* (Parisi & Antinucci, 1970; Zimmerman *et al.*, 1969; Carrow, 1969).

8.3.4. WH-questions

From February 1972 on, the earliest point at which I have all the WH-type questions recorded, Genie clearly and convincingly comprehends every WH-question type.

What

1.	November 1971.	M:	*What kind of soup?*
		G:	*Green pea soup.*
2.	December 1971.	M:	*What did we use?*
		G:	*Emery board.*
3.	January 1972.	M:	*What did you do?*
		G:	*Play.*
4.	January 1972.	M:	*What burned?*
		G:	*Stove.*
5.	February 1972.	M:	*What burned out?*
		G:	*Light.*

Where

1.	January 1972.	M:	*Where are these for?* (trash bags)
		G:	*Garbage.*
2.	January 1972.	M:	*Where were you today?*
		G:	*Big gym.*
3.	April 1972.	C:	*Where is M?*
		G:	*Airport.*

Who

1.	December 1971.	D	*Who gave those to you?*
		G:	*Judy.*
2.	January 1972.	M:	*Who do they belong to?*
		G:	*D.*

How

1.	February 1972.	D: *How should I reach it?*
		G: *Get ladder.*
2.	July 1973.	C: *How did you hurt your lip?*
		G: *Wall.* [She had smacked her face against the wall.]
3.	November 1973.	M: *How does it feel?*
		G: *Tickle.*

Why

1.	January 1972.	C: *Why is he bad?*
		G: *Gun.* [Because he had a gun.]
2.	October 1973.	C: *Why aren't you singing?*
		G: *Very sad.*

In contrast to the formal test, Genie responds to WH-questioning of the object almost 100% correctly in real life, as often and as consistently as with WH-questioning of the subject. She does not demonstrate any difficulty in understanding the transformed word order with *who, what, when, where, how,* or *why* questions.

8.3.5. Me/My versus You/Your

On the Possessive Pronouns Test, Genie does not reveal comprehension of either *my* or *your*, although her performance indicates that she may be beginning to comprehend them. What is interesting here is that her performance does not show any pattern of change or development, nor does it reveal any consistent misinterpretation for either *my* or *your*. This is in conflict with her apparent real-life comprehension.

In 1971 there was no evidence concerning comprehension of either word. But beginning in 1972, she showed a consistent confusion of first and second person possessive and object pronouns. She confused *my* and *your, me* and *you,* always interpreting *my* as *your,* etc.

1.	August 1972.	Mary (a friend): *You ate at my house*
		G: *My house* (pointing to herself).
		M: *You ate at my house.*
2.	February 1973.	G: *Very angry yell.*
		C: *Judy* [another friend] *yelled at you.*
		G: *Judy yell you.*
3.	February 1973.	G: *Play piano.*
		C: *Yes, I will play the piano for you.*
		G: For you (pointing to herself).
4.	February 1973.	Kim (a friend): *Those are my earrings.*
		G: *My earrings.*
		Kim: *Whose earrings are these?*
		G: *Kim.*

5.	August 1973.	C:	*I like Gail.*
		Gail (an adult friend): *I like you.*
		C:	*Who does Gail like?*
		G:	*Gail like you.*
6.	November 1973.	C:	*Whose jacket is that?*
		G:	*D. Genie jacket.*
		C:	*Is that your jacket?*
		G:	*Your jacket* (pointing to herself).
7.	March 1974.	G:	*Mama gave me camper truck.*
		C:	*That's because Mama loves you.*
		G:	*Mama love you* (pointing to herself).
8.	August 1974.	C:	*Do you want to stay here or come with me?*
		G:	*Come with me.*

(These examples may be simple echoes; the gestures accompanying the utterances suggest that they are not.) This confusion persisted despite repeated attempts by almost everyone around Genie to teach her the distinction.

Since summer, 1974, her use of these pronouns has changed. First, she began to demonstrate comprehension of first and second person subject pronouns.

1.	August 1974.	C:	*You were driving a tractor?*
		G:	*I driving tractor.*
2.	September 1974.	Ann:	*You're ignoring Curtiss.*
		G:	*I ignoring Curtiss.*
3.	February 1975.	N (Neal, her sign language teacher): *I have no books. Say that.*
		G:	*You no book.*

More significantly, she began making substitution transformations of object and possessive forms of first and second person pronouns.

1.	August 1974.	C:	*Do you want me to tell you?*
		G:	*Tell me.*
2.	September 1974.	M:	*You're gonna wipe your hand?*
		G:	*Wipe my hand.*
3.	August 1974.	Ann:	*Can you say "Nadine gave you a white cloth?"*
		G:	*Nadine gave me cloth.*
4.	February 1975.	M:	*Oh, the teacher gave you that at school.*
		G:	*Teacher gave me block.*
5.	April 1975.	G:	*M said not lift my leg in the dentist chair.*
6.	May 1975.	M:	[+sign] [+sign] [+sign] [+sign] *'Cause on Friday you're gonna meet your mother.*
		G:	*Meet my mother.*

Some confusion of *me* and *you* and *my* and *your* persist even at this writing; but there has been a marked change in her comprehension of these terms, a change not reflected in her formal test performance.

8.3.6.

There are other bits of anecdotal evidence that indicate "real-life" comprehension of linguistic elements Genie fails to comprehend in formal testing. She readily responds to "come here" imperatives, and issues "come here" commands of her own. She responds to sentences with time adverbs (days of the week, *tomorrow*, *later*, *in a little while*), showing comprehension of past and future time. There is even anecdotal evidence that Genie comprehends conditionals, which involve complex time relationships.

> D: *If you did not spit, what should we do?*
> G: *Get out coal mine* (referring to toys, which, as punishment, were placed in a closet called "the coal mine").

In real-life situations, Genie appears to comprehend almost everything that is said to her. In many instances there are clear nonlinguistic cues to help her to respond appropriately; but especially in the case of questions referring to nonpresent objects, events, and situations, there are instances where it seems that Genie understands the language involved—syntax, semantics, morphology, and phonology.

8.4. CONCLUSION

What, then, can be concluded regarding the extent of Genie's comprehension of English? The tests indicate one picture; anecdotal evidence indicates another. Recent neurolinguistic research (Zaidel, work in progress) suggests that the nondominant hemisphere for language understands far more language than had previously been thought, but understands language only outside of the rigors of formal testing, only when redundancies and extra linguistic cues remain available. It is possible that even normal adults as well as children call upon this "incomplete" or "gestalt" type of linguistic processing ability, making use of the entire context in which a sentence is spoken with all its redundancies and extralinguistic cues, for most of their everyday language processing. To the extent that this is true, Genie in effect comprehends everyday English. A formal test, however, reveals the deficiencies in the grammar which in everyday usage are compensated for by nonlinguistic factors, and through such testing we find that Genie's comprehension of English is incomplete.

9

Syntax, Morphology, Semantics: Production

9.0.

In this chapter I will discuss Genie's spontaneous production. Section 9.1 deals with syntax, Section 9.2 with morphology, and Section 9.3 with semantics.

9.1. SYNTAX

Before beginning an examination of the data, two points should be noted. First, Genie rarely speaks. For the most part, Genie spoke only when she was required to answer questions or express immediate needs, especially during the first $2\frac{1}{2}$ years covered by the data. Occasionally she commented on events or objects, but typically such comments were one-word utterances that I have not included in the following analysis. Because of the infrequency of Genie's spontaneous speech, every utterance in the data is important as evidence. At times, particular linguistic structures appear only once or twice in the data, but they cannot be disregarded on the basis of their low frequency of occurrence. Each novel utterance provides a glimpse of her abilities. Second, although Genie did not speak often, when she spoke, she frequently said the same sentence several times in a row. If something was on her mind, that is what she would talk about, and she persisted in the use of a single phrase to express her thought or need. Consequently, I did not record the immediate repetitions of an utterance unless the utterance contained new evidence. The data analyzed below, therefore, include only one token of each type.

Approximately 2,500 spontaneous two-word or longer utterances are on record. Rather than attempting to construct one grammar to generate all of these sentences (since they represent development over a period of years), the kinds of structures and syntactic relationships found in them will be examined.

9.1.1.   Two-word Utterances

In July 1971, Genie began to string two words together. She had used imitative two-word utterances previously; she had also used together what would be two independent words in adult English, but these represented one word in her speech (e.g., *nomore, stopit*). She had not, however, spontaneously strung two independent words together until July 1971. Examples of her first "sentences" are presented in (1) below.

(1)   a.   7/6/71   Jones['s] shampoo.
      b.   7/8/71   Yellow poster.
      c.   10/11/71   D. hurt.
      d.   10/14/71   Like powder.

9.1.1.1.   Two-word Noun Phrases

Before October 1971, all of the two-word utterances in my records were noun phrases, either (1) possessive structures: POSSESSOR + POSSESSED

TABLE 9.1
Examples of Genie's Modifier–Noun Sentences

Utterance	Modifier type
little marble	size
big teeth	size
black shoe	color
white skirt	color
more soup	quantity
lot bead	quantity
fat grandma	quality
bad gun	quality
two palm	number
two hand	number

(*Jones shampoo*; *Curtiss car*), (2) modifier + noun structures (*Yellow balloon*; *More soup*), or (3) compound nouns (*number one*; *number five*).

The modifier of modifier–noun utterances was one of several types: an adjective of size, a color term, and adjective of quantity, a number, or an adjective of descriptive quality. Examples are presented in Table 9.1.

9.1.1.2. Two-word Utterances with Verbs

In October 1971, Genie began to use verbs. She produced subject-verb and verb–object sentences. (See example [2].)

(2) a. 10/27/71 Mike paint.

    b. 11/24/71 Curtiss come.

    c. 12/1/71 Curtiss stamp.

    d. 10/14/71 Want milk.

    e. 10/14/71 Like powder.

    f. 11/17/71 Hurry Genie.

These sentences represented only a small portion of the two-word sentences on record prior to January 1972, however. The major portion of Genie's two-word utterances were noun phrases and two-word answers to yes/no questions (e.g., *Finished, yes*; *Ride, yes*). As time progressed, however, strings with verbs grew in frequency, and even her two-word utterances reflected a large variety of syntactic and semantic relationships (see Section 9.3.2).

9.1.2. Three(+)-Word Utterances

Genie had imitated three(+)-word phrases since July 1971, but did not begin spontaneously producing longer strings until late November 1971. The important aspect of these longer strings is that structures which stood as complete utterances in Genie's two-word strings were now part of the more elaborated structure of these longer sentences. Two-word noun phrases now appeared as subjects or objects, whether as part of strings totally of her own creation, or as part of trained rituals (see Section 9.1.11).

Her surface-structure constraints which had allowed only NP, or N–V, or V–N, to surface in her two-word strings now allowed combinations of these into two or three-term sentences:

NP–V

N–V–N

V–NP.

Thus all of the basic sentence constituents surfaced, as illustrated in example (3):

(3) a. 11/29/71 Genie love M.
    b. 12/8/71   Spot chew glove.
    c. 12/15/71 I want more soup.
    d. 12/27/71 I want more sandwich.
    e. 12/29/71 Mike['s] mouth hurt.
    f. 12/29/71 Four teeth pull[ed].

These three(+)-word strings were important for another reason. As time passed and Genie acquired more language, it was these longer strings that revealed what Genie had acquired and could produce. Until 1974, Genie spoke mainly in one- or two-word utterances, rarely making productive use of most of the linguistic knowledge she had acquired. It was these longer strings that continued to point up the disparity between her linguistic competence and performance (see Chapter 10, Section 10.10).

As more and more three(+)-word utterances were produced, the kinds of structures and relationships expressed in them grew in number. They will be presented and discussed in the context of the discussion below.

9.1.2.1.   Three(+)-Word Noun Phrases

Genie's ability to produce strings longer than two words in length was demonstrated in her production of three-word and longer noun phrases. As with her two-word noun phrases, her longer noun phrases were of two types: (1) modifier–noun structures and (2) possessive structures as shown in example (4).

(4) a. 3/13/72 Small two cup.
    b. 3/13/72 White clear box.
    c. 2/20/72 Sheila mother coat.
    d. 2/20/72 Sheila mother purse.
    e. 7/17/72 Little white clear box.

These strings always conformed to the same word order: Modifier(s) + Noun or Possessor + Possessed, although the order of modifiers was not always uniform.

Syntactic elaboration of the noun phrase took other forms as well, however.

9.1.2.1.1.   *Determiners*

Definite Article.   In spring of 1972, Genie used *the* spontaneously for the first time:

G: *I see elephant.*

M: *Where do you see elephants?*

G: *In **the** zoo.*

The appeared rarely except in imitation, however, until late 1973, when it began to occur with some regularity, always in object noun phrases, mostly objects of prepositions:

(5) a.   12/12/73   In the hospital.

   b.   10/16/73   Shut the door.

   c.   10/30/73   Apple in the bucket.

   d.   10/23/73   . . . in the back.

   e.   12/12/73   At the museum.

   f.   1/9/74   . . . on the bus.

Genie continued to use *the* solely in object position, almost exclusively in prepositional phrases until the fall of 1974 when she produced a subject noun phrase containing *the*: *The blue car in the garage* (9/25/74). Since that time she has returned to her previous pattern of restricted usage of this term.

   Indefinite Article. As with the definite article, it appeared that late in 1973 the indefinite article *a* was being used with some regularity (see [6] below for examples). Because of the phonological rule inserting a [ə]-like vowel between consonants, however (see **Rule 5, Chapter 7**), the interpretation of these *as* as articles is equivocal.

(6) a.   9/13/73   Elevator has [ə] door.

   b.   11/28/73   Have [ə] period.

   c.   12/12/73   I like elephant eat [i] peanut.

   d.   1/8/74   Drive [ə] locomotive.

Clear use of the indefinite article appeared about a year later when *a* was used in an utterance before a noun beginning with a vowel. It is likely that the whole set of sentences, of which the utterance in question was a part, contains several instances of the indefinite article. The set is presented below in example (7).

(7) a.   9/25/74   Mary have a office.

   b.   9/25/74   Mary have [ə] blue car.

   c.   9/25/74   Mary drive [ə] blue car.

   d.   9/25/74   Mary have a office.

Determiner "Nother." In the spring of 1973, Genie expanded her determiner category to include *nother*. Example utterances with [a]*nother* are presented in (8) below. *Nother* was always used to request an additional token of whatever object was named.

(8) a. 2/5/73   Nother penny.
     b. 3/5/73   Nother penny.
     c. 3/13/74   Nother basket.
     d. 6/5/74   Nother [sur]prise.
     e. 6/5/74   Nother big prize.
     f. 10/14/74 I want buy nother shoe box.

9.1.2.1.2. *Compound Noun Phrases*

In the fall of 1972 compound noun phrases appeared. In the first such compounds, the *and* did not surface:

(9) a. 11/29/72 Cat dog hurt.
     b. 9/11/72   (C: *Who's going away?*)
                   G: *Lyn Tom.*

In later compound noun phrases the *and* did surface:[1]

(10) 5/28/74   Dark purple and light pink.
      9/25/74   House and mouse.

At about the same time, she included compound noun phrases as part of full sentences (*I like M. and D. house.* 5/21/74). The syntactic importance of these compounds will be discussed in Section 9.1.10.3 as part of the discussion on recursion.

9.1.2.1.3. *Possessives*

As exemplified above, Genie began producing possessive structures as soon as she began combining words. Her early possessives were all noun phrases, either two- or three-word phrases, always following POSSESSOR–POSSESSED word order.

(11) a. 12/8/71   D.['s] back.
      b. 12/8/71   Curtiss chin.
      c. 12/15/71 M. bike.
      d. 12/28/71 Genie purse.
      e. 2/20/72   Sheila mother coat.

---

[1] Genie first produced *and* in speech only after she had learned the American Sign Language sign for *and*.

In summer 1972, Genie began to mark possession in subject–object strings with the *have* verb deleted:

(12) a. 6/26/72   Big elephant long trunk.
      b. 12/11/72   Mike blue car.

By December Genie began to produce the *have* in these subject–object sentences, but since she still spoke most frequently in one- or two-word strings, possession was most often expressed by a two-word NP as before. On occasion, however, a longer string expressing a genitive relationship appeared; and some of these did not delete the verb (*have*) signaling the possessive relationship between the subject and object. See (13).

(13) a. 12/11/72   Miss F. have blue car.
      b. 2/14/73   Bathroom have big mirror.
      c. 11/14/73   Grandma have present.
      d. 11/7/73   . . . animal have bad cold.
      e. 2/5/73   Mr. B. have flu.

Genie's acquisition of the morphological possessive marker *'s* is discussed in Section 9.2.4.

9.1.3. Predicate Nominatives

In the spring of 1972, predicate nominative sentences were first produced.[2] From the first, they appeared with some frequency, both Noun + Predicate Adjective strings, and NP + NP strings (see [14]). It became clear that Genie had strict Adjective–Noun word order within an NP, so that Noun–Adjective strings were part of the set of predicate nominative structures and not merely variable NPs.

(14) a. 1/24/72   Curtiss car big car.
      b. 3/27/72   Curtiss angry.
      c. 4/7/72   Tim tired.
      d. 5/8/72   Tooth hard.
      e. 5/29/72   Curtiss skinny.
      f. 7/24/72   Red car M. car.

---

[2] Actually there was an earlier string on record which may have been a Noun + Predicate Adjective structure (*Stocking white*; 11/4/71). It was the only such string on record during that time, however; and it was not clear whether it represented a predicate nominative structure or an NP with Adjective–Noun order reversed.

9.1.4. Negatives

A major syntactic development was the emergence of negative sentences in the very beginning of 1972. They took the form of NEG + S (although there was an instance of S + NEG on record during this period). The negative element that Genie used was *no more*. At first, negative sentences were all of the form NEG + Noun, but about March 1972, a negative utterance with a verb emerged (*No more take wax* ['Don't take wax out of my ear.']). This sentence was the only negative with a verb to appear for months; all others were NEG + noun sentences, as shown in (15):

(15) a. 1/17/72   Father no more.
      b. 2/20/72   No more take wax.
      c. 3/27/72   No more elevator.
      d. 4/7/72   No more pineapple.
      e. 2/2/72   No more meat.

As time progressed, negatives with verbs increased in frequency:

(16) a. 7/24/72   No more ear hurt.
      b. 1/22/73   No stay hospital.
      c. 1/22/73   No like hospital.
      d. 3/12/73   Not have orange record.
      e. 10/8/73   Not have floating chair.
      f. 10/17/73   Not take shopping.

As can be seen above, Genie's negative marker changed from *no more* to *no* to *not*. Rather than signaling any change in the syntax of negation, however, the shift from *no more* to *not* appears to represent acquisition of the adult

TABLE 9.2
Comparison of Genie's Negatives

Negative sentence	Intended meaning	Date
No more spit out.	'I won't spit anymore.'	11/14/73
No more floating chair.	'The floating chair isn't around anymore.'	12/5/73
Not have floating chair.	'We don't have the floating chair.'	12/5/73
No more shot arm.	'No more shots, please.'	3/27/74
Not spit bus.	'I didn't spit on the bus.'	3/13/74

meaning of *no more* and the concomitant separation of negative sentences into those signaling (*a*) completed existence of an object or rejection—where *no more* was used—from (*b*) other negative functions—where *not* was used. (See Table 9.2.)

Another indication that this shift indicated acquisition of the meaning of *no more* as used by adults, were the sentences *Have no more* and *not have more* (both June 5, 1974), both identical in meaning, and *No more penny*, meaning exactly that. Contrast *Have no more* and *Not have more* with *Not have* (June 5, 1974), which meant "You don't have one." (See Section 10.4.5 for further discussion of the semantics of Genie's negation.)

Until the fall of 1974, all of Genie's spontaneous negative sentences contained only sentence-external negation. In September 1974 we find a part-imitated, part-spontaneous internal negative:

(17)   9/25/74   C: *When people are sick, they don't feel well and they want to sit down.*

G: *Sick people not feel well.*

Later, in October, we find a fully spontaneous embedded negative:

(18)   10/9/74   G: *Cold go away. Curtiss have sick.*

M: *Is she sick now?*

G: *Curtiss not sick.*

All other instances of negation for months to come were at least surface sentence-external negatives:

(19)   a.   12/3/74   Not use own hand.
       b.   12/3/74   No more temper tantrum.
       c.   11/74   Not Akron.
       d.   3/19/75   Not spit.
       e.   10/30/74 Not speak.
       f.   3/17/75   Not wear glasses.

except for rehearsed sentences (*I did not spit* [10/9/74]). In all of these sentences the subject was deleted, however; so it is impossible to determine from these data whether or not the negatives were embedded in underlying form. Since there are no examples of negatives which include a subject and a verb in my data before fall 1974, I cannot determine when sentence-internal negation became part of Genie's grammar. After fall 1974, we find more examples of embedded negatives; so it does appear that the examples in the dialogue above actually represent the acquisition of internal negation, by the end of 1974, if not before.

In 1975, it became clear that Genie was using embedded negatives as shown in (20):

(20) a. 6/18/75 M. not like rub hard.
      b. 5/21/75 Ellen not work at school.
      c. 4/30/75 Genie not learn P.E. at school.
      d. 6/25/75 I do not have a red pail.

As with other aspects of Genie's production (see Sections 9.2.3, 9.2.7, and 9.2.14) there is either a waxing and waning of her production of well-formed negatives or variability in rule application.

(21) G: *Do **not** like bird at school.*
      C: *Is there a bird at school?*
      G: ***Not** bird at school.*
      C: *Is there a big bird at school?*
      G: ***Not** big bird at school.*
      C: *Is there a little bird at school?*
      G: ***Not** little bird at school.*
      (After a lapse of time)
      G: ***Not** real bird at school.*

These sentences were not instances where the subjects were deleted, for in order for that to be the case the subjects would have had to be the existential *there*—a linguistic element Genie has not acquired. They are, therefore, examples of external negation, co-occurring in time with the embedded negatives.

The acquisition of sentence-internal negation does not necessarily imply movement, of course. One can easily posit a base rule:

$$S \rightarrow NP \, (NEG) \, VP$$

such that the negative is generated internal to the sentence in the base itself, rather than requiring a transformational rule moving NEG from without to within the sentence. In Genie's case, we find no structures requiring movement at all—no passives, no particle separation, no subject–auxiliary inversion, no WH-fronting, etc. The only possible movement involved is affix-hopping:

$$-ing + verb \Rightarrow \emptyset \, 2 + 1$$
$$ 1 \quad\quad 2$$

within-word movement, not any rearrangement of sentence elements. Genie appears to be linguistically incapable of producing structures that involve such movement, possibly just because they require this kind of major surgery on the structure of sentences. All such constructions are absent from Genie's grammar, and in light of this it seems more plausible to posit embedded negatives in the base of Genie's grammar than a transformational rule moving NEG inside the sentence. (See Chapter 10, Section 10.2.9 and Chapter 11, Section 11.1.4 for further discussion of Genie's linguistic limitations.)

9.1.5. Locatives and Prepositions

Since Genie's acquisition of locative structures included the acquisition of prepositions they will be discussed together.

Locatives first appeared in two- and three-word sentences involving a locative noun, as in (22).

(22) a.   1/10/72   Cereal kitchen.
      b.   1/10/72   Play gym.
      c.   2/2/72   Cookie sleep car.
      d.   2/13/72   Stay bathtub long time.
      e.   4/7/72   Applesauce buy store.

At about the same time that these structures first appeared (about January 1972) we also found the first responses to WHERE questions (prior to that time, the few WHERE questions on record evoked only a repetition of the final words of the question):

(23) a.   1/10/72   M: *Where were you today?*
                      G: *Big gym.*
      b.   1/31/72   M: *Where are you going?*
                      G: *Going park.*
      c.   1/27/72   M: *Where did we get those books?*
                      G: *Library.*

Also in association with the emergence of locatives, the prepositions *in* and *on* first appeared. In each instance, it was in response to a question:

(24) a.   3/15/72   C: *Where does a curtain go?*
                      G: *On wall.*
      b.   4/2/72   G: *I see elephant.*
                      M: *Where do you see elephants?*
                      G: *In the zoo.*
      c.   1/31/72   M: *What did you do at the gym Wednesday?*
                      G: *Bounce on trampoline.*

Genie did not use *in* and *on* consistently, however. On the whole, no prepositions surfaced at all; and only occasionally did an *in* or *on* appear:

(25) a. Wax [in] ear hurt.
      b. Cereal [in] kitchen.
      c. Play [in] gym.
      d. C: *Where are you going to put the picture?*
          G: *Wall.*

The use of the prepositions *in* and *on* represented the first use of purely grammatical formatives (until their appearance, Genie's speech had consisted of content words alone); thus, in the expression of location a significant grammatical development had occurred.

In the first part of 1973, Genie began using prepositional phrases as adverbial modifiers of full sentences. During that same period, several other prepositions entered Genie's speech, specifically *at*, *behind*, and *front*.

(26) a. 1/15/73   Mama wash hair in sink.
      b. 2/22/73   Two valentine at school.
      c. 2/14/73   At school scratch face.
      d. 4/28/73   Dr. K. buy basket in hospital.
      e. 7/30/73   Back home M. waiting.
      f. 1/22/73   M. [in] front.
      g. 1/22/73   M. behind.

At was used exclusively with *school* but since *school* was used in other contexts, and *at school* was always used to mean *at school*, *at* appears to have been a separate locative preposition in these utterances. At a later time, *at school* appeared to become one word, since *school* never appeared without the word *at* in conjunction with it. When exactly *at school* became one word is difficult to determine.

Genie continued to acquire and use new prepositions. Curiously, however, late in 1973 she began to merge *on* and *in*, using *in* to mean both. This merger lasted for about a year, after which Genie appropriately used both *on* and *in*. Since her performance on formal tests indicated clear comprehension of both *on* and *in* from fall 1973 on, the use of [ĭn] for both prepositions probably represented a phonological merger and not a merging in any other sense. Some examples of her use of prepositions from late 1973 to late 1974 follow:

(27) a. 12/5/73   Wave to Mr. B.
      b. 12/12/73   Back picture.
      c. 12/12/73   At the museum.

    d. 12/12/73   Front picture.

    e. 12/23/73   Genie behind wheel.

    f. 10/1/73   In the floor.

    g. 12/5/73   Shopping in Friday.

    h. 12/12/73   In the hospital.

    i. 7/31/74   Wastebasket for car.

    j. 8/21/74   At camp.

    k. 10/30/74   On nose.

Before the latter part of 1974, locative prepositional phrases modified the subject noun phrase or the verb but never followed the object noun phrase. After that point, phrases modifying the noun phrase object emerged as well.

(28) a. 2/20/74   Swimming pool [is] in the hospital.

      b. 3/13/74   [Genie] not live in hospital.

      c. 3/27/74   Sick people in ambulance.

      d. 5/15/74   Big, huge fish in the ocean.

      e. 2/14/73   At school scratch face.

      f. 10/16/74   Pull bench [that was] in the gym.

      g. 11/20/74   Think about Mama [being] in bus.

      h. 9/25/74   Mary have blue car [which was] in the garage.

Genie's use of prepositional phrases continued to exhibit syntactic growth and complexity. In the first half of 1975 Genie used two prepositional phrases within one sentence and used a complex noun phrase in a prepositional phrase, both for the first time. Less importantly, *at school* was clearly no longer one word, for not only was *at* used with other nouns, *at school* was broken up. These developments are illustrated in (29).

(29) a. 5/6/75   I am thinking bout Miss J. at school in hospital.

      b. 5/2/75   Play with Curtiss in pretend dentist chair.

      c. 5/19/75   Thinking about toaster at old school.

9.1.6. Verb Phrases

In October 1971, Genie first began using verbs. From that point on, her verb phrases increased in variety and complexity.

9.1.6.1. Intransitive Verbs

Genie produced true intransitive verbs from the first. She also produced verbs which may or may not be used transitively.

(30) a. 11/24/71   Curtiss come.
       b. 12/1/71   Curtiss cough.
       c. 12/15/71   Curtiss stamp.
       d. 10/27/71   Mike paint.
       e. 2/21/72   Ear hurt.
       f. 3/6/72   D. shave.

9.1.6.2. Transitive Verbs

Genie also used transitive verbs from the first, sometimes with a required object, sometimes without.

(31) a. 11/24/71   Shake hand.
       b. 12/8/71   M. wash.
       c. 12/8/71   Chew glove.
       d. 12/15/71   Open soup.
       e. 12/15/71   Want soup.
       f. 2/22/72   Get ladder.
       g. 3/6/72   Shave beard.

As time passed, Genie's verb phrases grew in complexity, but she continued to delete direct objects, even when required for grammaticality and communication.

(32) a. 6/5/74   Not have.
       b. 7/2/73   Sally grab.
       c. 10/30/73   Genie bite.

9.1.6.3. "Serial" Verb Phrases

Another type of verb phrase which Genie produced, one which first appeared in early 1972, was what I have called "serial"-type verb phrases. These were strings of two or more (uninflected) verbs. Sentences with such verb phrases seemed to result from a rule like VP → V + VP. As with other structures, these serial VPs increased in length and complexity over time. See (33) below:

(33) a. 1/24/72   Want buy dessert.
       b. 2/10/72   Want stay.
       c. 10/16/72   Want go walk Ralph.
       d. 3/21/73   Like go ride yellow school bus.
       e. 5/21/73   Want go ride Miss F. car.

Some of these sentences appear quite complex, certainly semantically so (see Section 9.3.4.2 for a discussion of this point). Appearing as they did so early in Genie's acquisition of grammar, however, it seems unlikely that they represent great syntactic complexity. All of the verbs in Genie's serial strings share the same subject, always first person, almost always deleted. Moreover, some of the verb strings, especially those with *go* (*go ride, go walk*) involve *begin*-type verbs (Perlmutter, 1970) (like *start, stop*, etc.) which are typically followed by another verb. It is also possible that *go ride* and *go walk* are stored as single lexical items. The *want* and/or *like* of these strings act as concatenators. Rather than reflecting any underlying embedding or hierarchical structures, then, these serial VPs most likely result from a base rule allowing VP to be rewritten as V + VP, where certain verbs (*want* and *like*) will become the concatenating V to be attached to the ensuing VP; and any further verb strings (within the second VP) will be of the form [go + verb].

9.1.6.4. Two-word Verbs

In the early part of 1972, Genie began to produce two-word verbs. To date she has only used a few such structures; but they represent a distinctly English acquisition and, via particle separation, offer us one of several opportunities to look for movement in her grammar. For the most part they appeared as two-word commands, but one example in the data occurred in a long string as shown in (34):

(34) a. 6/14/72   Spit out gum.
      b. 10/30/73   Take off.
      c. 10/30/73   Tear off.
      d. 12/5/73   Leave on.
      e. 11/7/73   Take out coal mine[3] school bag.
      f. 2/20/74   Put together.

9.1.7. Imperatives

Probably because of psychological and social problems (feelings of powerlessness, lack of a self-concept, etc.), Genie did not issue imperatives for 2 years after she began to speak. Over that period of time she developed considerably. By spring of 1973, her self-awareness had grown and strengthened to the point where it was reflected even in language, through the introduction of first person pronouns (see Section 9.2.14) and commands into her speech.

---

[3] "Coal mine" was the name given to a storage closet in the foster home.

Although not accompanied by emphatic stress or imperative intonation or volume, the imperatives she produced were true commands to others to acknowledge her and her rights and desires.

(35) a. 2/27/73   Go way, Sam, finish story. [Go away, Sam, and let me finish the story.]

b. 3/8/73   Get out baby buggy. [Get out of my baby buggy.]

c. 7/2/73   Let go Sally. [Let go of me, Sally.]

d. 3/12/73   Play piano. [Play the piano for me, Curtiss.]

e. 9/13/73   Shut the door.

f. 11/14/73   Open cabinet. [Open the cabinet, Curtiss.]

9.1.8. Recursion

One of the most important aspects of human language is its recursive property by which, through compounding, embedding, and iteration, a finite set of elements can be recombined unlimitedly. Sometime around the end of 1972 Genie's grammar developed this special property.

9.1.8.1. Complementation

The earliest development in this area was the introduction of verb–complement structures. (See [36] below.)

(36) a. 12/6/72   Tell door lock. [Tell M. the door was locked.]

b. 1/29/73   Ask go shopping. [Ask M. to go shopping.]

Although the V + VP strings I have called serial-type structures could also be analyzed as verb + complement structures, they are not as syntactically or semantically complex as these other verb + complement utterances where the matrix subject and the embedded subject are not identical. In the serial-type strings the subject of all of the verbs is identical and always first person. They parallel the kind of strings involving catenatives (*wanna*, *hafta*, *gonna*) that one finds in child speech long before one finds any true verb + complement sentences (Fraser, Brown, & Bellugi, 1963; Limber, 1973).

In Genie's verb + complement utterances, the (deleted) subject of the matrix clause and the subject of the complement are not the same, nor is the subject of the complement ever first person. Although much of the underlying string is deleted from the surface in the early utterances of this type, these structures represent more elaborate and complex syntax than the serial-type sentences where more of the underlying form surfaces.

These verb + complement strings contributed importantly to the complexity of Genie's grammar. Until such strings appeared, there was no evidence of any recursion in the system of rules underlying Genie's speech. With the appearance of these strings, there was the first evidence that Genie had acquired the potential for generating sentences with no upper bound.

As time passed, Genie's complement structures grew more elaborate, with more of the underlying form appearing on the surface, as the examples in (37) demonstrate.

(37) a. 3/27/74   Beth help save money. [Beth helps me save up money.]

   b. 4/24/74   Talk Mama to buy[4] Mixmaster. [I'll tell Mama to buy me a Mixmaster.]

   c. 8/7/74   I want Curtiss play piano.

   d. 11/20/74 Think about D. swim in ocean. [I'm thinking about D. swimming in the ocean.]

   e. 11/20/74 I want think about Mama riding bus.

   f. 3/5/75   I want you open my mouth. [I want you to open your mouth.]

9.1.8.2. Embedding

The only sentences in the data which unequivocably involve embedding are of the simplest form, direct quotes.

(38) a. 6/10/75   Mr. W. say put face in big swimming pool.

   b. 3/12/75   Dentist say drink water.

   c. 4/23/75   Teacher say draw bird.

   d. 5/2/75   Teacher said Genie have temper tantrum outside.

An additional sentence (*M. say not lift my leg in the dentist chair* [5/14/75]) may involve an indirect quote, but Genie's confusion of *your* and *my* makes it unclear (see Section 9.2.14). A further sentence reported to me by M. appears to represent even more complex embedding: *Coffee on the table is spill*[ed] (4/29/75).

Early in 1975, Genie began using a new sentence structure, one not found in the adult English model. It was a structure where a noun not adjacent to sentence boundaries functions as both object of the verb to its left and subject of the verb to its right:

$$\text{Subject–verb–}\begin{Bmatrix}\text{object}\\\text{subject}\end{Bmatrix}\text{–verb–}\left(\begin{Bmatrix}\text{object}\\\text{subject}\end{Bmatrix}\text{–verb}\right).$$

---

[4] *To buy* is one word in Genie's speech. Her verb *buy* is pronounced *tobuy*. Thus, *to buy* is not an infinitivized form.

(39) a. 3/19/75   I want mat is present.

     b. 5/2/75   Father hit Genie cry longtime ago.

     c. 5/2/75   Genie upset teacher said outside.

     d. 5/2/75   Genie have Mama have baby grow up.

     e. 5/2/75   Ruth Smith have cat swallow needle.

     f. 5/2/75   Mama not have baby grow up.

In sentences (39a–e) the sentences would conform to English if they included relative pronouns after the noninitial nouns (e.g., *Genie have Mama who have baby who grow up.*). Sentence (39f), however, could not be "corrected" in this manner because of the scope of the negative. Sentences (39a–e), therefore, look like complex sentences involving relative clauses without relative markers. Sentence (39f) looks like either (1) a compound rather than complex sentence consisitng of *Mama not have baby, baby grow up* or (2) a structure identical to (39a–e), but with a necessarily different semantic structure. In either case, sentences (39a–f) imply a rule deleting a noun under conditions of identity. In (39a–e) the deletion has taken place without insertion of a relative to mark the underlying presence of the deleted noun. What results is a sort of serial sentence construction, where sentences are strung together much as VPs were strung together to produce strings like *I want go ride yellow school bus.* If these sentences are viewed as some sort of serialization of sentences they need not imply embedding or subordination. They nonetheless involve deletion of nouns under identity.

9.1.8.3. Iteration

In Section 9.1.2.1., I discussed Genie's acquisition of compound noun phrases. Almost all evidence of compounding in Genie's speech is found in her noun phrases. There is one sentence in the data that appears to have a compound verb phrase: *I want save money buy two rectangle box* (10/9/74). Without an *and*, however, it cannot be determined if the above structure represents a conjoined verb phrase or a *for–to* complement. There are no instances, except possibly for sentence (38f) above, of sentence conjunction in the data.

There is also a recorded example of syntactic iteration in the data: *Tomorrow big, big prize hula hoop* (2/3/74). Typically, iteration of this kind comes from repetitions of *very* (*very, very big prize*), so that Genie's repetition of the adjective itself is atypical. It is nonetheless an example of iteration.

9.1.9. Rituals and Nonsentences

There are a great number of sentences in the data that have not been covered in any part of the discussion above. These sentences require separate examination as they do not lend themselves to the kind of structural analyses possible for her more "normal" utterances. These sentences about to be discussed do not fall neatly into entirely separate groups; in certain cases they overlap. Where they overlap it will be pointed out, but for the purposes of the discussion to follow they will be separated into two groups: (1) rituals, and (2) nonsentences.

9.1.9.1. Rituals

Chapter 5, Section 5.4 provides background information on Genie's sentence rituals. These utterances are of two types: Those rituals she was trained to say (*Give me X*; *Help me X*; *I want X*; *May I have X*) and those she created (*X hurt*; and *I like X*).

The ritual phrases Genie was trained to say were systematically filled in: The *Help me* _____ rituals were always completed with verbs; the *Give me* _____ rituals were always completed with nouns, as were the *I want* _____ and *May I have* _____ rituals, as in (40):

(40) a. 2/72   Help me open.

     b. 1/12/72   Help me zip.

     c. 11/24/71 Give me soup.

     d. 11/24/71 Give me yogurt.

     e. 12/29/71 I want pea soup.[5]

     f. 12/15/71 I want cake.

     g. 11/21/73 May I have tray.

     h. 9/13/73   May I have blue shape.

These occurrence restrictions indicate a knowledge of constituent structure and syntactic categories.

The *I want* _____, *Give me* _____, and *Help me* _____ rituals were taught to Genie very soon after she began combining words. They fell into disuse within 6 months to a year, although Genie continued to use the verbs *give*, *want*, and *help* in novel strings. The *May I have* _____ rituals were introduced much later, toward the end of 1973, as part of an attempt (by Genie's foster parents) to get Genie to ask questions (see example [45].) They remain in Genie's speech as of this writing.

The rituals Genie has created are of two types: (1) _____ *hurt* (or *Hurt* _____), and *I like* _____ phrases. In the *hurt* rituals, the slot was always filled with a noun (see [41]), seemingly any noun in her vocabulary.

---

[5] *I want* in examples (40e) and (40f) was spoken as one word [əwã̄].

(41) a.   12/1/71   Doctor hurt.
    b.   12/14/71   Snow hurt.
    c.   1/10/72   Elevator hurt.
    d.   12/1/71   Hurt hospital.
    e.   12/1/71   Hurt cat.

The _____ *hurt* (and *hurt* _____) phrases were used for about a year, after which *hurt* was used only when the meaning of the word was intended. They were replaced by *I like* _____ phrases. The meaning and function of the phrases remained the same, however: an attempt to relate interpersonally through words, by mentioning a topic on her mind. As with the *hurt* phrases, any noun could follow the verb *like* (see [42] for examples). Though occasionally the noun happened to be something Genie really did like, these phrases rarely, if ever, meant what the words meant.

(42) a.   7/12/72   Like beach.   (She hated it then.)
    b.   12/6/72   Like floor.
    c.   12/6/72   Like ring.
    d.   1/8/73   Like pinky.
    e.   1/15/73   Like hanger.
    e.   3/19/73   Like egg carton.

With time, these ritual phrases "developed," i.e., became longer and more elaborate. As before, they merely stated topics of thought; but unlike before, their increased length at times led to the production of meaningless and/or ungrammatical strings:

(43) a.   5/14/73   I like D. right arm.
    b.   8/9/73   I like Mama Saturday.
    c.   8/9/73   I like laughing funny.
    d.   9/13/73   I like hurt finger.
    e.   12/5/73   I like hate school.
    f.   8/9/73   I like bed sick.
    g.   8/27/73   I like M. fix teeth.
    h.   9/26/73   I like. D. like you.
    i.   10/8/73   I like D. wave $\left\{ \begin{array}{l} \text{ing} \\ \text{in} \end{array} \right\}$ ocean.
    j.   11/7/73   I like animal have bad cold.
    k.   11/7/73   I like school is fun.
    l.   12/12/73   I like elephant eat peanut.

Genie's reliance on these rituals for verbal interaction grew to the point that between July 1973 and January 1974 over half of all of the spontaneous utterances in the data were *I like* ___ phrases. Since that time their frequency has decreased considerably, but they remain in use even at this writing and continue as one source of what I have called "nonsentences."

9.1.9.2. Nonsentences

In January 1972, Genie began to produce strings which appeared to lack any coherent internal structure. They may all have had meaning for Genie; but to the adults around her these strings appeared to be, on the whole, meaningless combinations of independent one- or two-word sentences. At least some of them could be said to possess S + S structure, but the resultant combinations were all ill-formed. These are illustrated in (44).

(44)
a. 6/26/72   Worr$\begin{Bmatrix} y \\ ied \end{Bmatrix}$ milk.

b. 5/29/72   Very angry clear water.

c. 1/10/72   Elevator hurt silly goose.

d. 6/12/73   Fred have feel good.

e. 6/4/73   Nancy blow balloon con.[6]

f. 7/23/73   Long time fix.

g. 9/10/73   Heart lady.

h. 9/13/73   Spit swallow.

i. 10/1/73   Maybe Dick.

j. 8/7/72   Swimming pool like Judy.

k. 10/16/72 Father hurt like Grandma.

l. 4/22/74   I supermarket surprise Roy.

Towards the middle of 1973, a new type of nonsentence emerged with Genie's attempts to respond to question models.

Genie's foster parents, noting that Genie did not ask questions, attempted to teach her to formulate WH-questions by modeling some simple questions for her. For example, when Genie would say,

G. *Curtiss come*

her foster mother would say,

M: *You're wondering when Curtiss is going to come. You want to know, "When will Curtiss come?" Say, "When will Curtiss come?" Instead of saying, "Curtiss come," ask "When will Curtiss come?"*

---

[6] Nancy, a friend, had called Genie a "con" for conning her into blowing up balloons for her.

In this manner, many of Genie's utterances that were construed to be questions in intent were rephrased as questions for her. Genie was then encouraged to imitate these questions and to reword her own utterances into questions (*Say it in a question. Ask me a question.*). Genie's attempts to formulate questions not only resulted in ill-formed utterances, but indicated that she was very confused as to what was expected of her. At times she included the answer as well as the question, put two types of questions into one phrase, or even turned utterances intended as statements into (abortive) questions, as shown in (45).

(45) a. 6/4/73   When Mike summer?
      b. 7/30/73   Where is doctor help Genie?
      c. 10/23/73   When enough money?
      d. 11/21/73   When is toy house?
      e. 10/6/73   Where is may I have ten penny?
      f. 5/29/74   I where graham cracker?
      g. 6/12/74   I where is graham cracker on top shelf?
      h. 6/5/74   Where is stop spitting?
      i. 6/5/74   Where is tomorrow Mrs. L.?

After about a year, attempts to "teach" Genie to ask WH-questions were stopped. These ungrammatical strings immediately disappeared.

Another type of nonsentence arose from attempts to teach Genie to use the copula. As with questions, Genie attempted to use the copula, even where inappropriate, in an effort to meet the demands upon her to "speak in sentences," a command which to Genie meant to insert a form of *be*. Although somewhat more successful than with questions, Genie's efforts usually produced ungrammatical strings.

(46) a. 9/13/73   Finger is soak.
      b. 9/13/73   Spit is swallow.
      c. 11/21/73   Picture is boy.
      d. 11/21/73   Is Akron.
      e. 2/5/74   Mr. B. is flu.
      f. 2/5/74   Glass is break.
      g. 5/8/74   Is stomach hurt.

Pressure to use *be* later resulted in sentences where progressive was marked by *be* alone, without the *-ing*.

(47) a. 1/16/74   Boy is pinch.
      b. 4/24/74   Mixmaster is shake.

    c. 6/19/74   Curtiss is dance.

    d. 4/24/74   Mama is feed you.

Genie did produce some well-formed strings containing copulas (*Car is wet* (1/15/74); *Big whale is wet* (1/15/74); *Glass is clear* (3/27/74)); and when the attempts at intervention were stopped, here again the resulting nonsentences disappeared from Genie's speech.

Although close to half of Genie's nonsentences would be eliminated if one were to ignore those she produced in response to intervention, the remainder set her apart from normals and constitute one of the most striking ways in which her language is abnormal.

9.1.10. Creative Language

In contrast to the many rituals and pat phrases Genie used so regularly (see 9.1.9 and 9.3), on occasion Genie demonstrated an ability to use her language very creatively:

(48)   9/26/73   To express the fact that she didn't want her trip to the mountains to last very long, Genie said, *Little bit trip.*

(49)   1/8/74   G: *Mother old.*
                     M: *No, mother's not old.*
                     G: *Mother new.*

(50)   5/3/74   G (counting): *Thirty-eight, thirty-nine, thirty-ten.*

(51)   10/30/74   M: *Who was at Grandma's house?*
                     G: *Grandpa. Grandfather is stay in bed. Very sick.*
                     C: *What's the matter with him?*
                     G: *Very bad sick.*

(52)   12/3/74   M: *How's the neck?*
                     G: *Feel better.*
                     M: *I told you it would feel better when you got to school.*
                     G: *Hurt.*
                     M: *It hurts? I thought it felt better.*
                     G: *Little hurt.*

9.1.11. Knowledge of Constituent Structure

We have already seen indications of Genie's knowledge of constituent structure, from the slot-filling restrictions present in her early rituals (Section 9.1.9.1). Her responses to WH-questions also demonstrate such knowledge.

For example, WHAT DOing-type questions always elicited a verb (WHAT questions a noun):

(53) a. 1/10/72   M: *What did you do?*
                    G: *Play.*

      b. 1/10/72   M: *What happened on the stove?*
                    G: *Burn.*

      c. 1/26/72   M: *What did you do at the park?*
                    G: *Climb.*

      d. 1/31/72   M: *What did you do at the gym Wednesday?*
                    G: *Bounce on trampline.*

      e. 3/15/72   C: *What do you use a towel for?*
                    G: *Wash.*

      f. 6/19/72   M: *What did you do at the big gym?*
                    G: *Work.*

      g. 7/26/72   M: *What will you do at school?*
                    G: *Play children.*

      h. 7/31/72   M: *What was the horse doing?*
                    G: *Eating grass.*

      i. 10/10/72 M: *What are you doing?*
                    G: *Color[ing] bell.*

      j. 11/29/72 M: *What did Nancy do?*
                    G: *Pick up.*

While WHAT-questions elicit nouns, and WHAT-DOing-type questions elicit verbs, WHAT KIND OF questions elicit adjectives or a subcategory of the topic questioned:

(54) a. 11/24/71 M: *What kind of soup?*
                    G: *Green pea soup.*

      b. 9/11/72   C: *What kind of food?*
                    G: *Cake.*

      c. 7/12/72   C: *What kind of car does M. have?*
                    G: *Red car.*

      d. 12/6/72   C: *What color should I bring?*
                    G: *Red.*

      e. 1/8/74   C: *What kind of pudding do you want?*
                    G: *Chocolate pudding. Yellow pudding.*

      f. 9/18/74   C: *When we get on the elevator, what number do we want?*
                    G: *Four.*

9.1.12. Word Order

With few exceptions, Genie demonstrated strict word order constraints. In noun phrases the order was

$$\text{Determiner–Modifier(s)–Noun}$$
$$\qquad 1 \qquad\quad 2 \qquad\quad 3$$

or

$$\text{Possessor–Possessed Noun.}$$
$$\qquad 1 \qquad\qquad 2$$

The order of modifiers was open to some variation, however, (cf. *little bad boy, small two cup, white big boat*). In verb phrases the order was consistently:

$$V-\begin{Bmatrix} VP \\ NP \end{Bmatrix}.$$
$$\text{NP}1 \quad\ 2$$

In sentences, the order was consistently,

$$\text{Subject–Verb–}\left(\begin{Bmatrix} \text{Complement} \\ \text{Object} \end{Bmatrix}\right).$$
$$\qquad\ 1 \qquad\ 2 \qquad\qquad 3$$

Contrast this strict use of word order in her speech with her comprehension problems in this area (Chapter 8).

9.1.13. Syntactic Features

From Genie's speech it was evident that she had acquired strict subcategorization features for nouns, verbs, and adjectives. Her grammar included at least the following features:

TABLE 9.3
Genie's Syntactic Features

For nouns	For verbs	For adjectives
[±Count]	[±Be+ing____]	[±Determiner__]
[±Determiner___]	[±Noun_____]	[±____Noun]
[±___Verb]	[±____Noun]	[±Copula___]
[±Verb____]		
[±Number]		

9.2.   MORPHOLOGICAL PRODUCTION

In this section Genie's acquisition of morphology will be examined. The grammatical morphemes listed in Brown (1973) as well as several others will be considered. I will discuss the presence or absence of each of these in Genie's speech, when they were acquired, and the order in which the grammatical morphemes were acquired. A comparison with the acquisition of morphology in normal children will be presented in Chapter 10, Section 10.3. Where material that this section covers has already been discussed, the pertinent section(s) will be referred to.

9.2.1.   In, On

See Section 9.1.7.

9.2.2.   -ing

The progressive inflection -ing first appeared in fall 1972. It has never occurred with a stative verb and has always signified ongoing action when assigned to a verb referring to present action. When assigned to a verb referring to action in the past, it is equivocal whether it has been used to signify ongoing (past) action; for example, *Boy is dropping penny* (9/13/73) refers to an incident where a boy dropped a penny, and Genie noticed him as he dropped it. *Beth walking pier* (5/15/74) refers to an outing at the beach with a friend, Beth, where Beth (and Genie) walked along the pier. The sentence *Beth walking pier* may refer to a memory of walking along the pier rather than the fact that Beth walked along the pier. All such examples are ambiguous:

Some examples of sentences with -ing follow.

(55)   a.   1/22/73   Waving hand.
       b.   3/19/73   Angry[,] pretending.
       c.   7/15/73   Genie laughing.
       d.   10/30/73 Miss C. biting.
       e.   1/8/74   Genie driving jeep.
       f.   3/13/74   Not wearing apron.
       g.   4/3/74   Tomorrow going school.

(See Section 9.2.11 for a discussion of *be* in *be* + *ing* constructions.)

9.2.3.   Plural

The plural marker first appeared in spring 1973. Both /z/ and /əz/ appeared, although each only once. In all of the data there are only five instances of phonologically marked plural in free speech: (*Bears have sharp claw; Five horses; Five rugs; Apples; Horses*) three /z/ plurals, and 2 /əz/ plurals (although one of the /z/ plurals underwent a phonological substitution: [rʌgd]). Since pluralization occurred so infrequently it is difficult to determine when Genie began assigning number to count nouns. She demonstrated full comprehension of plurals since summer 1972 and has shown equal comprehension with /s/, /z/, and /əz/ plural forms. In addition, in certain non-free speech situations she has demonstrated the ability to use the plural marker frequently. For example, note the following taken from a work session on plurals with her sign language instructor in February 1975:

N: *Here, have another card.*
G: *I have two cards.* [karz]
          [+plural sign]
   I have ten cards. [karz]
          [+plural sign]
G: *I have* [ə] *lot* [ə] *cards.* [karz]
          [+plural sign]
   You have lot [ə] *cards.* [karz]
          [+plural sign]
G: *I have* [ə] *two box*[es]. [bas]
          [+plural sign]
   I have cards box. [ba]
     [+plural sign]
   I have [z]   *boxes.* [bas·s]
     [+plural sign] [+plural sign]
   (Extremely long [s] with emphasis on the [s]).

   I like box. [ba]
G: *I have one book.*
   I you, you see two books. [bʊʔs]
          [+plural sign]
N: *I have no books. Say that.*
G: *You no book.* [bʊ]
G: *You have four balloon.* [bəlũ]
N: *Genie!!*
G: *You have four balloons.* [bəlũz]
          [+plural sign]
N: *Two.*
G: *Two balloon.* [bəlũ]
G: *I have two balloon.*
N: *Balloons.*
G: *Balloons.*
   [+plural sign]

(All of the spoken plurizations above were marked by the Signed English plural marker as well.)

Although fairly diligent in her application of plurals during the lesson, Genie demonstrates three aspects of her performance in this session.

First, as the lesson went on, she failed to mark plural except when prodded. She was able to do it; she simply did not. Her performance in the first part of the lesson differs markedly from that at the end of the lesson. The difference must have been motivation; it is surely not ability. We find then that lack of motivation or laziness masks Genie's true abilities.

Second, where Genie does mark plurals, final clusters are simplified. [Vrdz] → [Vrz], [ks] → [s], [Ṽnz] → [Ṽz]. These examples highlight Genie's difficulty with clusters. When pressured to produce a final consonant (the plural marker), Genie deletes the consonant immediately preceding it, if there is one. The only consonant which can remain is final [r], which is a liquid sonorant and not a true consonant. Otherwise, when not under pressure to produce a final consonant, Genie typically deletes it. When confronted with a final consonant cluster, she simplifies it by deletion of the final consonant in almost every instance (see Chapter 7). It is not surprising, then, that we find few examples of plurals in her speech. Only with nouns ending in vowels would we expect to find a surface plural marker in Genie's typical speech. Even in these words, because final consonants are so often deleted, it is not surprising, however, that plurals are unmarked.

The third phenomenon revealed in this session is Genie's mistaken application of the plural marker. It is not clear what Genie meant by *I have cards box*. It may even have been a speech error: *I have cards* [I mean] *box*. But *I have s boxes* clearly contains a grammatical error. Since it did not occur during
[+plural sign] [+plural sign]
free speech, it is difficult to know what significance such a mistake has; but it could indicate that Genie has not established the syntactic domain of the plural morpheme. It is possible then that were plurals to appear more frequently in Genie's speech, they might at times appear inappropriately. Since Genie's deletion of final consonants applies to verbs as well as nouns, there is no way to determine this.

9.2.4. Possessive

Possessive markers first appeared in spring 1973. More accurately, the first of two possessive markers in all the data appeared in spring 1973. The two are: *Sam's room* (3/12/73) and *Sam's big block* (11/7/73). It is unwarranted, perhaps, to claim from the data that Genie has acquired the possessive morpheme in productive speech; but as with plurals, final consonant deletion could account for the fact that possessive markers occur so rarely.

9.2.5. Third Person Present Singular /-s/

This morpheme has never appeared with a regular verb. It has only occurred with the verb *have* (i.e., *has*). It first appeared in fall 1973 and has appeared only a few times, afterward always with *have*. Its infrequent and ungeneralized application suggests that its occurrence may not represent marking of person, number, or tense; and so this morpheme has probably not been acquired. (It should be noted that Genie's pronunciation of *have* consistently includes the final consonant; therefore the presence or absence of /-s/ on the verb is not ambiguous.)

9.2.6. Past Regular

The regular past tense morpheme occurred in fall 1973, on the verb *break* [brekt]. It has not appeared in my data, since. It is possible, as with the plural and possessive morphemes, that the /-d/ past tense morpheme has been acquired, but does not surface because it is deleted to conform to Genie's phonological constraints on final consonants and consonant clusters. There are no regular verbs ending in a coronal consonant used to refer to the past in the data to determine if at least the [ə] of the [əd] morphophoneme required would appear on the surface as does the [ə] of the plural morphophoneme [əz] (*horses* [hórtə]). It appears that the past regular has not been acquired. (Note that Genie also does not comprehend past tense [see Section 8.2.14].)

9.2.7. Past Irregular

Past irregular also appeared for the first time in fall 1973. It occurred with several verbs: *say, make, give, see, buy.* In spring 1975 Genie first used the sign-language past time indicator with one of these verbs. It is not apparent, however, that even though these verbs appeared in their past forms and occurred in sentences describing past events, that they were actually inflected for past tense. It is possible that they were stored lexical forms not signifying tense.

It is also possible that the "sometime" occurrence of these past forms represents a waxing and waning in ability or a variability in the application of certain rules, much as is found in Genie's phonological output (see Chapter 7). For example, note the following exchanges:

2/12/75   G: *At school, teacher **give** block.*
        M: *Oh, the teacher gave you that at school.*
        G: *Teacher **gave** me block.*
           *Teacher **give** block.*

4/2/75   G : *Genie have yellow material at school.*
          M : *What are you using it for?*
          G : *Paint. Paint picture. Take home. Ask teacher yellow material. Blue paint. Yellow green paint. Genie have blue material, teacher said no. Genie use material paint. I want use material at school.*
          M : *You wanta paint it, or are you trying to tell me you **did** paint it?*
          G : ***Did** paint.*

5/14/75   G : *M.* **say** *not lift my leg in the dentist chair.*
          M. **said** *not lift my leg in the dentist chair.*

A conclusive determination of the presence or absence of past irregular in Genie's grammar cannot be made, and her acquisition of this morpheme remains questionable.

9.2.8. Articles

Articles first appeared in spring 1973. See Section 9.1.3.2 for discussion and examples.

It is not surprising that *the* appeared so early in Genie's acquisition of language because Genie concentrated on elaboration of the noun phrase, and determiners are early acquired NP elaborations (Brown *et al.*, 1969). What is surprising is that *the* did not occur in a subject noun phrase (where a verb appears on the surface) until spring of 1975—3 years after her first acquisition of this element.

9.2.9. Contractible Copula

The contractible copula first appeared in Genie's speech in fall 1973. It has only appeared in uncontracted form, and only the forms *am* and *is* have been produced. This morpheme has been used inappropriately as well as appropriately, although only the form *is* has been used grammatically. See Section 9.1.11.2 for discussion and examples. See (56) for examples of grammatical occurrences of the contractible copula.

(56) a.   1/15/74   Car is wet.
      b.   3/27/74   Glass is clear
      c.   4/74   Father is angry.
      d.   4/2/75   Teacher is boss at school.

9.2.10. Uncontractible Copula

The appropriate syntactic environments for the uncontractible copula (e.g., questions, comparatives) have never appeared in Genie's speech; thus the uncontractible copula has not appeared.

9.2.11. Contractible Auxiliary

There are three separate elements in this category: the *be* of *be* + *ing*, the *'ve* of *have* + *en*, and the *'ll* of *will* or *shall*. Only the first of the three has emerged in Genie's speech. The *be* of *be* + *ing* first appeared in fall, 1973. It has not been used consistently since that time, however; the *-ing* has continued to appear on the surface without an accompanying form of *be*. The reverse is true as well, however; the *be* of *be* + *ing* has appeared on the surface without its *-ing* counterpart. See Section 9.1.11.2 for examples.

Both *am* and *is* have occurred with *-ing*; neither form has ever been contracted. See (56) for examples.

(57)   a.   9/13/73   Boy is dropping penny.
       b.   11/14/73 I am slapping Spot.
       c.   1/15/74   Father is sitting top bus.
       d.   3/27/74   I like M. is laughing.
       e.   5/15/74   Mama is riding bus.
       f.   5/15/74   I is sitting.
       g.   6/19/74   Cat is scratching.

9.2.12. Uncontractible Auxiliary

The appropriate syntactic environments for the uncontractible AUX have not appeared in Genie's speech (e.g., subject–auxiliary inversion in questions), and therefore the opportunity to determine Genie's acquisition has never occurred.

9.2.13. Modals

Genie has not spontaneously produced any modals. She has produced *can*, *will*, and *may* in imitation and in trained phrases only.

9.2.14. Personal Pronouns

The only subject pronouns to appear in Genie's speech have been *I* and *you* (singular). *I* first appeared in spring 1973, and *you* first appeared in spring 1974. *You* has only occurred twice in the data. *It* has occurred three times, but only in sentences which were probable imitations.

At the same time Genie began to use *I* with an unreduced vowel, she also began to use *my* in her speech, although she consistently confused the meaning of *my* and *your* (e.g., *Your finger caught door* (2/22/73) [I caught my finger in the door]). Genie's use of *I* clearly signaled first person (i.e., was clearly another name for herself), but her use of other first and second person pronouns indicated confusion between them, confusion between *me* and *you*, and confusion between *my* and *your*. (See below for examples; further examples can be found in Chapter 10, Section 10.2.5.)

(Common occurrence) C: *I like you.*
                                       G: *Like you.* (Pointing to herself as she said *you*.)

9/12/74   M: *What's this?*
               G: *Towel.*
               M: *What're you gonna use it for?*
               G: *Wipe your hand.*
               M: *You're gonna wipe **your** hands?*
               G: *Wipe my hand.*

8/28/74   C: *Do you want to stay here or come with me?*
               G: *Come with me.*

2/26/75   G: *Your money.*
               M: *Is it my money? Give it to me.*
               G: *Genie money.*
               M: *Well, what do you say?*
               G: *My money.*

3/5/75   (Re what the dentist says to her.)
               G: *I want you open my mouth.*

Although at this writing Genie still frequently confuses first and second person object and possessive pronouns, there are indications that she is beginning to sort them out, or at least that she more regularly appears to comprehend and use them correctly.

2/12/75   G: *At school teacher give block.*
               M: *Oh, the teacher gave you that at school.*
               G: *Teacher gave me block.*

5/21/75   M: *'Cause on Friday you're gonna meet your mother.*
               G: *Meet my mother.*

5/14/75   G: *M. say not lift my leg in the dentist chair.*

Her performance with *my* and *your* and *me* and *you* may be another example of waxing and waning ability.

In conclusion it appears that only the subject marker *I* and possibly *you* have been acquired. No third person pronouns have appeared at all in Genie's spontaneous speech.

9.2.15. Relative Pronouns

No relative pronouns have been produced.

9.2.16. Indefinite Pronouns

No indefinites have been produced.

9.2.17. WH-words

WHEN and WHERE have been used in trained sentences and in ill-formed attempts to ask questions under social pressure to do so. No WH-words have occurred in spontaneous, well-formed strings in free speech conditions. See Section 9.1.11.2.

9.2.18. Conjunctions

Only *and* has been produced, and only in compound noun phrases. See Section 9.1.3.3.

9.2.19. Dummy DO

DO first appeared in spring 1975. It has been used only in negative sentences, and only with the subject *I* or in memorized commands. It has been used both appropriately and inappropriately. See (58) for examples.

(58) a. (Memorized) Do not spit.
     b. (Memorized) Don't bother people.
     c. 6/12/75 I did not sad.
     d. 3/17/75 I do not sick.
     e. 6/25/75 I do not have a red pail.
     f. 6/18/75 I do not have a toy green basket.

Because so much of Genie's use of DO is inappropriate, it is unclear whether she has acquired this morpheme.

9.2.20. Negative Terms

No more, no, and *not* have been used as negative markers, in that order. No other negative terms have appeared, nor has the negative morpheme /un-/ been produced.

9.2.21. Determiners

See Section 9.1.3.2.

9.2.22. Demonstratives

No demonstratives have been produced.

9.2.30. Order of Acquisition

The order of acquisition of the above grammatical morphemes in Genie's speech is presented in Table 9.4. Morphemes which have only questionably been acquired are included and are indicated by a (?) following the morpheme.

TABLE 9.4

Order of Acquisition of Grammatical Morphemes in Genie's Grammar

Morpheme	Rank order	Date acquired
negative marker		
on and *in*	1	Spring 1972
article (*the*)		
-ing		
me and *you* (?) (objects)	2	Fall 1972
Plural		
Possessive	3	Spring 1973
I		
third person singular irregular (?)		
past irregular (?)	4	Fall 1973
contractible copula		
contractible auxiliary		
you (subject) (?)	5	Spring 1974
Dummy DO (?)	6	Spring 1975

See Section 10.3 for a comparison with normals. All others are yet to be acquired.

9.3. SEMANTICS

At this writing there is no readily accessible system or procedure for coding or assessing semantic development in child language acquisition. Therefore, in detailing Genie's semantic development, I will simply single out particular aspects of this area of development and focus on those.

While Genie was isolated and immeasurably deprived during her years of confinement, she was not asleep. Her mind was alive, awake, and responding to her world. When she was discovered, Genie possessed no language, but her thoughts and ideation were not in an equal state of undevelopment. Semantic aspects of her language have reflected this fact. From her first vocabulary words on, Genie's semantic system was far more sophisticated than the syntactic system she manifested at every point in the course of my observation.

9.3.1. Vocabulary

Within a few months after entering the hospital, Genie began to acquire vocabulary. Her very early vocabulary is listed in Table 9.5.

TABLE 9.5
Genie's Vocabulary as of March 1971

Nouns	Verbs	Color words	Numbers
Mama	spit	red	one
Miss Jones	stopit	blue	two
Dr. K.	open	green	three
	blow	yellow	
		brown	

Even with a vocabulary of less than 20 words, Genie expressed a wide variety of concepts which included people, actions, colors, and numbers (compare with normals in Section 10.2.1.). Her vocabulary increased rapidly in all areas and soon included states as well as actions and perceptual qualities of objects as well as objects, themselves (see Table 9.6).

TABLE 9.6
Samples from Genie's Vocabulary as of May 1971

States	Actions	Qualities	Nouns
sleep	go	big	pillow
down	come	little	balloon
back ('away')	kick	silly	store
broken	pop		bed

Genie's vocabulary, largely differentiated from the beginning, developed even finer distinctions while she was still producing only two- and three-word sentences. Colors of objects were often expressed as *light green, dark blue*, and so forth; objects were often defined by two modifiers, and abstract adjectives such as *angry* appeared in her speech.

During the course of language acquisition, Genie's vocabulary grew and developed, but her use of vocabulary continued to reflect her predominantly visual cognitive style. She continued to focus on physical attributes of the world around her and developed a rich vocabulary of form and color as illustrated in Table 9.7. She used these words extensively in talking about

TABLE 9.7
Genie's Form and Color Vocabulary

Form terms	Color terms
round	gray
circle	clear
square	pink
rectangle	purple
triangle	black
star	brown
heart	gold
shape	red
	blue
	green
	yellow
	white

things she noticed or things she wanted to have. She never simply wanted a box, or beads, or a pillow; it had to be a *clear white plastic box*, or *light pink and red beads*, or *big green rectangle pillow*. The objects in her mental world were specific and detailed, and her vocabulary reflected this fact.

9.3.2. Semantic Functions and Functional Relationships

In 1971 Genie began to use verbs which, combined with nouns, expressed a variety of semantic functions and functional relationships found in normal child language: agency, action, object, location, agent–action, action–object, etc. After a year, she also began to express dative and instrumental function. Some examples of these functional relationships are presented in Table 9.8.

TABLE 9.8
Functional Relationships Expressed in Genie's Speech

Sample sentence	Function expressed	Date
Want milk.	action[a]–object	10/14/71
Mike paint.	agent–action	10/27/71
Wash car.	action–object	12/1/71
Big elephant long trunk.	possessor–object	6/26/72
M talk Nancy.	agent–action–dative	7/23/72
Applesauce buy store.	object–action–location	4/72
Call grandma telephone.	action–object–instrument	11/29/72
Curtiss give me valentine.	agent–action–dative–object	2/12/73

[a] 'Want' actually expresses a state and not an action.

In the summer of 1974 Genie appeared to acquire the benefactive, although it was not always overtly marked: *Wastebasket for car* (7/31/74); *Please play* [piano for] *me* (8/7/74); *Mama bought* [it for] *me* (8/21/74). Whenever Genie said the word *for* she signed it as well. It is possible that exposure to the sign for *for*, which in signing a sentence receives equal stress with the other signs of the sentence in contrast to its lack of stress in English speech, may have played a role in Genie's acquisition of this term and the semantic relationship it expresses.

In the sentences Genie produced, certain information was deleted. Often, the deleted material was semantically redundant or "given" information in relationship to the situation in which the sentence was uttered (e.g., "Genie" in *want milk*; or "cupboard" in *Mike paint* [this sentence was spoken as he was painting the cupboard]). Thus, Genie often supplied only the necessary information omitting all which the listener could supply from the context. Genie did not delete only redundant information, however; especially when she spoke of nonpresent events, deleted material included information that the listener did not share, pointing to a lack of conversational awareness on Genie's part (see Section 11.6 for further discussion of Genie's conversational competence). Nonredundant information was most frequently deleted from stereotypic utterances that Genie employed to refer to whole situations or events (see Section 10.4.1). These "pat" phrases were used whether or not her listener knew what they referred to. When the "pat" phrase was familiar to her listeners, the deleted information could be considered redundant. But Genie used the same phrases regardless of the listener's familiarity with the utterance or with her. Therefore, Genie frequently omitted clearly nonredundant information.

9.3.2.1. Adverbial Functions

About 6 months after Genie began combining words, she began to express location.

(59) a. 1/10/72 Cereal kitchen.
      b. 1/10/72 Play gym.
      c. 2/2/72   Cookie sleep car.
      d. 2/13/72 Stay bathtub long time.
      e. 4/72   Applesauce buy store.

Later she elaborated the expressions of location to include prepositional terms.

(60) a. 1/15/73   Mama wash hair in sink.
      b. 2/14/73   At school scratch face.
      c. 4/28/73   Dr. K. buy basket in the hospital.
      d. 10/10/73 At Woolworth big huge truck.
      e. 10/73   In the hospital, shot hurt arm.

Soon after Genie began expressing location, time adverbials appeared. Temporal nouns appeared first, followed by temporal adverbials.

(61) a. 2/13/73 Stay bathtub longtime.
      b. 9/13/72 See Mama Friday.
      c. 10/72   Monday Curtiss come.

    d. 10/73   After dinner have cookie.

    e. 1/8/74   After dinner use Mixmaster.

9.3.3. Semantic "Features"

In Genie's speech there appeared to be certain semantic constraints in her constructions. For example, in her earliest constructions, all agents were animate and objects inanimate. Within a year, objects could be either inanimate or animate, but agents remained animate. This suggests that she classified nouns as [± animate]. Her appropriate use of *lady*, *man*, etc. in the early part of 1973 reflects her ability to distinguish the gender of humans. When Genie began to apply the progressive *-ing* morpheme, this suffix was attached only to action verbs, indicating her classification of verbs into [± stative] classes.

Although for the most part Genie's speech showed appropriate use of the verbs *eat* versus *drink* (possibly reflecting a classification of nouns as [± edible]), in December 1973 she said "*I like eat milk* (12/12/73), violating a selectional restriction based on this "semantic feature."

To determine Genie's semantic classification system (which could reflect both her cognitive development and linguistic semantic feature system), a series of sorting tests was administered.

9.3.3.1. Semantic Classification Tasks

There were five classification tasks, testing the following features: (1) male/female, (2) human/nonhuman, (3) animate/inanimate, (4) edible/inedible, (5) part/whole. In each task, Genie was presented with a set of pictures and asked to identify each one. After correct identification of the pictures, Genie was asked to make two piles to "show me which ones belong together" (see Appendix I for further details).

Genie was first given these tests in January 1974. On every occasion she performed correctly on (1) male/female, (2) animate/inanimate, (3) edible/inedible, and in some instances was clearly able to verbalize her classification as well. For example, after a male/female sort:

C: *Why do these belong together?*
G: *Boy.*
C: *And why did you put these together?*
G: *Girl.*

and after an edible/inedible sort:

C: *Why do these belong together?*
G: *Food.*
C: *Why do these belong together?*
G: *Thing.*

At first, Genie had difficulty with the human/nonhuman sorting task and part (of body) versus whole (body) sorting task, failing to classify the pictures on the basis of these features; but by spring of 1974, Genie had no problem with any of the tasks and has since sorted appropriately on each task at every occasion.

9.3.4. Semantic Constructions

9.3.4.1. Noun Phrases

In addition to the functional relationships discussed above, several more sophisticated semantic constructions can be found in Genie's speech.

The first relatively complex constructions appearing in the data are the elaborate three- and four-word noun phrases Genie produced.

(62) a. Sheila mother coat.
      b. Small two cup.
      c. Little white clear box.
      d. Pretty blue car.
      e. White big boat.
      f. Sheila mother purse.

These noun phrases reveal Genie's attention not only to the object, but to two or three distinct and unrelated attributes of the object. She perceived, attended to, and expressed the features of size, number, and shape, separately and in conjunction with each other. Especially during the first year of her production of sentences, Genie appeared to focus more on details of objects than on the relationships between them. Although this selective attention might have reflected a static involvement with or perception of the world, Genie's complex noun phrases reveal perceptually richer and more developed cognitive structures than required to express agent–action–object strings. That is, perhaps, the reason that normal children do not produce modification structures, even simple ones, in their early two- and three-word sentences (Bloom, 1971).

9.3.4.2. Verb Phrases

Parallel with her semantically rich noun phrases, Genie produced serial-like verb phrases which reflect semantic richness in their expression of the action associated with the object noun. Rather than simply stating a verb phrase such as **like** *school bus*; or *ride car*; or *go* [to] *Ralph*['s] with a simple verb, Genie produced complex verb phrases much as she had done with noun phrases.

(63) a. 10/16/72   Want go walk [to] Ralph['s].
     b. 3/21/73   Like go ride yellow school bus.
     c. 5/21/73   Want go ride Miss F. car.
     d. 4/23/74   I enjoy ride train.

These "serial" verb phrases express intention and desire as well as more specific information regarding the action involved, all in one verb phrase.

9.3.4.3. Complex Relationships

When the structure of an utterance involves sentence embedding or complementation, the semantic interrelationships increase in complexity and number because relationships between sentences (as well as between constituents within the individual sentences) are involved. Genie's utterances revealed this complexity when she began to produce complex sentences. Although, as before, much semantic material was sometimes deleted, these complex intra- and intersentential relationships were overtly expressed in some of her sentences, as shown in Table 9.9.

TABLE 9.9
Examples of Complex Sentences

Sample sentence	Gloss	Date
Tell door lock.	'Tell them that the door was locked.'	12/6/72
Talk Mama to buy[a] Mixmaster.	'I should tell Mama to buy me a Mixmaster.'	4/24/74
Mr. W say, put face in swimming pool.	'Mr. W said put your face in the pool.'	6/10/74
I want Curtiss play piano.	'I want Curtiss to play the piano.'	8/7/74
Father make me cry.	'Father made me cry.'	8/20/74

[a]*to buy* was one word.

9.3.4.4. Causatives

Genie began expressing causation about a year and a half after her first sentences. Causative relationships were first expressed simply through relationships between phrases; later "causative" verbs (*feed, take*) were used; finally, the syntactic (*make X*) causative occurred, as illustrated in Table 9.10.

TABLE 9.10
Examples of Sentences Expressing Causation

Utterance	Gloss (when necessary)	Date
Mama give bath. Hurt.	'Mamma hurt me when she gave me a bath.'	1/24/73
Very sad, climb mountain.	'If you make me climb the mountain, I'll be sad.'	9/26/73
Take me shopping.		9/26/73
Mama feed me.	'Mama used to feed me.'	4/24/74.
Mixmaster make pudding.		1/8/74
Father take piece wood. Hit. Cry.	'Father used to take a piece of wood and hit me with it. It made me cry.'	8/20/74
Father make me cry.		8/20/74

9.3.4.5. If–Then Constructions

A sophisticated expression of causation occurs in *if–then* constructions. Although Genie does not use the terms *if* or *then*, she nonetheless has produced utterances of this type. Such utterances are further testimony to the sophisticated semantics of which she is capable. Note, for example, the following dialogue:

  11/24/74 G: *Neal come.*
      M: *Yes, Neal is going to come tomorrow. Neal makes you happy. He makes you happy. He's a friend of yours.*
      G: *Neal not come[,] happy. Neal come[,] sad.*

9.3.5. Responses to Questions

Genie's responses to questions demonstrates the extent of her reasoning, knowledge of the world, and semantic ability. For example,

  12/6/72 C: *How many sides does a triangle have?*
      G: *Three.*
      C: *How many sides does a circle have?*
      G: *Round.*
  7/30/73 M: *When can you have the Hershey bar?*
      G: *After dinner.*

1/8/74   M : *When is Curtiss supposed to come?*
           G : *Wednesday.*
2/22/72   D : *How should I reach it?*
           G : *Get ladder.*
1/15/74   M : *How did the car get wet?*
           G : *Raining hard.*
10/23/73   C : *Why aren't you singing?*
           G : *Very sad.*
           M : *Why are you feeling sad?*
           G : *Lisa sick.*
1/74   N : *Why do you think the boy looks sad?*
           G : *Spill milk.*
8/21/74   C : *Why do these belong together?*
           G : *Food.*
           C : *Why do these belong together?*
           G : *Thing.*

9.3.6. Semantic Play

Genie never exhibited any phonological play. She also never played with language syntactically. She spoke, for the most part, abnormally little, only when asked or expected to. Late in 1973, however, Genie surprised everyone by expressing, through speech, thought after thought. Temporarily fascinated with having things written down, Genie dictated the following to be written down one evening. All of the following occurred within a short space of time— words and phrases one after the other. Note how Genie uses semantic themes and explores them verbally. In some instances some free association appears to be going on, but in those cases what is particularly striking is the verbal coding of memories which took place long before Genie had language.

Lot friend . . . Ruth Smith . . . Mrs. F . . . Ralph . . . Grandma . . . Mama Grandma . . . Elizabeth . . . Sam . . . Andy . . . Judy . . . Mama . . . Curtiss . . . Laura . . . Billy . . . M. . . . Miss N . . . Carol . . . Miss U . . . Wendy . . . Father . . . Sam . . . Ann . . . Andy father . . . Father Bob . . . D. . . . Genie . . . Patty . . . D. . . . Lynn . . . Tom . . . Miss R . . . Rick . . . Peter . . . Spot . . . Baby . . . Nancy . . . Don . . . Miss J . . . Bert . . . Dennis . . . Fido . . . Cat . . . Mrs. L . . . Roy bus driver . . . Mr. B . . . Carl . . . Mike . . . Mike has blue car· . . . Train . . . Bus . . . Airplane . . . Blue burner . . . Stove . . . Boat . . . Chair swing . . . Take bath . . . Ocean hit back . . . Go shopping . . . Walk pier beach . . . Home . . . Go park . . . Go school . . . Go trip . . . Go hospital . . . Go Grandma house . . . I like potty chair . . . Work . . . Go eat . . . Drink . . . Go dress . . . Alone . . . Go diving . . . Climb mountain . . . Go ride . . . Ride bus . . . Ride boat . . . Airplane . . . Push cart . . . Go ride wagon . . . Ride cart . . . Ride horses . . . Ride van . . . Car have mirror . . .

Ride truck . . . Skate . . . Go walking . . . Ride sled . . . Ride wheelchair . . . Ride laundry box . . . I like a lot people . . . Ride jeep . . . Swimming pool have floating chair . . . Go ride floating chair . . . I like dancing . . . Ride pony . . . Ride helicopter . . . Ride elevator . . . Ride escalator . . . Ride bus up in the sky . . . Go camper . . . Eat beach . . . Eat in the park . . . Eat Hospital . . . Eat home . . . Eat at school . . . Eat restaurant . . . Eat camper . . . Ride merry-go-round . . . Ride box up in the box . . . Like M. back home . . . I like walking . . . Stair[s] . . . Walk on the floor . . . Ride baby buggy . . . Ride carriage . . . Catch ball . . . Rock back and forth . . . Curtains . . . Running . . . Ride fast . . . I like jumping . . . Father angry . . . Spit out . . . Car have mirror . . . Ruth Smith has skate board . . . I like Genie . . . Cut nail hurt father . . . Very angry make BM . . . Lady . . . Man . . . Boy . . . Girl . . . Eat go trip . . . Go zoo . . . Eat zoo . . . Go picnic . . . Eat big boat . . . Go big boat . . . Go doctor . . . Go farm . . . Eat farm . . . Go outside . . . Go dentist . . . Fix teeth . . . I want see Mama Saturday . . . Genie eat Saturday.

There have been a few other such sessions where Genie produced a monologue of some length. The other instances consisted primarily of recounting an event recently experienced or reflecting on her past. It is important to note that Genie's reflecting on her past through language not only involves reference to nonimmediate events and feelings, but also involves a verbal expression of entirely nonverbal memories.

9.3.7. Summary

This chapter has presented the linguistic elements and structures present in Genie's production of language in the areas of syntax, morphology, and semantics. In Chapter 8, Genie's receptive knowledge of language in these areas was discussed. Some aspects of Genie's acquisition are normal; some are not. Her language acquisition will be compared to normals in Chapter 10.

10

Genie in Relation to Other Children

10.0.

In this chapter, Genie's language acquisition will be compared to that of normal children acquiring a first language. In some instances, as a function of certain abnormal aspects of Genie's language acquisition, her linguistic behavior will also be compared with that of linguistically abnormal children.

The child language literature has focused largely on language production as opposed to comprehension. Moreover, children's comprehension is difficult to assess, and many of the methods and instruments which have been used toward this end are inadequate and/or poorly designed (de Villiers & de Villiers, 1974; Waryas & Ruder, 1974; Chapter 6 of this volume). Consequently I will focus primarily on acquisition as manifested through speech production. In addition, because of the maturational and physiological differences implicated in the age discrepancy between Genie and normal children who are learning language, because of the emotional trauma associated with the act of producing sound, and because of the physical effects of years of disuse of the vocal tract and laryngeal mechanisms, many aspects of phonology will not be included in this comparative section. Only those that constitute the basic structures of English and/or those which provide interesting contrasts with other studies will be discussed.

10.1. PHONOLOGY

Genie's acquisition of phonology parallels normal phonological development in several respects, for example, her deletion of final consonants, simplification of initial clusters, relatively late use of affricates, and deletion of unstressed syllables in polysyllabic words (Menyuk, 1971; Ingram, 1974). More generally, Genie, like normal children, is acquiring a phonological system— where the surface phonetic form is not identical with the underlying form of a lexical item, and where the difference between them can be accounted for by rules. For instance, [fʌ̃t] 'funny', is the phonetic realization of the phonological form [fʌni], which has undergone vowel nasalization, unstressed syllable deletion, and [n]-substitution; [fʌt] is the phonetic realization of the same form ([fʌni]) which has undergone only unstressed syllable deletion and [n]-substitution; or, for example, [to] 'stove' is the phonetic realization of the underlying phonological form [stov] which has undergone initial cluster simplification and final consonant deletion; and [sətóʷ] is the phonetic realization of the same phonological form which has undergone [ə]-insertion, final consonant deletion, and vowel diphthongization.

In addition, the kinds of consonant substitutions that we find in Genie's speech indicate that Genie, like normal children, is acquiring a feature-based phonological system (Menyuk, 1968). What is more, her performance on the Receptive Phonology Test and in rhyming sessions demonstrates that, like normal children, there are differences between her perception of phonological distinctions and the production of those distinctions (Shvachkin, 1948).

There are several differences between Genie's acquisition of phonology and phonological development in normal children, however. First, the sounds found in her early monosyllables and disyllables were of a far wider range and variety than found in comparable phonological units of normal children (Jakobsen & Halle, 1956; Jakobsen, 1962). Second, her disyllabic productions were not reduplications, partial or otherwise (Moskowitz, 1970). Third, intonation was absent from all of Genie's early speech (Bever *et al.*, 1965). Fourth, the degree of variability in Genie's phonological output is reminiscent of the output of language-disordered children, where oftentimes rules are not generalized and individual words may undergo specific rules applying to them alone (Salus & Salus, 1973).

10.2. SYNTAX

Like Genie's acquisition of phonology, her acquisition of English syntax, in some important ways, has been like that of normal children, and in other important respects different from that of normal children.

10.2.1. Lexicon

The early acquisition of vocabulary by normal children has been referred to as "nominalizing" because many normal children first acquire mainly nouns. Genie's early vocabulary included almost as many adjectives and verbs as nouns (e.g., *stopit, spit, go, blue, red, silly*).

It has been estimated that when normal children acquire from 30 to 50 words, they begin to construct two-word phrases. I was not able to measure Genie's vocabulary when she first put words together, partly because her language development was not yet under observation. Data from staff notes and from videotapes, however, indicate that Genie had a vocabulary of at least 100 to 200 words before she constructed phrases.

10.2.2. First Sentences

Genie's first sentences were almost all noun phrases. In contrast, the first (two-word) sentences of normal children are typically equational sentences (*Dat mine*) and strings involving relationships between subject–verb/object (Bloom, 1971).

10.2.3. Negation

It has been reported that normal children typically reveal a specific developmental sequence in the acquisition of the syntax of basic negation (Klima & Bellugi, 1966). Fairly rapidly (over a period of, perhaps, 1 to $1\frac{1}{2}$ years) the negative sentences found in their speech have been reported to develop from Stage 1 type sentences to Stage 3 type strings:

Stage 1:   *Sentence-external Negation*

Example: ***No*** *want milk.*

Description: Strings where a negative element such as *no* or *not* is appended to the sentence, usually to the beginning.

Stage 2:   *Sentence-internal Negation*

Example: *I **not** want milk.*

Description: The negative particle is embedded within the sentence rather than attached externally. Often, at this stage, other terms used to express negation appear: *can't, won't, don't*, although these terms may not be analyzed as negative forms of their positive counterparts, since *can, will,* and *do* do not occur.

Stage 3:   *Inclusion of Do-support*

Example: *I **do not** want milk.*

Description: The dummy DO appears to express the tense of the sentence. Contraction of the negative particle also appears (e.g., *He isn't drinking milk.*).

A simple progression from Stage I to Stage III may not adequately or accurately describe the acquisition of negation for many normal children, however. For example, it has been suggested that some children may mark noun phrase negation differently from verb phrase negation and may even use intonation as a negative marker (Lord, 1974). In contrast, Genie did not appear to make any distinction between noun phrase and verb phrase negation and had no intonation in her speech at all.

More significantly, reexaminations of early data (Bloom, 1970; Brown, 1973) suggest that Stage I negation possibly does not exist at all for many or even most children. Most of the sentences described as Stage I type sentences are actually (*a*) *no, S affirmative* sentences or (*b*) *No V* sentences where the subject is a deleted pronoun or a deleted existential subject. If these are removed from the original data one is left only with Stage II and III type structures.

In contrast, Stage I negation was unquestionably present in Genie's grammar. Genie still does not produce concatenations of the type *no, S affirmative*, still has not acquired existentials, and acquired "I" (her only productive subject pronoun) long after she began producing negative forms. All of her negative structures were Stage I type sentences for close to 3 years (*Not have floating chair*; *Not like school*; *No more meat*; *No more take wax*; *No more ear hurt*). In the acquisition of negative structures Genie thus differs from normals both by producing Stage I type sentences and by producing negatives with the same syntactic structure for 3 years—a very retarded rate of development.

In addition, since the point that Genie progressed beyond Stage I negatives, it has been difficult to determine which stage she has reached. It appears that she moved from Stage I negatives to a combination of Stage II and Stage III type negatives (*I do not have red pail*; *Ellen not learn P.E. in school*; *I do not sick*; *Curtiss not sick*). Modals and negative contractions do not appear in her speech at all, and her use of DO-support has occurred exclusively with "I" and, therefore, may represent a learned phrase rather than a productive use of DO. The absence of the grammatical features that differentiate Stages II and III from each other make it nearly impossible to ascertain which stage of development Genie has reached, and whether, at this point, her acquisition of negation parallels normal development more than before.

10.2.4. Interrogatives

Normal children begin asking questions almost as soon as they utter their first words (Brown, 1968, 1973). First through use of intonation, then through use of question words, and finally through use of question words and, where appropriate, with subject–auxiliary inversion, children formulate questions, ever approaching the well-formed interrogative structures of the adult model (Brown & Bellugi, 1964).

Genie has never asked a syntactically marked question. Her attempts to construct questions (in attempts to teach her to do so) have led to the most ill-formed, least English-like structures she has produced (e.g., *Where is may I have a penny?*; *Where is tomorrow Mrs. L.?*; *I where is graham cracker on top shelf?*). She can decode the linguistic structure of questions (cf. Chapter 8) and appears to know the constituent structure of the WH-question words she hears (Chapter 9), but is unable to produce spontaneous interrogatives.

Well-formed English questions involve movement rules, permutation of the elements of the sentence. Nowhere in Genie's speech do we find permutation of sentence elements. An inability to perform such complex linguistic operations may therefore account for the absence of well-formed questions from her speech, and lack of intonation can account for the absence of yes/no questions. Why however, does Genie not produce WH-questions of the form typical of early WH-questions of normal children: WHO that?, WHAT's that?, WHAT Mommy doing?, WHERE he going? WHO-questions often require a pronoun, either personal or demonstrative, and Genie does not use these elements; therefore we would not expect her to formulate such WHO-questions. Therein lies a possible clue as to why other WH-questions are also absent.

Not possessing intonation or permutation, Genie has no way to signal questions without the use of WH-words. It is only because questions represent such a basic sentence form that the absence of WH-words is so much more striking than the absence of certain other grammatical elements, however. It is in the absence of all of these elements considered together, that the explanation for Genie's lack of question words may lie. (See below.)

10.2.5. Proforms

WH-words are grammatical proforms representing some noun or noun phrase. Proforms, in general, are absent from Genie's speech.

Genie does not use third person pronouns. Attempts to teach her third person pronouns have not been successful. For example, note the following exchange:

Sign language teacher: *Give me a "he" sentence. Start it with "he" and tell me about the boy in the picture.*

G: *The boy signing is he cookie.*

Relative pronouns, indefinite pronouns, and demonstratives are also absent from Genie's speech. The only apparent proforms present in her speech are

I, you, and *me* (*it* has occurred twice, but occurred in strings that were esentially imitations of sentences she had heard).

You and *me* have consistently been confused; Genie has not been able to correctly sort out the correct usage of these terms, although she has been working on this since fall 1972, and there have been continuous attempts to help her to learn the difference. Her confusion and difficulty with these terms appear to parallel problems that autistic and schizophrenic children demonstrate with these pronominals (Needleman, 1974; Cunningham, 1966). Perhaps the acquisition and appropriate usage of *me* and *you* involve clear psychological separation of one's self from others, a self-awareness and separation Genie and other emotionally disturbed children do not have. In any case, Genie cannot be said to have acquired the pronouns *me* and *you* and, although she has on occasion used both correctly, that leaves *I* as the only proform Genie may possess (see Chapter 9).

Essentially, then, Genie's grammar lacks a system of deixis and the individual elements comprising such a system. WH-question words may be absent, therefore, because they are part of a class of elements that Genie has not been able to acquire: deictics.

In addition, however, there is an even larger range of elements that Genie has not yet acquired—and perhaps cannot acquire at all. WH- words and other deictic elements are only part of this larger set. The larger set of elements, which cover all of the aspects of syntax missing from Genie's grammar, are those that carry a minimal semantic load and are almost completely syntactic in makeup: deixis, permutation rules, and AUX elements. WH-words, then, may be absent because they are part of a system of deixis and the whole deictic system is absent from Genie's grammar. A system of deixis may be absent, however, because it is part of a broader range of syntactic elements that are absent from Genie's grammar. The absence of these particular aspects of syntax is also found in other groups acquiring language. See Chapter 11 for a discussion of this phenomenon and its implications.

10.2.6. Word Order

Genie's utterances, like those of normal children acquiring English, follow strict word order: Modifier–Noun, Possessor–Possessed, Subject–Verb–Object, Preposition–Noun Phrase. There are exceptions to S–V–O word order, but as with data on normal children (Brown *et al.*, 1969), such order reversals are rare.

Order between more than one noun modifier has not always conformed to the adult model in Genie's speech (*small two cup*; *Big, two, square pillow*), but such examples are even rarer than Subject–Verb–Object reversals.

Unlike normal children, Genie appears to have problems in decoding certain word order problems. Whereas normal children appear to manifest a developmental sequence in interpreting actives and passives (Bever, 1970), Genie has not manifested such a sequence and shows particular problems interpreting reversible actives. De Villiers and de Villiers (1974) report that very young normal children (Stage I children) manifest similar problems with reversible actives, so problems in this area may be a sign of an immature stage of language acquistion in addition to other problems.

10.2.7. Rate of Acquisition of Syntax

It has often been noted how rapidly normal children appear to acquire language, especially speech. In approximately $2\frac{1}{2}$ years, children with no language production at all, develop practically the full range of grammatical structures found in the adult language, although not everything (McNeil, 1970). Children's first "syntactic" stage, the two-word stage, normally lasts for only a few weeks; and then not long afterward a sort of explosion occurs, and the change and growth becomes so rapid and wide-ranged, it is difficult to keep track of or describe.

> There is a very early stage where in the child's production of speech you do not find many of the mechanisms, and there is a slightly later stage in which you find so many of the mechanisms you cannot begin to describe them, and the transition between these two stages seems fairly rapid [Chomsky, 1967, p. 86].

Genie's linguistic development, especially her speech development, has been quite slow, extremely slow compared to normals. Her two-word stage lasted for 4 months; negative sentences remained in the same state of development for almost 3 years. Despite the fact that Genie has acquired many grammatical morphemes, her speech remains largely telegraphic—4 years after she began putting words together. The great explosion has simply not occurred.

A retarded rate of development is a feature of language disorder. The acquisition time from level I to level V is nearly two and a half times longer for a language deviant child than for normals (Morehead & Ingram, 1973).

10.2.8. Imitation

Although there is much imitation in child speech, especially in the earliest stages, normal children do not essentially speak in imitation of the sentences they hear nor do they acquire language primarily by imitation.

Like normal children, Genie is not learning language by imitation. Her production of sentences such as those in example (1) through (3) below are evidence of this fact.

(1)   Small two cup.

(2)   Big two square pillow.

(3)   Fred have feel good.

Further evidence that Genie is not learning language primarily through imitation is shown by the sentences in examples (4) through (9):

(4)   Where is tomorrow Mrs. L.

(5)   I like M. fix teeth.

(6)   Boy is picture.

(7)   I like animal have bad cold.

(8)   Very angry clear water.

(9)   Angry burn stove.

The sentences given above, examples (4)–(9), are, however, different from those produced by normal children. Normal children rarely distort word order, but more importantly, the sentences normal children produce are reduced or unpermuted versions of grammatical strings. Sentences such as examples (4)–(9) are neither reduced nor unpermuted versions of grammatical sentences; they are ill-formed—both syntactically and semantically. Some ([8] and [9]) are reminiscent of the S + S + S-type structures that language-disordered children have been observed to produce (Menyuk, 1969; Lee, 1966), that is, strings of words apparently lacking in internal structure. Others ([4]–[7]) appear to combine disjoint and unrelated sentence fragments. All fail to communicate any meaning they might at some level be attempting to encode.

10.2.9.   Rules

When syntactic rules are considered, two important differences between Genie and normal children emerge. The first is in the kinds of rules used in the grammar of production. In the very early speech of normal children we find only reduction/deletion rules aside from base rules (Bloom, 1970). An underlying three-term sentence is reduced to a two-term sentence on the surface, especially when one of the terms is redundant information, as illustrated in Table 10.1. Genie has used rules of this type, as shown in Table 10.2. In (a) and (c), for example, since Genie was speaking, the subject was redundant and therefore deletable.

Soon after normal children begin using sentences, however, deleted elements decrease in number, and more and more of the basic constituents of the sentence appear on the surface. Not so with Genie. Throughout the period of observation, Genie has continued to delete subjects, verbs, or objects, whether redundant or recoverable. The only change is that these reduction/deletion

TABLE 10.1
Deleted Redundancies in Normal Child Language

Child's sentence	Redundant term included	
Eve lunch.	*Eve* $\left\{\begin{array}{c}\text{having}\\\text{eating}\end{array}\right\}$ *lunch.*	(Brown & Bellugi, 1964)
Want more.	*Stevie want more.*	(Braine, 1963)
Horsie flower.	*Horsie eat*(s) *flower.*	(Bowerman, 1973)

TABLE 10.2
Deleted Redundancies in Genie's Speech

Genie's sentence	Less reduced form
a. *Want soup.*	*Genie want soup.*
b. *Give me more.*	*Give me more soup.*
c. *Like powder.*	*Genie like powder.*
d. *Play piano.*	*Curtiss play piano.*

rules may have been obligatory (since redundant terms never surfaced), whereas they have become optional as the recent sentences in examples (10)–(19) indicate (date of utterance is listed with each sentence). The deleted elements may also, of course, not have been generated at all.

(10) 8/7/74 I want play piano.
(11) 8/7/74 I want Curtiss play piano.
(12) 9/26/73 Take shopping.
(13) 9/26/73 Take me shopping.
(14) 6/19/74 To buy present.
(15) 6/19/74 M. to buy present.
(16) 8/7/74 I want play piano.
(17) 8/7/74 I want Curtiss play piano.
(18) 3/27/74 Draw shot.
(19) 3/27/74 Genie draw shot.

As normal children acquire more language, other kinds of rules appear: substitution rules, addition rules, permutation rules. The only possible substitution rule present in Genie's grammar is the substitution of *I* for *Genie*. However *I* may be generated in the base, and her sentences with *I* probably do not require substitution at all. The only addition rules present in Genie's grammar are the rules affixing morphological markers to nouns and verbs. These rules are optional in her grammar as shown in examples (20)–(23):

(20)	a.	6/19/74	Curtiss is dance.
	b.	6/19/74	Curtiss is dancing.
(21)	a.	1/8/74	Genie drive jeep.
	b.	1/8/74	Genie driving jeep.
(22)	a.	10/1/73	I like five rug.
	b.	10/1/73	Five rugs.
(23)	a.	10/30/73	Apples.
	b.	10/30/73	Apple in the bucket.

The only possible permutation rule in Genie's grammar is a rule moving *-ing* after the verb. There are no rules permuting sentence constituents. The remainder of Genie's grammar can be accounted for by reduction and/or deletion.

The second major difference between Genie's grammar and the grammars of normal children acquiring a first language is in the variability of rule application. Most of Genie's rules are optional; sometimes they apply, sometimes they do not. This variability in rule application, coupled with the preponderance of reduction and deletion, produces a surface syntax that often masks the underlying grammar. In other words, Genie's speech seldom reveals the amount and range of linguistic structures and elements she has acquired. There is a great disparity between competence and performance when it comes to her production. A competence–performance disparity is also found in language-disordered children (Menyuk, 1964; Eisenson & Ingram, 1972); the waxing and waning quality of syntactic ability that great rule variability produces has also been found in developmentally aphasic children (C. Baltaxe & D. Meyers, personal communication).

10.3. MORPHOLOGY

Children's early sentences have been described as "telegraphic" (Brown & Bellugi, 1964) because they lack many of the grammatical formatives that we omit from a telegram message. The analogy is overextended since tense, modals, plurals, and possessives all would appear in a wired message but do not appear in early child utterances. The early sentences that Genie produced also lacked morphology and were "telegraphic." But in contrast to normal children,

Genie's utterances continued to appear "telegraphic," even long after exceptional utterances revealed that she had acquired much of the morphological machinery omitted from these "telegraphic" strings. Phonological rules such as final consonant deletion and final cluster deletion account for some of these ommissions (e.g., plurals, possessives, past tense endings), but not all.

In any case, it has been proposed (Brown, 1973; de Villiers & de Villiers, 1973) that English morphology is acquired in a certain developmental sequence across children who are learning English as a first language. It has also been proposed that children learning English as a second language and adults learning English as a second language also acquire these elements in a specific order, although the order is somewhat different for each group (Bailey *et al.*, 1974; Dulay & Burt, 1973).

Table 10.3 presents a comparison of proposed normal order of acquisition of English morphological elements with Genie's order of acquisition of English morphology. The correlation between Genie's rank order of acquisition and Brown's suggested order is fairly high (rho = .6).

TABLE 10.3
Comparison of Order of Morphological Acquisition

Brown's (1973) order		De Villiers and de Villiers (1973) order		Genie's order	
-ing	1	plural	1	on and in,	
in, on	2-3	-ing	2	article	1-2
plural	4	past irregular	3	-ing	3
past irregular	5	articles	4	plural, pos-	4-5
possessive	6	contractible	5	sessive	
(uncontractible	7	copula		third person	6-10
copula)		possessive	6	irregular,	
articles	8	third person	7	past regular,	
past regular	9	contractible		past irregular,	
(third regular)	10	auxiliary	8	contractible	
(third irregular)	11			copula,	
(uncontractible	12			copula,	
auxiliary)				contractible	
contractible	13			auxiliary	
copula					
contractible	14				
auxiliary					

10.3.1. The Noun Phrase

Normal children appear to elaborate the noun phrase by marking number and definiteness early (Brown *et al.*, 1969; Menyuk, 1971). Plural and definite modifiers such as demonstratives, and definite quantifiers, such as *more* and *another*, appear early on in the child's development of the noun phrase. Articles and indefinite modifiers appear later.

In contrast, articles and the quantifier *more* appeared in Genie's early noun phrases, but not number or demonstratives. (Demonstratives have never appeared.) Although Genie concentrated on noun phrases in her early speech, she produced mainly adjectives, sometimes two or three of these, with nouns, i.e., content words only.

Looking at the acquisition order of noun phrase morphology, Table 10.4 shows how Genie compares with normals.

TABLE 10.4
Order of Acquisition of Noun Phrase Morphology

Brown's (1973) order		De Villiers and de Villiers (1973) order		Genie's order	
plural	1	plural	1	article	1
possessive	2	article	2	plural,	2–3
article	3	possessive	3	possessive	

10.3.2. The Verb Phrase

There are some striking differences in Genie's acquisition of verb phrase elements and structures. Prevalent in the development of the verb phrase in normals is the presence of catenatives: *wanna, gonna, hafta* (Brown, 1973). Genie has never used catenatives. She has, however, used "serial" type sentences (e.g., *I want go walk* [to] *Ralph*['s]; *I like go ride Miss F. car*). Although Genie's "serial" verb phrases are much more complex structurally (both semantically and syntactically), neither involve a hierarchy of sentences, even though they involve what look like complex verb phrases on the surface. Both catenative constructions and Genie's "serial" verb phrases probably arise from a VP → V + VP phrase structure rule.

Also noticeably different is Genie's acquisition of the contractible copula and modals. Typically, in normal children contractible copulas first appear in contracted form (*That's mine; Where's Daddy?; It's innere*). At this stage the *'s* probably does not represent more than an unanalyzed feature of the noun phrase (Brown, 1973). Next, the contractible copula appears in its full form, and only afterward does it appear in contracted form once again. Genie has never used a contracted form of the copula, perhaps because of final consonant deletion.

Modals appear in full form before contracted form, as well (excluding the forms *won't* and *can't* which appear earlier in negative sentences; these are probably not related to their affirmative modal counterparts). What is strikingly different here, however, is their total absence from Genie's speech.

Contractible AUX has also never appeared in Genie's speech in contracted form. In summary, then, Genie's acquisition of the constituent AUX is decidedly different from normal, much of it not yet having been acquired.

Table 10.5 shows how Genie's acquisition of verb phrase morphology compares to normals in rank order.

TABLE 10.5
Comparison of Order of Acquisition of Verb Phrase Morphology

Brown's (1973) order		De Villiers and de Villiers (1973) order		Genie's order	
-ing	1	-ing	1	-ing	1
past irregular	2	past irregular	2	past regular,	2
past regular	3	contractible	3	past irreg-	
third person	4	copula		ular, contrac-	
irregular		third person	4	tible copula,	
contractible	5	contractible	5	contractible	
copula		auxiliary		auxiliary	
contractible	6				
auxiliary					

10.4. SEMANTICS

10.4.1. Vocabulary

The early spoken vocabulary of normal children is typically a set of concrete nouns, often overgeneralized in semantic representation and real-life application (Clark, 1973). In contrast, Genie's early vocabulary included color words, numbers, and adjectives expressing size and qualities (such as *funny*, *silly*) as well as concrete nouns and action verbs (see Chapter 9). Moreover, Genie did not overextend the meanings of any lexical items in her vocabulary.

Whereas, at least in the view of some (Schlesinger, 1974), a child learns to categorize much of the world by learning the meanings of words, Genie's early use of words reflected categorizations that were already well developed. From data on videotapes it was clear that Genie learned individual items of clothing as well as the term *clothes*; individual animals as well as the term *animal*; individual people as well as the term *people*; individual forms as well as the term *shape*; individual vehicles as well as the category vehicle; individual foods as well as the term *food*. She never used these terms inappropriately and demonstrated an ability to differentiate between objects resembling each other closely in form and functions (*nail* vs. *screw*, *poster* vs. *picture*, *jacket* vs. *coat*).

The early acquisition of vocabulary in normal children often serves the function of labeling in the sense of naming or pointing out the existence of objects (Dore, 1975). Genie rarely uses words as labels in the above sense (except when called upon to do so). In contrast, however, she appears to use whole phrases as labels. In referring to past situations or events, or in referring to present situations or events that are similar to past occurrences, Genie attaches entire phrases as labels.[1] This use of phrases as labels is reminiscent of the language of autistic and schizophrenic children (Baltaxe & Simmons, 1975)[2] and contributes to the esoteric quality and pragmatic abnormality of Genie's speech.

10.4.2. Semantic Functions

Unlike normal children, whose first sentences involve the expression of agency, action and patient (Bloom, 1970), Genie's first sentences expressed

[1] This use of phrases as labels for situations does not refer to perserverations, where one phrase is repeated continuously in reference to an event that holds particular importance or anxiety for Genie (e.g., instances of fear where she has spilled or broken something [*Glass is broken*], [*Juice is spill*], or instances of agitation over an upcoming event [*not Doctor*]).

[2] Although, like Genie, autistic children are reported to use entire phrases as labels, unlike Genie, they are hypothesized to do so because they lack the capacity to recognize or express functional relations (Baltaxe & Simmons, 1975). Genie's ability to express and understand functional relationships in sentences is evident throughout all but the earliest stages of her linguistic development.

only modification and possession. Within months, however, Genie, too, began to express the variety and range of semantic functions found in normal child language (see Chapter 9).

In the acquisition of adverbial functions, "locative" precedes "time" and "manner" in normal first language acquisition (Brown *et al.*, 1969). Like normals, Genie expressed location first, but time adverbials (*tomorrow*, *Friday*, *Monday*) entered Genie's speech within months after locatives first appeared. Manner adverbials have yet to appear.

10.4.3. Semantic Relations

Like normal children, once Genie began to use verbs, she began to express the same kinds of semantic relationships found in early child speech—whether or not a verb actually appeared on the surface: agent–action, action–object, agent–object, agent–action–object, action–dative–object, agent–action–instrumental, agent–action–dative–object (see Section 9.3.2). Also, like normal children, Genie often omitted what might be termed unnecessary or redundant information; unlike normals, she also frequently omitted necessary information.

10.4.4. Semantic Features

Like normal children (Brown, 1969; Bowerman, 1973) Genie used the feature [±animate] to mark nouns for semantic function—with animacy reserved for agents, inanimacy for objects. Also like normal children (Brown, 1973) Genie never misapplied -*ing* to a stative verb, although stative verbs (e.g., *love*, *like*, *want*) frequently occurred in her speech. Her acquisition and use of the feature [±stative], therefore, also appear normal. Other features apparent in normal acquisition, however, have not been evident in Genie's grammar, at least not in the normal fashion: [±human], for example, has not been evident at all as part of Genie's semantic feature system, and [±female] has only been apparent through her use of gender-marked nouns. Both of these features are evident in normal acquisition through the acquisition of pronouns, but Genie has not acquired the relevant pronouns.

10.4.5. Negation

Bloom (1970) has proposed that there is a universal order in the emergence of negative functions: (1) nonexistence, (2) rejection, (3) denial. From normal child language data I have examined and from other evidence, it appears that the semantics of negation in child language is not nearly as clean-cut as Bloom suggests (Lord, 1974). Genie's use of *no* even at the point where all of her utterances were single-word utterances corresponded to each of the above semantic functions, no one clearly appearing before the other, and, at times, more than one seemingly functioning in the same *no*. These one-word negatives were almost all prompted either by questions, requests, or verbal and nonverbal suggestions (like food being placed in front of her), and so may have been semantically structured for her. Her spontaneous two- and three-word negatives were not so structured, however, and they nevertheless also express all three proposed negative functions, no one clearly preceding another (all of these were produced in the spring of 1972):

TABLE 10.6
Some of Genie's Early Negatives

Genie's utterance	Probable intended meaning	Semantic function
a. *No more father.*	*Father is not around anymore.*	Non-existence
b. *No more meat.*	*I don't want any meat.*	Rejection
c. *No more ear hurt.*	*My ear does not hurt anymore.*	Denial

Again, as with the one-word negatives, some utterances are difficult to classify according to the categories above. For example:

(24)   No more take wax. 'Stop taking the wax out of my ear, please.'

(25)   Not take shopping. 'I am thinking about the fact that Curtiss is not going to take me shopping.'

Neither of these examples has clearly just one negative semantic function.

10.5.   COMPREHENSION/PRODUCTION

Great rule variability in syntactic production also produces a large difference between Genie's comprehension and production of English—far greater than normal. There is a gap between comprehension and production for normal children as well, a gap that is not always unidirectional (i.e., comprehension does not always precede production) (Bloom, 1974); but that gap is never as great as we find with Genie. Normal children do not comprehend the full range and elaboration of a specific grammatical construction before producing any form or reflection of that construction in their speech. Normal children do not, for example, comprehend all WH-question forms before ever producing any (Ervin-Tripp, 1970; Brown, 1973); nor do normal children comprehend all tense and aspect forms before producing any (Carrow, 1969; Lee, 1969). In fact, there are cases where production of a form or some reflection of it precedes comprehension (e.g., tag questions (Brown *et al.*, 1969), certain WH-questions (Ervin-Tripp, 1970)). In Genie's case, therefore, the disparity between her comprehension and production of WH-questions, comparative, superlative, complex sentences, complex negation, pronouns, quantifiers, and prepositions is abnormal. Such a large gap (also not unidirectional—cf. her use of progressive as compared with her comprehension of progressive aspect) is only found with severely language-disordered children (Eisenson, 1972; Ingram, 1969). The disparity between comprehension and production is so great that one would draw very different conclusions regarding Genie's linguistic abilities and knowledge by examing only one and not the other. The disparity between comprehension and production suggests two independent systems, one underlying comprehension, one underlying production.

10.6.   COMPETENCE/PERFORMANCE

Genie's language performance often does not reflect her underlying linguistic ability. In production she rarely makes use of certain rules (pluralization, for example) or produces certain structures she is capable of producing (e.g., complements, embeddings). In comprehension, she manifests waxing and waning performance for some aspects of language (e.g., *me* versus *you*, future with *going to*). Whereas normal children appear to continually make use of the range and variety of linguistic elements and rules they have acquired in both comprehension and production, Genie does not. Especially in production, but in comprehension as well, Genie often manifests less linguistic ability than her underlying competence would allow.

The term competence has been used for the most part in relation to a highly abstract idealized model of grammar, and when we speak and understand, factors other than our knowledge of the language system play a role. Chomsky (1975) suggests the necessity to:

> distinguish between the grammar and a system of information processing perhaps not specific to language, and to account for actual behavior in terms of the interaction of these systems [p. 141].

Whereas such nonlinguistic factors cause speech errors, false starts, and so forth in normals, the great disparity between competence and performance in Genie's language behavior indicates more serious and detrimental (abnormal?)

intervention of coding and decoding processes not specific to language, processes not simply related to the extent of her linguistic knowledge.

10.7. CONCLUSION

Genie's language is far from normal. More important, however, over and above the specific similarities and differences that exist between Genie's language and the language of normal children, we must keep in mind that Genie's speech is rule-governed behavior, and that from a finite set of arbitrary linguistic elements she can and does create novel utterances that theoretically know no upper bound. These are the aspects of human language that set it apart from all other animal communication systems. Therefore, abnormalities notwithstanding, in the most fundamental and critical respects, Genie has language.

Part III

NEUROLINGUISTIC ASPECTS

11

Neurolinguistic Aspects

11.1. THE CRITICAL PERIOD

Genie's case has direct bearing on the question of a "critical age" for language acquisition. The concept of critical periods was introduced by ethologists, who in the study of the origin and development of species-specific behavior, noted that with respect to certain aspects of development there were periods in which an organism had to be appropriately stimulated in order for certain behaviors to develop normally. Research with goslings and birds (Hess, 1958, 1964), chicks (Tinbergen & Perdeck, 1950), chimpanzees (Riesen, 1947), rats (Levine, Alpert, & Lewis, 1958), and so forth, provides support for this concept.

Critical periods in the maturation of humans have also been proposed. Levine (1957), for example, has posited critical periods for the development of specific emotional responses, e.g., stress. Lenneberg (1967) proposed a critical period for the development of human language. He suggested that language is a function of brain maturation and develops "from mere exposure" to a linguistic environment (appropriate stimulation) only during a critical period—from about the age of 2 years to puberty.

Lenneberg suggests that before age 2, language acquisition is not possible because the brain is not sufficiently mature; and after puberty, natural language acquisition is not possible because the brain is physiologically mature, cerebral organization (lateralization) of all higher mental functions is complete, and cerebral plasticity is lost. For language to develop, the necessary requirements are only two: (1) a human brain and (2) sufficient exposure to language during this critical period between the age of 2 years and puberty.

Experimental deprivation has been a principal source for determining the validity of claims regarding critical periods and appropriate stimulation (Held & Bossom, 1961; Rosenzweig, 1971). Such experiments on humans, however, have not and cannot be carried out for obvious reasons. "Experiments in nature"—tragic alterations of the normal human condition not purposefully induced by the scientific community—provide us with our only means of studying such hypotheses re human development. Genie is such an experiment in nature, providing us with a case of "experimental" deprivation with which to examine the validity of Lenneberg's claims.

It is true that we do not know all of the details of Genie's past; specifically we do not know exactly how much language input she received. The information we do have, however, strongly suggests that Genie did not, in fact, receive sufficient linguistic input to develop language. Several factors indicate this. First, Genie was reported by her mother to have begun to speak words close to the time she was confined (20 months), and then to have stopped shortly after her confinement. If this is true, then Genie's "loss" of speech may have reflected a "loss" of adequate stimulation or input.[1] Second, the amount of linguistic input during her isolation was extremely limited as discussed in Part I. Third, although Genie may have begun acquiring language before her isolation, when she emerged from isolation, she did not have language (see Chapter 8). Other, nonverbal abilities (form discrimination, color matching abilities, form–puzzle solving abilities, imitative abilities) were evident, but language was absent. Her confinement did, therefore, allow for the development or retention of some cognitive/perceptual abilities, but did not appear to permit the development of language. One may then assume that Genie is a test case for Lenneberg's hypothesis in that she emerged from isolation without having received adequate linguistic stimulation during the period from age 2 to puberty.

There are two versions of Lenneberg's critical age hypothesis that can be extracted from his writings: (1) a strong version—a human being cannot acquire a first language naturally (by "mere exposure") after puberty, and (2) a weak version—*normal* language acquisition cannot occur naturally beyond the critical period.

---

[1] The mother's report that Genie had started to speak words before her confinement, if true, would be strong evidence against a diagnosis of mental retardation for Genie, since no mentally retarded child begins to talk at the age of 20 months. In fact, language delay (delay of the onset of speech) is one of the most discussed and accepted characteristics of mental retardation (Graham & Graham, 1971; Karlin & Strazzulla, 1952; Lenneberg, Nichols, & Rosenberger, 1964). What is more, because the nervous system is not sufficiently mature as suggested by Lenneberg (1967) or because the emergence of language depends on cognitive structures developed during the sensorimotor stage as suggested by Sinclair (1971), the onset of speech for normal children does not usually occur until close to 18 months of age. If Genie, therefore, actually did speak some words before her confinement at the age of 20 months, she began her years of confinement as a cognitively and linguistically normal child.

The "strong" version, that natural language acquisition cannot occur after puberty, can be dismissed in this case. As demonstrated in Part II, Genie is acquiring language from "mere exposure."

The "weak" version, that natural language acquisition cannot develop normally after puberty, cannot be dismissed. To be sure, no one has yet defined exactly what the course of "normal" language acquisition is. Not every aspect of language has been examined in terms of its acquisition, nor is the course of linguistic development entirely uniform across children. There are, nonetheless, certain features of language acquisition that mark abnormal development, features reportedly found in language-disordered children's linguistic development, or in cases of adult brain damage.

These features of abnormal language development include (1) a larger than normal comprehension/production disparity (Ingram, 1969), (2) a large competence/performance distinction (Eisenson & Ingram, 1972; Leonard, 1972), (3) abnormal variability in rule application (Salus & Salus, 1973; Baltaxe, C. and Meyers, D., personal communication), (4) stereotypic speech (Menyuk, 1971; Lee, 1966), (5) a retarded rate of development (Morehead & Ingram, 1973), and (6) in certain cases, failure (perhaps inability) to acquire specific syntactic forms and mechanisms always present in normal grammatical development. Genie's language reflects all of these characteristics.

11.1.1. Comprehension/Production

As described in Part II, Genie's comprehension and production are abnormally disparate. In comprehension she manifests knowledge of most of the basic structures of English, whereas in production she does not. (See Chapters 8, 9, and 10 for a full discussion.) Such a gap between the two is a sign of highly abnormal language acquisition (Ingram, 1969; Lenneberg, 1962).

11.1.2. Competence/Performance

The difference between Genie's competence and performance is abnormally large and is also a sign of language disorder (Leonard, 1972; Menyuk, 1964). (See Section 10.6 for discussion.)

11.1.3. Variability

As detailed in Part II, an abnormal degree of variability of rule application is present in Genie's speech. To be sure, there is rule variability in the grammars of normal children and adults as well; but both the extent and unpredictability of variability in Genie's grammar and the length of time such variability has persisted are abnormal and reflect language disorder.

11.1.4. Stereotypic Speech

Language-disordered children are reported to produce a considerable amount of stereotypic speech, S + S + S type and others (Menyuk, 1971; Lee, 1966). Genie's speech is filled with stereotypic utterances: rituals, formula-like utterances, sentences as labels for whole situations (see Chapters 9 and 10 for discussion).

11.1.5. Retarded Rate of Development

Like language-disordered children (Morehead & Ingram, 1973), the rate of Genie's linguistic development is far slower than that found in normal children (see Chapter 9).

11.1.6. Gaps in Acquisition

As discussed in Part II, there are certain aspects of language that Genie has not acquired. They are all syntactic: (1) proforms of all kinds—WH-words, relative markers, pronouns, indefinites, demonstratives, "pro-verbs" (*do* as a referential VP); (2) movement rules—inversion of sentence elements such as in subject–auxiliary inversion, WH-fronting, and so forth; (3) AUX—tense inflections (except for those that occur with individual lexical items, which are probably part of the lexical entries themselves), modals, aspect markers (except *be* + *ing*). AUX, the sentence constituent with the least semantic content, the constituent most dependent on syntactic factors alone, remains by far the least developed in Genie's grammar.

11.1.7.

There are three other groups that to date have not demonstrated the ability to acquire these very features of language: (1) left-hemispherectomized adults whose right hemispheres are left to acquire language in adulthood (Hillier, 1954; Smith, 1966; Zollinger, 1935), (2) children in the earliest stage of language acquisition (Bloom, 1970, 1973; Braine, 1963; Brown, 1973; Miller & Ervin, 1964), and (3) chimpanzees attempting to learn language (Brown, 1973; Fleming, 1974; Gardner & Gardner, 1969; Russell & Russell, 1971).

The first two groups represent human beings attempting language acquisition before or after the critical age—at inappropriate times in the maturation of the organism (Stage I children, for example, before they are maturationally equipped to do so). The third group—nonhuman attempts to acquire language—parallels human attempts when such attempts are (1) not carried out by cortex predisposed or "programmed" to process language in the normal brain or (2) outside of the appropriate maturational stage.

It is as if there are specific limitations to how much and what aspects of language "nonlanguage" area cortex, or the immature cortex can acquire. "Nonlanguage" cortex in humans may be the right hemisphere in general, and possibly the left hemisphere outside of the appropriate maturational state in development. In chimpanzees it is possibly the cortex in general. Such cortex can acquire vocabulary (Bellugi & Brown, 1964; Bloom, 1970; Brown, 1973; Gardner & Gardner, 1969; Gazzaniga & Hillyard, 1971; Hillier, 1954; Smith, 1966), simple two-, three-, and four-word utterances (Bowerman, 1973; Brown, 1973; Gardner & Gardner, 1971; Hillier, 1954; Linden, 1974; Russell & Russell, 1971; Smith, 1966), negatives (Bellugi & Brown, 1964; Bloom, 1970; Gazzaniga, 1970), and, in general, greater semantic than syntactic abilities (Bloom, 1970; Bowerman, 1973; Fleming, 1974; Gazzaniga, 1970; Greenfield et al., 1973; Zaidel, 1973). None of the groups above has been reported to have acquired proforms,[2] movement rules, or AUX elements. Genie's acquisition of language, therefore, resembles that of (1) humans attempting to reacquire language utilizing their right hemispheres, (2) humans attempting to acquire language in the "noncritical" period, or (3) other species acquiring language.

11.2. GENIE AS A RIGHT-HEMISPHERE LANGUAGE LEARNER

As stated above, Genie's language acquisition in some ways resembles the reported language acquisition abilities of adult right hemispheres. There are additional comparisons between Genie's language and the language of right hemispheres to those previously discussed.

Gazzaniga (1970) reported that the right hemispheres he studied had word-order discrimination problems; specifically, they could not discriminate a reversible active such as "The boy kissed the girl" from its reversed counterpart "The girl kissed the boy." Denis and Whitaker (1976) examining the linguistic abilities of childhood hemispherectomies also found word-order discrimination problems in the right hemispheres, but not in the left. Genie, as determined by her performance on the Active Voice Test (see Chapter 8), exhibits word-order discrimination problems as well.

Zaidel (1973, in press-a) found the vocabulary competence of the right hemisphere of his split-brain subjects to be only slightly below that of their

---

[2] Chimpanzees are reported to use the signs for "me" and "you" and "that," but these merely involve pointing (to oneself or to the listener or to the object referred to) and so cannot be considered abstract proforms, such as the spoken pronouns "me," "you," or "that." Chimps are also, however, reported to ask questions. Although their questions may not include proforms, they are unquestionably utterances marked as questions and therefore include at least one syntactic element absent in Genie's grammar.

left hemispheres, as judged by their scores on the Peabody Picture Vocabulary Test (PPVT). Zaidel further found that their relatively good scores on the PPVT contrasted with their poor scores on the Token Test, a measure of the ability to comprehend nonredundant spoken commands (Zaidel, 1977). (The "average" right hemisphere performed above the 11-year-old level on the PPVT, while the average right-hemisphere performance on the Token Test was approximately at the 4-year-old level.) The three cases of adult left hemispherectomy in the literature also had higher vocabulary abilities then syntactic competence (Zollinger, 1935; Hillier, 1954; Smith, 1966); and comparing PPVT scores with Token Test scores on another left hemispherectomy (symptoms at 8 years and surgery at 10), Zaidel (1977) reports far higher vocabulary performance (8.1 years) than Token Test performance (3.0 years). Denis and Whitaker (1976) also report relatively better right-hemisphere vocabulary ability (as measured by the PPVT) than syntactic abilities (as measured by a series of tests) with their childhood right hemispheres. Although Genie's performance on the PPVT is low (see Table 11.1), it is more advanced than most other aspects of her grammatical performance. In this respect as well, therefore, she resembles right hemispheres reported in the literature.

Denis and Whitaker report that the childhood left hemispherectomies had better receptive semantic than syntactic abilities. Genie, too, demonstrates better semantic than syntactic abilities (see Chapter 9).

All of the adult right hemispheres (both split-brains and left hemispherectomies) reportedly have far better comprehension that speech. Genie, too, has much better comprehension than speech.

In many ways, then, Genie's language abilities resemble the language acquisition abilities of right hemispheres: better vocabulary than syntax; better semantic than syntactic ability; word-order comprehension problems;

TABLE 11.1
Peabody Picture Vocabulary Test Scores

Date tested	Genie's score
3/5/71	no score
4/9/71	no score
4/22/72	below all norms
9/17/72	2.9 – 3.2 years
5/8/73	4.4 years
2/74	5.7 years
1/31/76	5.10 years

better comprehension than speech.[3] Although detailed examination, especially of adult right hemispheres, has not yet been carried out so that more detailed comparisons with Genie cannot be made at this time, Genie fits the picture of right hemisphere language that has emerged so far.[4]

Linguistically, then, Genie looks like a right-hemisphere language learner. There is even stronger evidence, however, that Genie is indeed using her right hemisphere to do language. This evidence comes from three sources: dichotic listening tests, tachistoscopic tests, and evoked response tests, discussed in 11.3.

11.3. LATERALIZATION

In his "critical period" hypothesis, Lenneberg (1967) tied the "critical period" to the lateralization of language (localization of language to one hemisphere of the brain). Based on clinical evidence of recovery from aphasia and of language acquisition after hemispherectomy for infantile hemiplegia, Lenneberg concluded that lateralization was complete at puberty, accounting for the loss of brain plasticity at that point. Although leaving any relationship between lateralization and plasticity unexplained, recent work (Krashen, 1972, 1973; Krashen & Harshman, 1972; Molfese, 1972; Witelson & Pallie, 1973) has shown that lateralization of language is complete long before puberty, by age 5 or before. Nonetheless, since by the age of 5 years normal children have acquired native competence in their language, the question of the relationship between language lateralization and language acquisition remains an interesting one to explore. The development of lateralization may still, to some degree, reflect the optimal or critical period for first language acquisition to occur, namely, when it normally does.

Again, Genie presented an opportunity to examine the relationship between language lateralization and language acquisition. Would she, since she already had a mature brain even though she did not possess language, have a "fixed," lateralized representation for the few words she knew and manifest the same degree of lateralization throughout; or, would Genie become lateralized as she acquired language, i.e., would lateralization parallel the development of language? Moreover, if Genie did manifest language lateralization, would her language be lateralized to the left hemisphere as in normal right-handers (Genie is right-handed) or might some abnormal pattern

---

[3] Denis and Whitaker's childhood right hemispheres did not reportedly exhibit better comprehension than speech (although speech was not specifically studied), and in this respect Genie differs markedly from childhood right hemispheres.

[4] There is one blatant exception. Genie possesses no "automatic" speech (Jackson, 1932). See Section 11.5 for a discussion of this point.

of lateralization and cerebral organization appear since Genie was beyond the proposed critical period?

To answer some of these questions, investigations into Genie's cerebral organization were undertaken. There were three experimental techniques utilized: dichotic listening, tachistoscopic, and evoked response. (A description of all the dichotic listening and tachistoscopic tests is given in Appendix II.)

11.3.1. Dichotic Listening

The technique referred to as dichotic listening has been used for 15 years to investigate lateralization. It has been used with normal children (Knox & Kimura, 1970; Berlin, C. I., Hughes, Lowe-Bell, & Berlin, H., 1973) and on normal and brain-damaged adults. Detailed explanations of the technique and how it works can be found elsewhere (Kimura, 1961, 1963, 1967); the technique will be reviewed here briefly.

The technique involves presenting simultaneous competing auditory stimuli, one to each ear, usually at the same intensity. Although there are two auditory pathways connecting each ear to the brain (ipsilateral—same side connection, and contralateral—opposite side connection), the cross pathways dominate in dichotic listening (Kimura, 1961), and the ear contralateral to the hemisphere best able to perceive and/or process the stimuli performs slightly better than the ipsilateral ear. Two points to keep in mind are (1) for normal right-handed adults there is a slight right-ear advantage on verbal stimuli (hypothesized to reflect left-hemisphere processing) and a slight left-ear advantage for nonverbal stimuli (hypothesized to reflect right-hemisphere processing), and (2) the ear advantage found using dichotic listening on normal adults is slight.

Genie was given dichotic listening tests on both verbal and nonverbal auditory stimuli. The verbal test consisted of fifteen pairs of words, each pair preceded by the binaural instructions: "Point to the _____." Genie had to point to objects and pictures representing the words. All the words on the test were part of Genie's productive and receptive vocabulary, and the voice on the dichotic tape was my own.

Verbal dichotic listening tests were administered on four separate occasions over a period of 1 year and 3 months. On three of these occasions a single pair of dichotic words was presented at a time; on the last occasion two pairs of words were presented together, one pair immediately following the other, separated by 0.5 seconds.

On each occasion Genie was first tested monaurally (i.e., stimuli were presented to one ear at a time). She had no difficulty whatever in responding correctly to stimuli in either ear, in every instance performing at 100% accuracy.

In Tables 11.2–11.4 below the results of the verbal dichotic listening tests are presented.

TABLE 11.2
Dichotic Listening Results Using Single Pairs of Words Presented Dichotically

Date	Number of pairs presented	Number correct	
		Right ear	Left ear
3/27/72	29	6	29
5/10/72	15	1	15
8/16/72	30	5	30

TABLE 11.3
Dichotic Listening Results Using Two Pairs of Words Presented Dichotically

Date	Number of pairs presented	Number correct	
		Right ear	Left ear
6/3/73	28	0	28
Controls[a]	28	23.5	21.4

[a]N = 21, right-handed adults with normal hearing; p <.025, one tail.

TABLE 11.4
Comparison of Genie's Dichotic Listening Results with Other Classes of Subjects[a]

Subjects	Percentage correct		
	Better ear	Weaker ear	
Normal subjects	60.3	51.9	(Curry, 1968)
Genie	100.0	16.0	
Right hemispherectomized	99.0	24.3	(Berlin *et al.*, 1972)
Split-brain	90.7	22.2	(Milner *et al.*, 1968)

[a]From Fromkin, Krashen, Curtiss, Rigler, & Rigler (1974).

The results are unusual in two respects. First, the direction of ear advantage is unexpected for a right-hander (Genie is right-handed): Genie's left ear outperformed her right ear on every occasion. Secondly, the degree of ear advantage is abnormal: Genie's left ear performed at 100% accuracy, while her right ear performed at a level below chance. (Contrast the normal ear advantage with Genie's in Table 11.4.) The degree of ear advantage resembles that found in split-brains and hemispherectomies, where (because only contralateral pathways are functional in dichotic listening) only one hemisphere is functioning. (See Table 11.4.)

With regard to lateralization, Genie's dichotic listening results indicate strong lateralization for language,[5] even though Genie had not yet acquired a great deal of language, nor had her language acquisition run its course. In her case, then, language lateralization was not developing in parallel to her language acquisition. It is questionable whether Genie's results should or can be related to the question of the relationship between language lateralization and language acquisition in normals, however; for the dichotic results indicate language lateralized to the right hemisphere in Genie, whereas it is the left hemisphere that is predisposed for language in normals (Molfese, 1972; Witelson & Pallie, 1973). Since it is the left hemisphere which is predisposed for language in normals, and language is lateralized to the left in right-handed normals, Genie's case can only be regarded as abnormal in this respect and without implications for the relationship between lateralization and acquisition as it normally occurs. Genie's case does, however, have implications for that relationship when normal development is prevented (not by surgery or specific brain disease).

The dichotic results correspond to our finding that Genie's language resembles right-hemisphere language. The dichotic listening tests indicate that her language *is* right-hemisphere language. Thus, Genie's case may indicate that after the "critical period," the left hemisphere can no longer assume control in language acquisition, and the right hemisphere will function and predominate in the acquisition and representation of language. The inability of the left hemisphere to process language after the "critical period" may be accounted for by a kind of functional atrophy of the usual language areas, brought about by disuse (due to inadequate stimulation) or suppression. In Genie's case this would explain why her right-ear scores on the verbal dichotic listening tests were so abnormally low. The undeveloped language areas prevented the flow of language impulses from the left primary auditory recognition area to the right hemisphere.

Genie's results on the verbal dichotic tests not only revealed right-hemisphere language processing, they also resembled results obtained from

---

[5] At least for vocabulary, the only aspect of language tested in these experiments.

individuals in whom only one hemisphere functioned for such a task; namely, split-brains and hemispherectomies. To determine if Genie was one of the rare right-handed individuals with crossed dominance, or was rather functioning to some degree like an individual with only one hemisphere, nonverbal dichotic listening tests were administered.

Environmental sounds were presented dichotically on four separate occasions. On three of these a single pair of sounds was presented, and on the fourth, two pairs of sounds were presented, one pair directly following the other separated by 0.5 seconds. In each case Genie had to point to a photographic representation of the sound. The photographs were taken in her foster home, and both sounds and pictures depicted objects that were part of Genie's daily environment.

As before, each stimulus was presented monaurally to each ear prior to dichotic presentation, and Genie performed at 100% accuracy on each occasion. The results of the environmental sounds dichotic tests are presented in Tables 11.5 and 11.6.

The results show that Genie does not have crossed dominance. Her right hemisphere appears to process nonverbal as well as verbal auditory stimuli. Once again the degree of ear difference in Genie's results is greater than normal,

TABLE 11.5
Dichotic Listening Results with Single Pairs of Environmental Sounds Presented Dichotically

	Number of pairs	Number correct	
Date	presented	Right ear	Left ear
8/2/72	20	12	18
8/16/72	20	14	19
6/3/73	20	14	20

TABLE 11.6
Dichotic Listening Results with Two Pairs of Environmental Sounds Presented Dichotically

	Number of pairs	Number correct	
Date	presented	Right ear	Left ear
6/3/73	28	15	27

although it is nowhere as extreme as her results with verbal stimuli. It is only language stimuli that appear to be blocked from crossing the corpus collosum.

This result together with the other dichotic listening results suggests a picture of Genie as an individual who does all mental functioning with her right hemisphere. Thus it appears that language acquisition beyond the critical period has implications for cerebral organization in general.

Attempts to further determine if Genie's cerebral organization corresponded to our preliminary findings were undertaken.

11.3.2. Tachistoscopic Tests

Tachistoscopic experiments have been used to measure and ascertain laterality. The technique has been described in detail elsewhere in the literature (Geffen, Bradshaw, & Nettleton 1972), and I include here only a brief description.

Each eye has a left half-field (connected to the right hemisphere) and a right half-field (connected to the left hemisphere). A tachistoscope, which is a split-screen viewer, makes use of the fact that visual hemi-fields are linked with contralateral areas of the cortex. When the eyes are fixated at the center of the field and, via T-scope, stimuli are briefly exposed in the right or left half-field, the opposite hemisphere is stimulated. Visual stimuli presented tachistoscopically are flashed at one-tenth of a second or less, too fast for eye movements to occur. In this manner, two images may be projected simultaneously, one to the left hemi-field and one to the right.

To test our hypothesis that Genie was using her right hemisphere for both language and nonlinguistic cortical functions, we administered two types of T-scope tests, language and nonlanguage.

11.3.2.1. Language T-Scope Test

As Genie could not read, the most obvious visual linguistic test, reading, could not be used. We decided to use rhyming words as a test of linguistic processing. Work with split-brains had already shown that rhyming was a strongly left-lateralized ability (Levy, Trevarthen, & Sperry, 1972),[6] so we felt it would be a viable means for testing language lateralization with Genie. To ensure that Genie could do the task and to familiarize her with it, three separate sessions were devoted to assessing her ability to recognize when words rhyme. (See Part II, Section 7.1 for details of these sessions.) Her per-

---

[6] In fact, our first T-scope exercise with Genie was to administer the chimeric figures tests used with split-brains, including faces, rhymes, and antlers. For this attempt we were permitted both the materials and laboratory used in the model split-brain experiments. Unfortunately, Genie perseverated in her responses to such a degree as to render the results inconclusive.

formance on all three occasions indicated strongly that Genie had sufficient rhyming ability to permit its use as a means of testing hemispheric specialization for language.

On February 2, 1975, we administered a rhyming task via tachistoscopic presentation. Pictures of objects, whose names were part of both Genie's receptive and productive vocabulary, were used. Five rhyming word triplets comprised the test stimuli: (1) *pear/bear/chair*, (2) *hat/cat/bat*, (3) *tie/eye/pie*, (4) *bee/key/tree*, and (5) *toes/nose/rose*. Each member of each triplet occurred as both test stimulus and response array choice, and all possible pairings were used. Each stimulus occurred in both visual fields and the entire stimulus set was presented twice, for a total of sixty stimulus trials. The response array consisted of three picture choices; the position of the correct choice in the array was randomized throughout. (See Appendix II for more complete details.) Each stimulus was flashed for 75 milliseconds.

Out of 60 trials, Genie made 28 errors, 11 left visual field (LVF) errors, 17 right visual field (RVF) errors. The difference was not significant (.097, one tail, on the Fisher exact test), but the trend of errors again suggests right-hemisphere processing for language.

11.3.2.2. Nonlanguage T-Scope Test

The nonlinguistic task administered to Genie was a dot location task. Our task was patterned after a more elaborate dot location test (Kimura, 1969), to test spatial location abilities (normally lateralized to the right hemisphere).

We presented a 16-square grid, the center of which corresponded to the central fixation point of the split-screen. (See Figure 11.1.) Thus, half the grid flashed to the RVF, half to the LVF. Each dot stimulus was located within a different square on the grid; thus there were sixteen separate dot stimuli. The

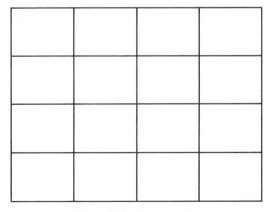

Figure 11.1. T-scope grid.

stimulus set was presented four times for a total of 64 trials, 32 trials in each visual field. For half the trials Genie responded by pointing with her left hand, for the other half with her right hand. The response array consisted of an empty grid four times larger than the tachistoscopically presented grid. Genie had to point (with a pointer) to the square on the grid corresponding to the square in which the stimulus dot appeared. Tachistoscopic presentation was at 30 milliseconds.[7]

Genie made 24 errors out of 64 trials, 12 errors with each hand. There were 16 LVF errors, 8 RVF errors. This difference was significant ($p = .03481$, one tail, $= <.05$) using the Fisher exact test. These results indicate left hemisphere dominance for spatial location.

The tachistoscopic tests, therefore, in part supported our hypothesis, in part conflicted with it. The asymmetry reflected using auditory stimuli was clearer than with visual presentation, however; and since the experimental factors were perhaps not as well controlled in the T-scope tests, the findings are not conclusive.

11.3.3. Evoked Potential Studies

Evoked response is the brain's electrical reaction to a single stimulus. In contrast to EEG experiments, stimuli are fairly short and are repeated several times, the responses then being averaged.

Brown, Marsh, and Smith (1973) at the UCLA Brain Research Institute have used evoked response to study cerebral asymmetry and the representation of language in the brain. Using homophones in differing grammatical contexts (e.g., "*Fire* is hot" and "*Fire* the gun"), they have been able to demonstrate that the evoked response is different for the same word used in different grammatical contexts and that in normal right-handed adults these waveform differences are lateralized to the left hemisphere. At the present time, it remains unclear exactly what the differences in waveform represent. There are several possibilities, none of which can be proved given the present state of the art. Brown et al. (1973) suggest that the response differences reflect the lateralization of linguistic processing. Brown and Marsh, using their technique, conducted two pilot studies on Genie, (1) a language task, and (2) a (visual) facial recognition task. In each study, four electrodes were placed over the cortex, two over the left, and two over the right. The electrodes were located approximately over Broca's area and Wernicke's area on the left, and over homotopic loci on the right.

---

[7] This duration was used because slower durations did not produce sufficient errors to detect hemispheric differences in her performance.

In the language study, two homophones were used in differing contexts: "I *sock* Bobo" and "My *sock* is red." The facial recognition task used composite drawings differing only in one or two features (nose, mouth, eyes, etc.). The pilot data from both tests were analyzed by Brown and Marsh. In both the homophone task and the facial recognition task, these data showed greater right-hemisphere than left-hemisphere involvement.[8] If Brown and Marsh are right in their interpretation, these results are consistent with our dichotic listening results and thus strengthen our hypothesis that Genie is using her right hemisphere for nonlanguage cortical functions as well as for language.

11.4. GENIE AS A RIGHT-HEMISPHERE THINKER

Our lateralization studies, although not sufficiently extensive or varied to be conclusive, indicate that Genie is using her right hemisphere for language and nonlanguage processing. This corresponds to our general observational impression that Genie is better at abilities that are normally (in right-handed individuals) controlled by the right hemisphere, than at abilities normally controlled by the left. Reflecting on Genie's general cognitive behavior, one notes that she is visually and tactilely oriented, excellent at remembering faces, good at finding her way around in real space, and good at gestalt recognition. As a result, we attempted to test our hypothesis—that Genie is better at abilities localized in the right hemisphere in right-handed normals—by administering tests that tap various cognitive and perceptual abilities.

11.4.1. Tactile Perception

"Normal" cerebral organization—language in the left hemisphere, visuo-spatial in the right—is defined mainly for right-handers. Genie's unusual brain organization (as indicated by her performance on tests of laterality), is, therefore, unusual to a large extent because she is right-handed.

Several factors evidence her right-handedness. First, Genie prefers to use her right hand. She writes, eats, cuts, draws, and performs all of her daily fine motor acts with her right hand as principal manipulator. Second, on the Localization of Tactile Stimuli Test, a section of the Southern California Sensory Integration Test (Ayres, 1972), Genie performed better on her left (nonpreferred) hand. Results from other tactile stimulation tests (e.g.,

---

[8] With Genie, right anterior leads showed the greatest lateralization effect, whereas in normals (males, at least) it is the left anterior lead that shows the greatest lateralization effect (Brown *et al.*, 1973).

Carmon & Benton, 1969; Benton, Levin, & Varney, 1973) indicate that it is the nondominant hand which is more sensitive to tactile stimulation, a finding that makes Genie's test performance indicative of right-handedness. Third, Genie's left hand outperformed her right on the Finger Identification Test of the Southern California Sensory Integration Test. Results from other tests of this nature (e.g., Metzig, Rosenberg, & Ast, 1975; Metzig *et al.*, in press) indicate a superior performance with the nondominant hand.

11.4.2. Gestalt Perception

Very early in our experience with Genie, we noticed her extraordinary ability to gestalt numbers. When asked to get five napkins, or when asked how many trays there were in a pile, for example, Genie responded immediately, without counting, and always correctly. She would simply reach into a drawer and pull out the number of items requested.

Genie responded faster than we could count. It was as if she had the tactile image of what three, four, five, or whatever, "felt" like, and the visual image of what one through seven looked like. (Her ability to gestalt numbers stopped at seven.)

In contrast, she did not know how to count in serial order, and it took over 2 years of work to get her to count at all successfully. This cognition of numbers (one through seven) reflected a more general well-developed gestalt perception ability as evidenced by her performance on tests specifically designed to tap this ability. In each of the tests that follow, the ability to perceive an apparently disorganized or unrelated group of parts as a meaningful whole is tested.

11.4.2.1.   Street Gestalt Test (Street, 1931)

In June, 1972, Genie was given the Street Test, which is comprised of 12 silhouettes, parts of which have been obliterated from view. The subject must ascertain the whole from the remaining portions of the picture and state what the picture represents. A normal adult performance is 7 correct. Genie scored 7 and 9 on two separate testing sessions, this despite the fact that two of the pictures portrayed items not within Genie's life experience at that time: a locomotive and an old-fashioned, wood-burning stove. Genie named the stove correctly. (We have no explanation for her correct answer to the stove picture.) Thus Genie's performance was comparable to or better than that of a normal adult.

11.4.2.2.   Harshman Figures

On February 19, 1975 Genie was given the Harshman Figures Test, a test similar in design to the Street Gestalt Test. There are 22 items on the test, one of which (an octopus) was not presented to Genie because of her unfamiliarity with the object. Genie received a score of 18 correct. Based on two different normative samples of adults, Group 1, males between the ages of 21 and 35 years; and Group 2, adults of both sexes between the ages of 17 and 50 years, her performance approached the ceiling of the test. With respect to Group 1 Genie scored approximately two standard deviations above the mean (12.8) (SD = 4.3). With respect to Group 2, she performed between one and two standard deviations above the mean (12) (SD = 5).

Her above normal performance might even have been higher had she known what an octopus was.

11.4.2.3. Thurstone Closure Speed Test

On March 5, 1975 Genie took the Thurstone Closure Speed Test (Thurstone & Jeffrey, 1956), a gestalt perception test consisting of 24 pictures to be identified within a total of 3 minutes. The test is a measure of the speed with which the subject can integrate apparently unrelated parts into a meaningful whole. Genie was asked to identify only 22 of the 24 pictures because two of the pictures depicted situations unfamiliar to her (boxers fighting and a baseball umpire and catcher). Genie missed only 3 out of 22. Her actual score (19 correct) placed her in the 86th percentile; her extrapolated score (3 errors) placed her in the 95th percentile. In either case her performance easily placed her in the well above average adult range.

11.4.2.4. Mooney Faces

The Mooney Faces Test (Mooney, 1957), considered to be the most reliable and widely used test of gestalt perception (Lansdell, 1968), involves gestalt facial recognition. The test consists of 70 black and white pictures, 50 of which are silhouette-type drawings of real faces, 20 of which are drawings of "false" faces. The subject must identify, in each instance, whether a picture is that of a real or false face, and upon classification of a face as real, must point out several specific facial features (eyes, nose, mouth, chin, etc.) on the face. (This is done to eliminate correct answers by guessing.) Only after a subject has correctly indicated specific facial features is the classification of a real face counted correct.

There are ten questionable items, considered so because few people are able to classify them. Normally, the test is given with only the remaining 60 pictures. (The test has also been simplified further, with presentation of only 50 pictures, in some studies.)

Genie was shown all 70 pictures. She classified 50/50 real faces correctly—a 100% correct performance. She classified 14/20 false faces correctly—a 75% performance. Genie missed no questionable items. The only items she missed were those faces, which, although not realistic faces, could easily have been either masks or caricatures. It is possible that had I been able to communicate to her that only *realistic* faces were to be counted as faces, she would not have misclassified any. I did not successfully communicate this aspect of the test, however. Despite this fact, Genie's performance is, to my knowledge, the highest performance reported in the literature for either child or adult on this test.

11.4.2.5.

In summary, Genie appears to have above normal gestalt perception ability. Although her ability to count appears to have supplanted her ability to gestalt numbers to some degree, Genie continues to demonstrate well-developed ability to perceive things holistically. When asked to describe what she did in gym class, for example, she often resorts to drawing a picture of the activity, a picture including just enough detail to provide a clear gestalt of the activity she failed to adequately describe through language. Gestalt perception is hypothesized to be predominantly a function of the right hemisphere (Nebes, 1971; Bogen, Dezure, Tenhouten, & Marsh, 1972); therefore the results of observations and test findings support the hypothesis presented in 11.4.

11.4.3. Part–Whole Judgments

Another reportedly right-hemisphere ability is the ability to project the whole when presented with only a part. This ability is probably directly related to gestalt perception. In gestalt tests, apparently unrelated parts are presented and the whole must be generated from the given information. In part–whole tests a coherent but single part is presented, and the whole must be projected from the single part.

11.4.3.1.   Arc/Circle Test (Nebes, 1971)

This test which has been used on split-brains and normal adults, consists of the tactile presentation of Plexiglas arcs which must be matched to one of three Plexiglas circles differing in size. The model circles are visually presented and labeled before the test is begun, then are removed from view but can be referred to tactilely throughout the test. The arcs are never presented visually. Four degrees of arc are presented and tested for each circle (280°, 180°, 120°, and 80°), and the stimulus presentations are divided into three parts separated by a 2-minute break between periods during which the subject may re-view the model circles to refresh his/her memory. There are forty-five stimuli in all. The subject must use only one finger to touch the materials.

The Nebes Arc/Circle Test was administered to Genie on May 29, 1975. Normally the test takes from one-half hour upward, often as long as 45 minutes to an hour. Genie took only 13 minutes to do the entire test, including the two required 2-minute breaks. She missed only 7 out of 45 items; and of the 7, 6 were the most difficult arc-types (80°), the remaining one was the second most difficult (120°). Although there are no norms for this test, Genie's performance is among the best reported to date (Nebes, 1971; Harshman, Crawford, & Hecht, 1975). Here again, testing has confirmed the hypothesis that Genie is good at abilities tapping predominantly the right hemisphere.[9]

11.4.4. Sequential Order

The ability to perform sequences and to remember sequences is hypothesized to be a predominantly left-hemisphere ability, so much so that the left hemisphere is at times referred to as a "sequencer," or as a *sequential* thinker, in contrast to the right hemisphere which is a *simultaneous* thinker (Luria, 1966). The ability of the left hemisphere to perform sequences and judge sequential ordering has, in fact, been suggested as one of the reasons that language is subsumed by the left hemisphere (Krashen, 1972). Moreover, individuals with left-hemisphere damage who have deficits in left-hemisphere abilities are noted to have sequencing problems (Carmon & Nachson, 1971; Efron, 1963).

11.4.4.1.

We observed that Genie was slow to perform certain motor acts involving sequencing (e.g., tying shoes), but she was slow to move in general. One area where Genie shows marked sequencing problems, however, is counting. After years of coaching, teaching, and game-playing, and so forth, counting is still laborious and slow for Genie. She counts only on command and requires cueing and encouragement to proceed. Although Genie is clearly deficient in this area, counting ability has not been specifically tested. We have, however, administered a few sequential ordering tests.

11.4.4.2. Knox Cube Test

The Knox Cube Test uses a wooden base with four cubes extending upward, each one inch apart. Experimenter and subject both use unsharpened pencils. The experimenter sits facing the subject and taps out a sequence on the cubes with the pencil tip. The subject must copy the sequence immediately following its presentation. The sequences increase in length until the subject misses three sequences in a row. The entire test, including instructions, is nonverbal.

---

[9] There is some doubt as to whether or not the Arc/Circle Test actually tests part–whole judgment. Whatever cognitive ability it is that is tapped in this test, however, it appears to be a right-hemisphere function (Nebes, 1971, 1974).

Genie was given the Knox Cube Test twice (each complete test requires two test administrations). On January 24, 1973 and March 12, 1973 her combined score was at the 6 year-old level; on May 21, 1975 and June 4, 1975 she scored at the $7\frac{1}{2}$-year-old level. Although her Knox Cube scores are higher than her scores on many verbal tests (see Section 11.4.8), they fall significantly below those she attains on specifically right-hemisphere tests, where she performs at or above normal adult levels.

11.4.4.3. Illinois Test of Psycholinguistic Abilities (ITPA)
Subtests on Sequential Memory

The ITPA has nine subtests, two ·of which involve sequential memory: (1) auditory sequential memory, and (2) visual sequential memory. The auditory memory subtest is a digit span test, beginning with the presentation of two digits, increasing the span with each presentation. The visual sequential memory test consists of chips (or tiles), each with a design drawn upon it. A model picture of a design sequence is presented for 5 seconds, then withdrawn; and the subject must recreate the sequence with the chips, from memory. The designs (except for the first two—a square and a circle) are not easily encoded verbally. The sequences increase in length from two designs up to a maximum of eight.

Genie took the ITPA subtests on four separate occasions. Table 11.7 shows the results.

Better with visual than auditory sequences, Genie performed poorly on both subtests, showing poor ability with sequential memory regardless of modality. Both the visual and auditory sequential memory subtests have been shown to depend on left hemisphere processing (Zaidel, 1973), so Genie's poor performance on both modalities is again consistent with our hypothesis that she is poor at abilities not controlled predominantly by the right hemisphere.

TABLE 11.7
ITPA Sequential Memory Subsets

Date tested	Auditory-sequential memory	Visual-sequential memory
2/2/71	not administered	3 years, 1 month
1/27/73	unscorable	4 years, 11 months
5/8-9/73	2 years, 10 months	5 years, 4 months
2/74	3 years, 5 months	5 years, 4 months

11.4.5. Facial Recognition

Facial recognition is an ability which is hypothesized to be controlled by the right hemisphere (Rondot & Tzavaras, 1969; Levy *et al.*, 1972). In general, this may be because recognition of faces may be resistant to analytical verbal description and may thus involve a gestalt-like strategy.

Observationally, Genie appears to have excellent ability in this area. Her memory for faces has impressed all who know her. In meeting someone she has not seen for several years or in looking at photographs of people she has met even only once, Genie never fails to immediately recognize the person and name him or her, or to verbally describe some image associated with that person. One would thus expect Genie to perform well on a formal facial recognition task.

Genie's performance on the Mooney Faces Test attests to her ability to recognize a visual pattern as a face if it is such. An additional test assessing the ability to differentiate between faces was also administered.

11.4.5.1. Benton Facial Recognition Test
(Benton, Van Allen, de S. Hamsher, & Levin, 1975)

The Benton Facial Recognition Test involves matching faces from a sample array to a model. The test has three parts: (1) matching of identical, front-view photographs—the subject must identify the one photograph in an array of six which is identical to the model face; (2) matching of front-view with three-quarter-view photographs—the subject must locate the model front-view photo three times in a display of six three-quarter-views; and (3) matching of front-view photographs under different lighting conditions—the model photo is a front-view of a face taken under full lighting conditions; the subject must locate the model face three times in a display of six front views taken under different lighting conditions.

On December 11, 1975 Genie was administered this test. She achieved a score of 32, a score below all norms for children and adults without brain damage. She performed at the lower end of the scale for those with right-hemisphere lesions, and at the bottom for those with left-hemisphere lesions. The results are given in Table 11.8.

Genie's performance on this reportedly right-hemisphere task appears surprising. One would expect her to do better than she did. Closer examination of the data on brain-damaged adults, however, shows that there are two groups who perform poorly on this test namely, right-hemisphere lesions and aphasics. Why both groups should do poorly on this task has not yet been explained; but it might be the case that this test requires a contribution from both hemispheres, the left-hemisphere contribution involving some ability or mechanism for which aphasics manifest a deficit. (The left-hemisphere contribution might be the need for abstracting or for transformation from one form to another.) Other facial

TABLE 11.8
Performances on the Benton *et al.* Facial Recognition Test

Normals		Brain-damaged	
Age (or grade)	Mean score		
Kindergarten	33.0	Left hemisphere	
1st grade	35.7	lesions	42.5
2nd grade	37.5	Right hemisphere	
3rd grade	38.1	lesions	33.3
4th grade	40.0		
5th grade	40.0		
16-55 years	45.7		

recognition tests may not require a left-hemisphere contribution, therefore the disparity between these particular test data and others. What is important regarding Genie is that although facial recognition is generally a right hemisphere ability, the Benton *et al.* test appears to require some contribution from the left hemisphere; and thus Genie did not perform as well as expected.

This variance in her performance on tests using both hemispheres as opposed to tests tapping predominantly the right hemisphere is manifest in other tests as well (see 11.4.6).

11.4.6. Visual Memory

11.4.6.1. Memory for Designs (Graham & Kendall, 1960)

On October 1, 1975, Genie was administered Graham and Kendall's Memory for Designs (1960) Test. The test consists of simple geometric designs without meaningful associations. The subject views each design for 5 seconds; then the design is withdrawn, and the subject is asked to reproduce it. There are 15 items on the test, and points are subtracted for easily identifiable errors, with rotation or reversal of the figure heavily penalized. No penalty is given for incomplete or forgotten designs, as Graham and Kendall report that such errors were frequent among normals. Orientation errors, however, were frequent among brain-damaged patients. Based on performance data, Graham and Kendall suggest that the task involves skills utilizing both sides of the brain, including the ability to perform a sequence of behaviors, attention to and retention of the pattern, and the reproduction of the pattern via a complex motor act.

TABLE 11.9
Memory for Designs Comparative Scores

Category	Raw score
Normal	0-4
Borderline	5-11
Brain damage	12+

Genie's performance on this test was scored by two raters independently. Her scores were 9 and 8. Table 11.9 presents the interpretation of raw scores on this test.

Genie's performance places her in the borderline range. (Noteworthy, however, is the fact that Genie made no reversals or rotational errors. The nature of her scores, therefore, indicates the absence of brain damage; and Graham and Kendall claim that their test is very sensitive to organic brain damage.) Her low score on this test differs from her excellent performances on "true" right-hemisphere tasks and points out her difficulty on tasks that are generally thought to involve both hemispheres.

11.4.6.2. Visual Retention Test

The Visual Retention Test is similar to the Memory for Designs Test in that it involves the presentation of simple geometric designs, each exposed for a short duration then withdrawn from view, with the subject asked to reproduce it. The test administration may take several forms, all of them with corresponding scoring norms. On September 17, 1975 and October 8, 1975 Genie was given the Visual Retention Test. The test administration took the form of 10 seconds of exposure for each design with immediate reproduction from memory on the part of the subject. Genie was given two different forms of the test. On Form E (September 17, 1975) she achieved a score of 4 correct, 13 errors. On Form C (October 8, 1975) her correct score was 2, her error score 10. Both of these scores place her in the "grossly defective" range based on adult norms. Her score of 4 correct places her in the "high average" range for 8-year-old normal children, "average" range for 9-year-olds, "low average" for 10-year-olds, "borderline" for 11-year-olds, and "defective" for 12-year-olds and up. Her error score of 10 places her in the "average" range for 8-year-olds, and in the "defective" range for 11 years and up.

In studies examining the differences between right- and left-hemisphere performance on this test (e.g., Heilbrun, 1956), two groups were found to do worse than others: (1) right-sided brain damage, and (2) aphasics, although in neither case was the difference statistically significant. These findings suggest that like the Memory for Designs Test and the Facial Recognition Test, this test appears to involve both hemispheres of the brain; Genie does not perform well on such tests.

11.4.7. Raven Coloured Progressive Matrices

On January 9, 1975, Genie was given the Coloured Progressive Matrices Test. This nonverbal test involves the presentation of patterns with a section missing. The subject has to select which of the choices corresponds to the missing piece. Genie's overall score was 29. Because she was outside of the age range appropriate for the test, the level of her performance can only be extrapolated. Raven norms indicate that a score of 28 is at the 50th percentile for 11-year-olds, and 25% of $10\frac{1}{2}$-year-olds attain a score of 29 or more points.

Work with split-brains suggests that the Raven test taps both cerebral hemispheres (Zaidel, personal communication). It is possible that certain items (the easiest and earliest items in each set) may be solved by gestalt-like methods (with the right hemisphere), while the more difficult items require analytic solutions (by the left hemisphere). Such an explanation would account for Genie's overall poor performance, but good performance on specific items.

11.4.8. Disembedding

Disembedding involves holding a configuration in mind despite distraction (e.g., from a complex and overlapping background). Several studies have reported the superiority of the left hemisphere in such tasks (Teuber, Battersby, & Bender, 1960; Russo & Vignolo, 1967), but others report right hemisphere superiority on similar tasks (De Renzi & Spinnler, 1966). There is much evidence, however, that this ability involves a contribution from both hemispheres (Poeck, Kerschensteiner, Hartse, & Orgass et al., 1973; Zaidel 1973; Teuber & Weinstein, 1956). One would, therefore, not expect Genie to perform well on tasks involving this ability.

11.4.8.1. Figure–Ground Perception Test

The Figure–Ground Perception Test consists of two subparts, each part containing eight test items. Each item consists of complex designs in which three figures are delineated. Extraneous lines are also present, and the subject must select from an array of six pictures, the three which are hidden in the test item. The first part consists of "hidden" objects; the second part consists of "hidden" geometrical designs.

Genie was given this test on June 28, 1973 and February 19, 1975. On both occasions she scored at the 10.11-year-old level. Interestingly, she performed well on the object section but was unable to perform the geometric design section. The geometric design section more closely parallels disembedding tasks described in the literature cited (see Section 11.4.8) than the section involving common objects. Genie's inability to perform successfully on this portion of the test thus corresponds to our prediction that she will do poorly on tests involving both cerebral hemispheres.

11.4.9. Summary

Our hypothesis that Genie is a "right-hemisphere thinker," better at abilities normally localized and primarily controlled by the right hemisphere, is supported. Genie performs far better on specifically right-hemisphere abilities, such as gestalt perception and tactile part–whole judgments, than on left-hemisphere abilities, such as sequential memory and disembedding. Although the differences between her performance on verbal as opposed to nonverbal tasks are substantial, the disparate scatter in her ability appears more one of right versus left and/or left plus right ability. Genie performs better in the visual/tactile than in the auditory modality (as shown in Table 11.10, for example) and better, in general, on nonverbal than on verbal tasks. Since she also performs poorly on nonverbal and visual tasks tapping left-hemisphere functions, however, one must conclude that Genie is not simply a nonverbal, or visuo-spatial thinker, but primarily a right-hemisphere thinker, relying on and proficient in cortical abilities subsumed primarily by the right cortical hemisphere.

TABLE 11.10
ITPA Test Scores

Visual/tactile	5/73	2/74	Auditory	5/73	2/74
Visual sequential			Auditory sequential		
memory	5.4	5.4	memory	2.10	3.5
Visual reception	6.7	5.2	Auditory reception	2.11	5.0
Visual association	5.9	7.2	Auditory association	4.11	5.3
Visual closure	8.0	6.6			
Manual expression	5.3	5.10	Verbal expression	3.8	3.8

11.5. RIGHT-HEMISPHERE SPEECH

In normal righthanders there are certain aspects of language which are suggested to be bilaterally represented or possibly even right hemispheric in nature and localization (Jackson, 1932; Van Lancker, 1975). They are referred to as "automatic" or "nonpropositional," and include obscenities, profanities (swear words in general), and rituals such as "How are you?", "I don't know," and "What's happenin'?". It appears from the data that Genie is using her right hemisphere for language; yet interestingly, Genie does not have any "automatic" or "right-hemispheric" speech. Those aspects of language normally represented in the right hemisphere or bilaterally represented are absent, even though Genie uses her right hemisphere for language.

"Automatic" speech seems to fall into two categories: social, and affective. Examples of social automaticisms are expressions such as rejoinders ("hi," "bye," "please") and ritual questions and statements ("How are you?", "I'm fine."). In addition, I think, use of the vocative; summoning someone by name, would fall into this category. Genie lacks all of these.

Attempts to teach Genie to use rituals and rejoinders spontaneously have failed. She is, of course, capable of memorizing phrases and has done so to please others. Thus, she has learned the routine of responding with a belabored "I am fine" to a "How are you?" addressed to her by someone pressuring her to answer. She typically, however, ignores the question.

A good example of Genie's inability to incorporate automatic language into her speech has occurred with the vocative. Genie used to grab hold of someone's face and direct it toward herself when she wanted that person's attention. A great effort was made to teach her to use the more socially acceptable method of calling someone's name. In response to these efforts, Genie learned to use the person's name. Despite many daily examples of the vocative, however, Genie's interpretation of the instruction "If you want me, call my name" has been to say, "Call (person's name)." Genie apparently does not even comprehend what producing a verbal summons involves, though she responds to her own name being called.

Automatic language with mainly affective expressive function (swearing-and-the-like) evokes a marked response from Genie (e.g., great laughter, nonverbal attempts to have such exclamations repeated) but is not part of Genie's own speech, and no attempts have been made to teach her to use such language.

The absence of automatic language from Genie's speech seems to reflect an emotional and social disorder rather than a linguistic one. In many respects Genie remains an unsocialized person, and she manifests her lack of appropriate social functioning linguistically as well. Typically, language has many social uses—teasing, greetings, information seeking, arguments, etc. Moreover, verbal interaction (social use of language) requires the conversational participants to perform and be sensitive to a range of social behaviors in accompaniment with the actual spoken message. One has obligations as a conversational partner which include acknowledgments of assertions and summonses, agreement or disagreement with yes/no questions, and many others. Acknowledgment of having received a message (whether it contains an assertion, question, command, or summons, etc.) is an integral part of the conversational interaction. It may be verbal or nonverbal (e.g., Assertion: "John isn't feeling well." Response: "Yes, I know." "Uh-huh," a head shake, a questioning gaze with eyebrow lift), but it must be there for normal communicative interaction to take place.

Genie fails to acknowledge questions, statements, request, summonses, and so forth, much of the time. She can, of course, and does at times acknowledge communication addressed to her (especially if the topic holds some special interest for her). Genie very often acts as if she has not been spoken to, however. In fact, Genie's appropriate sociolinguistic behavior is extremely limited. She does answer questions, although at times she merely repeats part of the proposition she wishes to affirm in yes/no questions as do some autistic children (Kanner, 1943; Needleman, 1974). Genie also makes repairs in instances where her message has not been understood (through verbal acts such as repetition, elaboration of the original utterance, or use of sign, or through nonverbal acts such as pointing or drawing). In addition, she holds onto topics through repetition of a word or phrase, despite continued attempts of others to switch topics. Nonetheless, in total, Genie performs few normal or appropriate acts and, in large measure, appears to be conversationally incompetent. Verbal interaction with Genie consists mainly of someone's asking Genie a question repeatedly until Genie answers, or of Genie's making a comment and someone else's responding to it in some way (performing their obligation as a conversational partner). Except for those instances where Genie exerts control over the topic through repetition, verbal interaction with Genie is almost always controlled and/or "normalized" by the person talking to Genie, not by Genie.

It is not surprising, I think, that Genie displays incompetence in this area. Her failure to perform many of the behaviors requisite for successful conversational interaction is most probably a result of her social and psychological deprivation. Genie grew up in an environment devoid of verbal interaction. Never or practically never having witnessed the performance of these sociolinguistic behaviors, she did not develop them.

Recent research (Keenan, 1974, 1975) has shown that the elements of conversational competence develop during and are part of what a normal child acquires during the course of language acquisition. If this is so, one would expect individuals with developmental social and psychological disturbance to display problems in this area. Recent research suggests that this may be so. Autistic children, for example, evidence inability to answer or even acknowledge yes/no questions addressed to them (Needleman, 1974) and display general and pervasive impairment in the social and communicative functions of language (Fay, 1973; Rutter, Greenfield, & Lockyer, 1967).

Work with retardates, on the other hand, has shown that this aspect of language behavior can develop in the absence of a great deal of linguistic competence. Working with Down's syndrome adults, Sabsay (1975) has shown that these individuals may possess a surprising degree of communicative competence, even though they lack much grammatical ability. It appears, therefore, that communicative competence may be a separate aspect of linguistic functioning, one not dependent on most other linguistic abilities, but rather dependent on the absence of social and/or psychological disturbance. Genie's lack of competence in this area, therefore, is probably not a function of her more general linguistic limitations. Her conversational incompetence is instead a manifestation of her social and psychological impoverishment and abnormality.

11.6. SUMMARY AND CONCLUSIONS

From our observations and testing, Genie appears to be a right-hemisphere thinker. Most importantly, she uses her right hemisphere for language. Genie's language is abnormal in specific ways. Her language resembles that of other cases of right-hemisphere language as well as the language of those generally acquiring language outside of the "critical period." Her case, therefore, supports Lenneberg's "critical period" hypothesis and furthermore suggests specific constraints and limitations on the nature of language acquisition outside of this maturational period.

The fact that Genie has right-hemisphere language may be a direct result of the fact that she did not acquire language during the "critical period." It suggests that after the critical period, the left hemisphere may no longer be able to function in language acquisition, leaving the right hemisphere to assume control.

The similarities between Genie and (1) right-hemisphere language cases, (2) other cases of language acquisition outside of the critical period, and (3) chimpanzees, suggests that all of these groups have something in common. I have labeled it "nonlanguage area language"—language of cortex not predisposed for language or outside of the appropriate state of maturation.

In addition to language, Genie performs other cortical functions with her right hemisphere and is more proficient at abilities lateralized to the right in normal right handers than in abilities involving both hemispheres or lateralized to the left. In general, Genie is an "appositional" thinker, visually and tactilely oriented, better at holistic than sequential, analytic thinking. Although she lacks the aspects of language normally associated with the right hemisphere (automatic language) due to social and psychological factors, Genie is both linguistically and nonlinguistically a right-hemisphere functioner.

APPENDIX I

Comprehension Tests

1. SIMPLE NEGATION

Purpose: To determine if Genie comprehended the distinction between negative and affirmative in simple sentences. The full and contracted negative forms were used and tested.

Materials: Three pairs of pictures identical except for the presence or absence of some element:
- (1) a girl with shoes on
  a girl without shoes on
- (2) a rabbit with a carrot
  a rabbit without a carrot
- (3) a balloon with a string
  a balloon without a string

Presentation: After Genie had identified all of the test vocabulary, the pictures were set before her in pairs.

Test Items:
1. *Show me* The girl is wearing shoes.
2. *Show me* The bunny does not have a carrot.
3. *Show me* The balloon has a string.
4. *Show me* The bunny has a carrot.
5. *Show me* The girl is not wearing shoes.
6. *Show me* The balloon does not have a string.
7. *Show me* The girl is wearing shoes.
8. *Show me* The bunny doesn't have a carrot.
9. *Show me* The balloon has a string.

10. *Show me*   The bunny has a carrot.

11. *Show me*   The girl isn't wearing shoes.

12. *Show me*   The balloon doesn't have a string.

2. SIMPLE MODIFICATION

Purpose: To determine if Genie could successfully and consistently process a modification structure consisting of a single adjective plus a noun.

Materials: Plastic shapes, all of the same color (red): 1 large circle, 1 large square, 1 large triangle, 1 medium circle, 1 medium square, 1 medium triangle, 1 small circle, 1 small square, 1 small triangle.

Presentation: After Genie identified the shapes, the test items were administered. The shapes were arranged as follows: All of the circles were placed in a vertical row, all of the squares were placed in a vertical row next to the circles, and all of the triangles in a vertical row alongside the other two. The shapes were arranged so that the horizontal rows did not have the same sized shape along them; e.g., a large circle stood next to a small square which stood next to a medium triangle in one horizontal row, etc.

Test Items: 1. Point to the big circle.

2. Point to the little triangle.

3. Point to the little square.

4. Point to the big triangle.

5. Point to the big square.

6. Point to the little circle.

3. COMPLEX MODIFICATION

Purpose: To determine if Genie could successfully and consistently process a modification structure consisting of two adjectives plus a noun.

Materials: Plastic shapes, one set red, one set yellow:

1 large red circle	1 large yellow circle
1 large red square	1 large yellow square
1 large red triangle	1 large yellow triangle
1 medium red circle	1 medium yellow circle
1 medium red square	1 medium yellow square
1 medium red triangle	1 medium yellow triangle
1 small red circle	1 small yellow circle
1 small red square	1 small yellow square
1 small red triangle	1 small yellow triangle

Presentation: After Genie identified the shapes, the test items were administered. The shapes were arranged as follows: The three red circles, squares, and triangles were lined up in vertical rows interspersed between vertical rows of yellow circles, squares, and triangles. They were aligned in such a way so that no horizontal row had shapes all of one uniform size.

Test Items: 1. Point to the big red circle.

2. Point to the little red triangle.

3. Point to the little yellow circle.

4. Point to the little red square.

5. Point to the big yellow square.

6. Point to the big red triangle.

7. Point to the little yellow triangle.

8. Point to the big red square.

9. Point to the big yellow circle.

10. Point to the little red circle.

11. Point to the little yellow square.

12. Point to the big yellow triangle.

4. PREPOSITIONS *IN, ON, UNDER*

Purpose: To determine Genie's comprehension of the prepositional terms *in*, *on*, and *under*.

Materials: A dish, a button, a pencil, and two glasses, one of which was turned upside down.

Presentation: Genie first had to identify the test vocabulary by pointing to the objects named. Then the test items were presented and the objects placed in their original positions after each test item.

Test Items: 1. Put the button on the glass.

2. Put the button in the glass.

3. Put the dish under the glass.

4. Put the button under the dish.

5. Put the pencil in the glass.

6. Put the dish on the glass.

5. PREPOSITIONS *BEHIND, IN FRONT OF, BESIDE,* AND *NEXT TO*

Purpose: To determine Genie's comprehension and interpretation of the prepositional terms *behind, in front of, beside,* and *next to*.

Materials: A set of three pictures:
a house in front of a tree
a tree in front of a house
a house next to a tree

Presentation: After Genie identified the relevant vocabulary, the test items were administered.

Test Items: 1.   Show me the house that is next to the tree.
                   2.   Show me the house that is behind the tree.
                   3.   Show me the house that is in front of the tree.
                   4.   Show me the tree that is beside the house.
                   5.   Show me the tree that is in front of the house.
                   6.   Show me the tree that is behind the house.
                   7.   Show me the house that is beside the tree.

On occasion, a missed test item was repeated.

6. PREPOSITIONS *IN, ON, NEXT TO, UNDER, OVER, IN BACK OF, IN FRONT OF, BEHIND, BESIDE*

Purpose: To test Genie's comprehension of several common English prepositions and the relationships between objects that they represent.

Materials: Five nesting cubes (plastic boxes of different sizes and colors).
                  Colors: orange, yellow, green, blue, white
                  Order of sizes, starting with the smallest:
                      orange, green, yellow, blue, white

Presentation: After Genie had identified the colors, the test items were presented. The two boxes involved for each item were placed closest to Genie. I sat beside her. The cube openings were placed in various positions. Item no. 1 from set no. 1 was presented, then item no. 1 from set no. 2, then item no. 1 from set no. 3, item no. 1 from set no. 4, item no. 1 from set no. 5. Then item no. 2 from each set in turn was presented, followed by items 3–10 from each set. After each item, the boxes were returned to their original position.

Test Items:

Set No. 1:   1.   Put the orange box in the yellow box.
                  2.   Put the green box on the white box.
                  3.   Put the yellow box in the white box.
                  4.   Put the yellow box on the blue box.
                  5.   Put the green box in the white box.
                  6.   Put the blue box on the white box.
                  7.   Put the yellow box on the white box.
                  8.   Put the yellow box in the blue box.
                  9.   Put the orange box on the yellow box.
                 10.   Put the green box in the white box.

Set No. 2:   1.   Put the blue box under the yellow box.
                  2.   Put the green box over the orange box.

      3.   Put the white box under the green box.

      4.   Put the yellow box under the orange box.

      5.   Put the blue box over the green box.

      6.   Put the blue box over the yellow box.

      7.   Put the white box over the green box.

      8.   Put the blue box under the green box.

      9.   Put the green box under the orange box.

    10.   Put the yellow box over the orange box.

Set No. 3:   1.   Put the white box in back of the blue box.

      2.   Put the green box in front of the white box.

      3.   Put the orange box in back of the yellow box.

      4.   Put the yellow box in back of the blue box.

      5.   Put the green box in front of the blue box.

      6.   Put the green box in back of the white box.

      7.   Put the white box in front of the blue box.

      8.   Put the yellow box in front of the blue box.

      9.   Put the orange box in front of the yellow box.

    10.   Put the green box in back of the blue box.

Set No. 4:   1.   Put the yellow box beside the blue box.

      2.   Put the blue box behind the orange box.

      3.   Put the green box behind the white box.

      4.   Put the yellow box beside the white box.

      5.   Put the blue box beside the orange box.

      6.   Put the orange box behind the green box.

      7.   Put the yellow box behind the blue box.

      8.   Put the green box beside the white box.

      9.   Put the yellow box behind the white box.

    10.   Put the orange box beside the green box.

Set No. 5:   1.   Put the orange box next to the white box.

      2.   Put the green box in the blue box.

      3.   Put the yellow box next to the blue box.

      4.   Put the blue box in the white box.

      5.   Put the orange box next to the green box.

      6.   Put the green box next to the blue box.

      7.   Put the blue box next to the white box.

      8.   Put the orange box next to the white box.

      9.   Put the yellow box in the blue box.

    10.   Put the orange box in the green box.

7. SINGULAR VERSUS PLURAL IN NOUNS

Purpose: To determine if Genie comprehended the distinction between the (unmarked) singular form and the (marked) plural form of nouns. All three regular plural endings were tested: /s/, /z/, /əz/.

Materials: Pairs of pictures were used—a single object on one picture, three of the identical objects on the other. The objects pictured included:

(a) /s/: pots, carrots, jackets, hats, books, cups

(b) /z/: balloons, pails, turtles, trees, umbrellas

(c) /əz/: boxes, roses, noses, dishes, horses

Presentation: After Genie identified all of the test vocabulary in a subtest, the pictures from one of the three subtests were placed before her. All three subtests were tested in each session.

Test Items:

(a) /s/:   1. Point to the carrots.

             2. Point to the book.

             3. Point to the cup.

             4. Point to the jackets.

             5. Point to the hat.

             6. Point to the pot.

             7. Point to the books.

             8. Point to the cups.

             9. Point to the carrot.

          10. Point to the hats.

          11. Point to the pots.

          12. Point to the jacket.

(b) /z/:   1. Point to the balloons.

             2. Point to the turtle.

              3. Point to the pail.

             4. Point to the trees.

             5. Point to the turtles.

             6. Point to the balloons.

             7. Point to the umbrella.

             8. Point to the tree.

             9. Point to the pails.

          10. Point to the umbrellas.

(c) /əz/:   1. Point to the nose.

             2. Point to the boxes.

    3. Point to the dishes.

    4. Point to the horses.

    5. Point to the rose.

    6. Point to the dish.

    7. Point to the noses.

    8. Point to the box.

    9. Point to the horse.

   10. Point to the roses.

Note: Before August, 1972, only five pairs were presented at a session.

8. CONJUNCTION/DISJUNCTION

Purpose: To test Genie's knowledge of the meaning of the conjunctions *and* and *or*, and to test her comprehension of the functional distinction between them.

Materials: A key, a spoon, a watch, a pencil, a button.

Presentation: After Genie identified all of the test items, they were placed in a row in front of her. After each response, the items were placed back in their original positions.

Test Items: 1. Point to the key and the pencil.

                   2. Point to the spoon and the watch.

                   3. Point to the watch or the button.

                   4. Point to the button or pencil or key.

                   5. Point to either the spoon or the watch.

                   6. Point to the pencil and the button.

                   7. Point to the key and watch and spoon.

                   8. Point to the button or the pencil.

                   9. Point to the spoon and the pencil.

                 10. Point to the spoon or the pencil.

Note: Before August, 1972, only items 1, 2, 3, 5, 7, and 9 were included.

9. POSSESSIVE PRONOUNS

Purpose: To assess Genie's comprehension of the personal possessive pronouns of English.

Materials: A picture of a boy and a girl standing together, dressed in coats and hats. Our bodies.

Presentation: The picture was placed before Genie. After she identified all of the test vocabulary, she was told that sometimes she would point to the picture, sometimes to herself, sometimes to Curtiss.

Test Items: 1.   Point to his hat.

　　　　　　　 2.   Point to her shoes.

　　　　　　　 3.   Point to his hand.

　　　　　　　 4.   Point to her neck.

　　　　　　　 5.   Point to your nose.

　　　　　　　 6.   Point to my chin.

　　　　　　　 7.   Point to their hats.

　　　　　　　 8.   Point to her hair.

　　　　　　　 9.   Point to their noses.

　　　　　　 10.   Point to our noses.

　　　　　　 11.   Point to their mouths.

　　　　　　 12.   Point to your mouth.

　　　　　　 13.   Point to our mouths.

　　　　　　 14.   Point to my mouth.

On occasion, test items 1–4 were presented last to determine whether initial focus on the picture affected Genie's performance.

10.   COMPARATIVE

Purpose: To determine Genie's comprehension of the comparative morpheme /-er/.

Materials: Two white buttons, only slightly different in size. Two strips of paper, almost the same length.

Presentation: First the buttons were placed before her and item 1 was asked; then the strips of paper were placed before her and item 2 was asked. The procedure was repeated for items 3 and 4.

Test Items: 1.   Which button is smaller?

　　　　　　　 2.   Which paper is longer?

　　　　　　　 3.   Which button is bigger?

　　　　　　　 4.   Which paper is shorter?

11.   SUPERLATIVE I

Purpose: To determine Genie's comprehension of the superlative morpheme /-est/.

Materials: Five white buttons, all small and similar in size. Three strips of paper, all the same width, each varying $\frac{1}{2}$ inch in length from the next one in size.

Presentation: The buttons were placed before Genie, and then item 1 was asked; then the papers were placed before her and item 2 was asked. The procedure was repeated for items 3 and 4.

Test Items 1. Point to the smallest button.

2. Point to the shortest paper.

3. Point to the biggest button.

4. Point to the longest paper.

Note: All of the adjectives involved were already known to be part of Genie's receptive vocabulary.

12. SUPERLATIVE II

Purpose: To further determine Genie's comprehension of the superlative morpheme.

Materials: The same array of objects as was used in the Simple Modification test (Test 2).

Presentation: The objects were arranged exactly as in Test 2 above. Genie was asked to identify the shapes, then the test was presented.

Test Items: 1. Point to the littlest red circle.

2. Point to the biggest red triangle.

3. Point to the biggest red square.

4. Point to the littlest red triangle.

5. Point to the biggest red circle.

6. Point to the littlest red square.

13. COMPARATIVE AND SUPERLATIVE

Materials: Seven circles—all different in size from one another, arranged in random order with respect to size.

Presentation: The circles were placed before Genie. Pointing to a circle other than the smallest or largest one, I asked test item 1. Repeating the procedure, but pointing to a different circle, I asked item 2. This procedure was repeated for items 3 and 5. Test items 4 and 6 were presented without pointing.

Test Items: 1. Point to one that's bigger.

2. Point to one that's smaller.

3. Point to one that's bigger.

4. Point to the smallest circle.

5. Point to one that's smaller.

6. Point to the biggest circle.

14. TENSE/ASPECT

Purpose: To test Genie's comprehension of the following elements of the tense/aspect system in English:
progressive
future with *will*
future with *going to/gonna*
past tense
(finish + VP)

Materials: Six sets of pictures, three pictures to a set: (pictures taken from Milton Bradley—four Scene Sequence cards)
(1) a.   girl about to open an umbrella
     b.   girl in act of opening an umbrella
     c.   girl with a fully opened umbrella

(2) a.   boy preparing to brush his teeth
     b.   boy in act of brushing his teeth
     c.   boy finished brushing his teeth

(3) a.   candle about to be lit
     b.   candle being lit
     c.   candle that is lit

(4) a.   a pitcher next to an empty glass
     b.   a pitcher pouring juice into a partially filled glass
     c.   a pitcher next to a full glass

(5) a.   an untied shoe
     b.   a shoe being tied (the hands are just finishing the job)
     c.   a tied shoe

(6) a.   a boy about to blow up a balloon
     b.   a boy blowing up a balloon
     c.   a boy with a balloon that has just burst

Presentation: Each picture set was presented individually to Genie, while I told a "story" about the pictures in the set. For example, for Set 1 I said, "What's that green thing that girl has? Yes, it's an umbrella. That girl has an umbrella because it's raining. Here, (pointing to [1a]) the girl hasn't opened the umbrella yet, not yet. Here (pointing to [1b]), what's she doing? Here (pointing to [1c]), she's all done. The umbrella's open." For Set 2, I said, "This boy is getting ready to brush his teeth. There's his toothbrush, there's his toothpaste. Here (2a) he has not brushed his teeth yet, not yet. Here, (2b) what's he doing? And here (2c), he's all done."

After we went through each set, I presented them one at a time to Genie, as I read the test items.

Test Items: 1.   *Show me*   The girl opened the umbrella.

                 2.   *Show me*   The boy will blow up the balloon.

                 3.   *Show me*   He is lighting the candle.

                 4.   *Show me*   She's going to/gonna pour the juice.

                 5.   *Show me*   He finished tying his shoe.

                 6.   *Show me*   He will brush his teeth.

                 7.   *Show me*   She is opening the umbrella.

8. *Show me*   The boy blew up the balloon.

9. *Show me*   He's gonna light the candle.

10. *Show me*   She poured the juice.

11. *Show me*   He will tie his shoe.

12. *Show me*   He finished brushing his teeth.

13. *Show me*   She's gonna open the umbrella.

14. *Show me*   The boy is blowing up the balloon.

15. *Show me*   He lit the candle.

16. *Show me*   She is pouring the juice.

17. *Show me*   He's gonna tie his shoe.

18. *Show me*   He brushed his teeth.

19. *Show me*   The girl finished opening the umbrella.

20. *Show me*   The boy is gonna blow up the balloon.

21. *Show me*   He will light the candle.

22. *Show me*   She finished pouring the juice.

23. *Show me*   He is tying his shoe.

24. *Show me*   He's gonna brush his teeth.

25. *Show me*   The girl will open the umbrella.

26. *Show me*   He finished blowing the balloon.

27. *Show me*   He finished lighting the candle.

28. *Show me*   She will pour the juice.

29. *Show me*   He tied his shoe.

30. *Show me*   He is brushing his teeth.

15.   *BEFORE* AND *AFTER*

Purpose: To determine the extent of Genie's comprehension of the terms *before* and *after*, both when the verb phrases follow true temporal order and when they do not.

Materials: Genie's body.

Presentation: Genie had first to identify her eye, ear, nose, cheek, chin, pinky, and bottom. Then the test items were presented. At times, the test was administered twice in one session.

Test Items: 1. Touch your nose before you touch your ear.

2. After you touch your eye, touch your chin.

3. Touch your nose after you touch your cheek.

4. Before you touch your pinky, touch your ear.

5. Touch your bottom before you touch your nose.

6. Touch your cheek before you touch your eye.

7. Touch your ear after you touch your bottom.

8. Touch your chin after you touch your pinky.

9. Before you touch your cheek, touch your nose.

10. After you touch your ear, touch your eye.

16. *SOME, ONE, ALL*

Purpose: To Test Genie's comprehension and interpretation of the quantifiers *some, one,* and *all*.

Materials: Five plastic circles, of different colors (red, yellow, blue)
                  Five plastic squares, of different colors (red, yellow, blue)
                  Eight plastic triangles, of different colors (red, yellow, blue)
                  A dish
                  A cigar box

Presentation: After Genie identified the test vocabulary, all of the items were placed before her, on the table.

Test Items: 1. Put all of the circles in the dish.

                  2. Put some of the squares in the box.

                  3. Put one of the triangles in the dish.

                  4. Put some of the circles on the table.

                  5. Put one of the squares in the dish.

                  6. Put all of the squares on the table.

                  7. Put one of the circles in the box.

                  8. Put all of the triangles in the box.

                  9. Put some of the triangles on the table.

17. PRONOUNS

Purpose: To test Genie's comprehension of subject and object pronouns, including reflexive and reciprocal object pronouns.

Materials: Pictures of children sitting and eating or being fed from a bowl.
                  a. a boy eating by himself
                  b. a girl eating by herself
                  c. a girl feeding a boy
                  d. two boys feeding each other
                  e. a boy feeding a boy
                  f. a boy feeding a girl
                  g. two boys feeding themselves
                  h. a boy and a girl feeding each other

Presentation: Genie had first to identify the children as boys or girls. All of the pictures were set before her and then the test items presented. Genie was instructed to point to the picture I was talking about.

Test Items: 1. She is feeding him.

2. The girl is feeding herself.

3. He is feeding the girl.

4. They are feeding themselves.

5. The boy is feeding a boy.

6. He is feeding her.

7. The boys are feeding each other.

8. He is feeding himself.

9. The girl is feeding the boy.

10. He is feeding him.

11. She is feeding herself.

12. She is feeding the boy.

13. They are feeding each other.

14. The boy is feeding himself.

15. He is feeding the boy.

16. The boy is feeding the girl.

17. The boys are feeding themselves.

18. WORD ORDER

A. Active versus Passive

Materials: A set of three pictures:
a girl pulling a boy in a wagon
a boy pulling a girl in a wagon
a girl and a boy pulling a wagon

Presentation: Genie had to identify which of the pictured children were boys, which were girls. Then, with all of the pictures in front of her, the test items were presented.

Test Items: 1. *Point to*   The girl is pulling the boy.

2. *Point to*   The girl is pulled by the boy.

3. *Point to*   The boy pulls the girl.

4. *Point to*   The boy is pulled by the girl.

5. *Point to*   The girl is being pulled by the boy.

6. *Point to*   The boy is pulling the girl.

B. Active Voice Word Order

Materials: Two set of three pictures:
(1)   a girl pulling a boy in a wagon
a boy pulling a girl in a wagon
a girl and boy pulling a wagon

(2)   a girl pulling a boy's hair
      a boy pulling a girl's hair
      a boy and girl pulling their own hair

Presentation: Genie had to identify which were the girls and which the boys in each picture. Then picture set no. 1 was placed before her and test item no. 1 presented. Next, picture set no. 2 was placed before her and test item no. 2 was presented. The test continued in this fashion until all of the items were presented.

Test Items: 1.   *Point to*   The girl is pulling the boy.

2.   *Point to*   The boy is pulling the girl's hair.

3.   *Point to*   The girl and boy are pulling the wagon.

4.   *Point to*   The girl is pulling the boy's hair.

5.   *Point to*   The boy is pulling the girl.

6.   *Point to*   The boy and girl are pulling their own hair.

Note: On occasion, a missed test item was repeated.

19.   WH-QUESTIONING OF SUBJECT VERSUS OBJECT

Materials: Four blocks, two blue, one green, one yellow, were placed as follows:

yellow	blue
blue	green

Presentation: Genie had to identify the colors involved. Then the test items were presented. (Points as well as spoken answers were accepted.)

Test Items: 1.   What is on blue?

2.   What is blue on?

3.   What is under blue?

4.   What is blue under?

20.   COMPLEX SENTENCE PROCESSING

Purpose: To test Genie's comprehension of complex sentences, both those with a relative clause modifying the subject noun phrase, and those with a relative clause modifying the object noun phrase.

Materials: Two sets of pictures:

(1)   a.   a boy smiling booking at a frowning girl turned away from him
      b.   a smiling girl looking at a frowning boy turned away from her
      c.   a frowning girl looking at a smiling boy turned away from her
      d.   a frowning boy and a smiling girl turned away from each other

(2)   a.   a boy sitting on a chair looking at a girl who is also looking at him
      b.   a boy sitting on a chair but turned away from the girl
      c.   a girl sitting on a chair looking at a boy looking back at her

Presentation: Genie had to identify which were the boys and which the girls, which ones were looking at each other, which ones were frowning, and which smiling. Then Set 1 was placed before her and test item 1 presented; then Set 2 was placed before her and test item 2 read; then Set (1) was set before her and test item 3 read. The test continued in this manner until all the test items had been read. Genie was instructed to point to the picture I was talking about.

Test Items: *Point to*:
1. The boy is looking at the girl who is frowning.
2. The girl who is sitting is looking at the boy.
3. The boy who is frowning is looking at the girl.
4. The boy who is sitting is looking at the girl.
5. The girl who is frowning is looking at the boy.
6. The boy is looking at the girl who is sitting.
7. The girl is looking at the boy who is frowning.
8. The boy who is looking at the girl is sitting.
9. The boy who is smiling is looking at the girl.
10. The girl who is looking at the boy is sitting.
11. The boy is looking at the girl who is smilling.
12. The girl is looking at the boy who is sitting.
13. The girl who is smiling is looking at the boy.
14. The girl is looking at the boy who is smiling.
15. The boy who is looking at the girl is frowning.
16. The girl who is looking at the boy is smiling.

Test items 15 and 16 were added to the test in June 1974. Some of the missed items were repeated on occasion.

21. COMPLEX NEGATION

Purpose: To test Genie's comprehension of negation in complex sentences (scope of negation); i.e., negation of either the main clause or the embedded clause.

Materials: *Four pictures*:
(1) a red book on a black chair
(2) a red book on a black table
(3) a blue book on a black chair
(4) a blue book on a black table

Presentation: Genie was asked, for each picture, *Is the book red or blue? Is it on a table or a chair?* After she had answered correctly the test items were presented. Genie was instructed to point to the picture I was talking about.

Test Items: 1. The book that is not red is on the table.
2. The book that is on the table is not blue.

    3.   The book that is red is on the table.

    4.   The book that is red is not on the table.

    5.   The book that is on the table is not red.

    6.   The book that is not blue is on the table.

    7.   The book that is not on the table is red.

    8.   The book that is blue is not on the table.

    9.   The book that is blue is on the table.

   10.   The book that is not on the table is blue.

   11.   The book that is on the table is red.

   12.   The book that is on the table is blue.

22. RELATIVE TERMS

Purpose: To test Genie's comprehension of the relational terms:

top	bottom
down	up
in	out
off	on
around	through
left	right
near	far
big	little
come	go
under	over
tall	short
here	there
to	from
thick	thin
front	back
high	low
wide	narrow

Materials: Milton Bradley Space Relationship Cards.

Presentation: The cards were placed in a pile and either the (a) or (b) items presented by going through the pile one at a time. The remaining items (whichever set was not presented) were presented after several intervening tests or at another session altogether. Genie was asked to point to _____ .

Test Items: (a) *Items*   (b) *Items*

	(a) *Items*		(b) *Items*
1.	top (slide)	1.	bottom (slide)
2.	down (birds)	2.	up (birds)
3.	in (window)	3.	out (window)
4.	off (diving)	4.	on (diving)
5.	around (rope)	5.	through (rope)
6.	left (hands)	6.	right (hands)

Test Items: (a) *Items*   (b) *Items*

	(a) *Items*		(b) *Items*
7.	near (ducks)	7.	far (ducks)
8.	big (caveman)	8.	little (caveman)
9.	up (seesaw)	9.	down (seesaw)
10.	out (cage)	10.	in (cage)
11.	come (boy and girl)	11.	go (boy and girl)
12.	under (dogs)	12.	over (dogs)
13.	on (squirrels)	13.	off (squirrels)
14.	little (lion)	14.	big (lion)
15.	tall (flower)	15.	short (flower)
16.	there (boxes)	16.	here (boxes)
17.	to (cars)	17.	from (cars)
18.	go (bus)	18.	come (bus)
19.	over (cars)	19.	under (cars)
20.	thick (bread)	20.	thin (bread)
21.	front (boy)	21.	back (boy)
22.	low (planes)	22.	high (planes)
23.	wide (clocks)	23.	narrow (clocks)
24.	here (cows)	24.	there (cows)
25.	far (stars)	25.	near (stars)
26.	short (urns)	26.	tall (urns)
27.	bottom (cat and dog)	27.	top (cat and dog)
28.	thin (trees)	28.	thick (trees)
29.	right (cars)	29.	left (cars)
30.	from (shoppers)	30.	to (shoppers)
31.	back (trucks)	31.	front (trucks)
32.	through (puddles)	32.	around (puddles)
33.	narrow (doors)	33.	wide (doors)
34.	high (buildings)	34.	low (buildings)

23. *MORE* VERSUS *LESS*

Purpose: To test Genie's comprehension of the terms *more* and *less*.

Materials: Plastic shapes of different sizes, colors, and thicknesses:
5 small squares
1 big square
5 small circles
1 big circle
5 small triangles
4 big triangles

Presentation: A different number of items was placed in each hand. Genie had to point to one
hand or the other according to the test question.

Test Items:

	Left hand	Right hand	Test question
1.	4 small squares	1 small square	Which has more?
2.	3 small circles	1 small circle	Which has more?
3.	4 small squares	1 big square	Which has less?
4.	5 small circles	1 big circle	Which has more?
5.	3 mixed triangles	6 mixed triangles	Which has more?
6.	1 small square	2 small squares	Which has more?
7.	4 small squares	1 small square	Which has less?
8.	3 small circles	1 small circle	Which has less?
9.	2 small triangles	1 big triangle	Which has more?
10.	5 small circles	1 big circle	Which has less?
11.	3 small triangles	6 mixed triangles	Which has less?
12.	3 small triangles	2 small triangles	Which has more?
13.	1 small square	2 small squares	Which has less?
14.	2 small triangles	1 big triangle	Which has less?
15.	3 small triangles	2 small triangles	Which has less?
16.	4 small squares	1 big square	Which has more?

24.   *MOST, MANY, FEW, FEWEST*

Purpose: To test Genie's comprehension of the relative adjectives *few* and *many* in their
standard and superlative forms.

Materials: Four pictures of apple trees: one with only one apple, one with two apples, one
with five apples, one with eight.

Presentation: All four pictures were placed in a row. Genie had to point to one of the four in
response to each test question. The test was repeated after several intervening tests.

Test Items: 1.   *Which tree has few apples?*

2.   *Which tree has many apples?*

3.   *Which tree has the fewest apples?*

4.   *Which tree has the most apples?*

Scoring: For *few*, the selection of either the tree with one apple, or the one with two apples,
was counted correct. For *many*, the selection either of the tree with five apples, or
the one with eight apples was counted correct.

25. SEMANTIC CLASSIFICATION TESTS

Purpose: To test Genie's ability to classify items on the basis of certain semantic features, some of which are said to be reflected in English syntax. The features tested were:

(1) Edible/inedible

(2) Human/nonhuman

(3) Male/female

(4) Animate/inanimate

(5) Body part/Whole body

Materials: Pictures, taken mostly from Milton Bradley Picture Flash Words for Beginners. These pictures were supplemented by pictures cut out from magazines and educational workbooks.
Two dishes.

Presentation: The pictures for an individual classification test were presented to Genie, one at a time. Genie had to identify the items pictured, by telling me in words what was on each picture. Then she was instructed to make two piles and *put together the ones that go together; show me which ones belong together. Put some in here and some in here* (pointing to the two dishes). Then the pictures were given to Genie, repeating, *Put together the ones that belong together*. Genie then had to sort them into two groups. The items sorted on each test were as follows:

Part/Whole

Materials: Ten pictures, five of body parts, five of full-bodied humans.

Part		Whole	
1.	feet	1.	girl
2.	hand	2.	boy
3.	leg	3.	man
4.	eye	4.	woman
5.	nose	5.	baby

Animate/Inanimate A

Materials: Twenty pictures, ten of animals, ten of objects.

Animate		Inanimate	
1.	duck	1.	broom
2.	monkeys	2.	clock
3.	pig	3.	letter
4.	kitten	4.	wood
5.	horse	5.	box
6.	elephant	6.	book
7.	rabbit	7.	chair

Animate	Inanimate
8. squirrel	8. balloon
9. cow	9. bed
10. dog	10. door

Animate/Inanimate B

Materials: Forty pictures, ten of humans, ten of animals, and twenty of objects.

Animate	Inanimate
1. children	1. broom
2. party	2. clock
3. baby	3. letter
4. girl	4. wood
5. mother	5. box
6. queen	6. book
7. boy	7. chair
8. father	8. balloon
9. farmer	9. bed
10. king	10. door
11. duck	11. floor
12. monkeys	12. paper
13. pig	13. dish
14. kitten	14. basket
15. horse	15. wagon
16. elephant	16. key
17. rabbit	17. hat
18. squirrel	18. car
19. cow	19. table
20. dog	20. window

Edible/Inedible

Materials: Twenty pictures, ten of edible items, ten of inedible items.

Edible	Inedible
1. bread	1. radio
2. fish	2. kite
3. pear	3. drum
4. apple	4. horn
5. orange	5. tree

	Edible		Inedible
6.	pie	6.	rain
7.	cake .	7.	sun
8.	eggs	8.	fire
9.	corn	9.	top
10.	milk	10.	gun

Human/Nonhuman

Materials: Twenty pictures, ten of humans, ten of animals.

	Human		Nonhuman
1.	baby	1.	duck
2.	party	2.	monkeys
3.	girl	3.	pig
4.	mother	4.	kitten
5.	children	5.	horse
6.	queen	6.	elephant
7.	boy	7.	rabbit
8.	father	8.	squirrel
9.	farmer	9.	cow
10.	king	10.	dog

26. RECEPTIVE PHONOLOGY

Purpose: To test Genie's ability to comprehend fine phonological distinctions.

Materials: Thirty-nine pairs of pictures (some taken from magazines or educational material, some originally drawn) on colored pieces of construction paper.

Presentation: Each pair was presented to Genie, one at a time, and either the A or B items were read. Genie had to point to the word I was saying. The remaining items (A or B) were given after several intervening tests or at a separate testing session.

Test Items: Each item was preceded by the instructions, *Point to . . .*

	A	B
1.	pie	tie
2.	bee	pea
3.	vase	face
4.	fox	socks
5.	hill	heel

	A	B
6.	cat	cap
7.	bell	bear
8.	sheep	ship
9.	sub	tub
10.	bag	back
11.	pen	pin
12.	toe	two
13.	hen	head
14.	mail	nail
15.	bud	mud
16.	cup	cap
17.	bun	bud
18.	man	men
19.	ball	bowl
20.	boat	goat
21.	goat	coat
22.	pear	bear
23.	bird	beard
24.	meat	beet
25.	clock	lock
26.	rain	train
27.	stair	chair
28.	glass	grass
29.	rake	lake
30.	king	key
31.	mop	map
32.	wing	swing
33.	cone	comb
34.	broom	room
35.	stop	top
36.	top	pot
37.	lamp	lamb
38.	stool	spool
39.	clown	cloud

APPENDIX II

Dichotic Listening and Tachistoscopic Tests

I. DICHOTIC LISTENING TESTS

A. Words

1. The test stimuli for all dichotic word pairs consisted of six words: *pig*, *car*, *boy*, *baby*, *mirror*, *table*.

2. The presentation of monaural words was used as a warm-up for all word tapes.

3. On 3/27/72, 5/10/72, and 8/16/72 single pairs of words were presented dichotically.

4. On 3/27/72 29 pairs of words were presented.

5. The response array consisted of a small toy pig, a small toy boy doll, a small baby doll, a small mirror, a picture of a car, and a picture of a table.

6. Genie was asked to point to the objects or pictures corresponding to what she heard.

Test Stimuli for 3/27/72

a. *Warm-ups (word set presented twice)*
   pig
   car
   boy
   baby
   mirror
   table

b. *Dichotic Pairs*

	Left ear	Right ear
1.	pig	mirror
2.	car	baby
3.	boy	table
4.	baby	pig
5.	table	car
6.	mirror	boy
7.	car	mirror
8.	pig	boy
9.	table	baby
10.	boy	car
11.	pig	table
12.	baby	mirror
13.	car	pig
14.	mirror	table
15.	boy	baby

The headset was reversed, and 1–14 were presented again, this time originally left-ear items going to the right ear and originally right-ear items going to the left ear.

	Left ear	Right ear
16.	mirror	pig
17.	baby	car
18.	table	boy
19.	pig	baby
20.	car	table
21.	boy	mirror
22.	mirror	car
23.	boy	pig
24.	baby	table
25.	car	boy
26.	table	pig
27.	mirror	baby
28.	pig	car
29.	table	mirror

7. On 5/10/72, 15 pairs of words were presented dichotically. The warm-up words were presented in the same order as 3/27/72.

Test Stimuli for 5/10/72 (Dichotic Pairs)

	Left ear	Right ear
1.	pig	mirror
2.	car	baby
3.	boy	table
4.	baby	pig
5.	table	car
6.	mirror	boy
7.	car	mirror
8.	pig	boy
9.	table	baby
10.	boy	car
11.	pig	table
12.	baby	mirror
13.	car	pig
14.	mirror	table
15.	boy	baby

8. On 8/16/72, 30 pairs of words were presented dichotically. Warm-up words were the same as on 3/27/72.

Test Stimuli for 8/16/72 (Dichotic Pairs)

	Left ear	Right ear
1.	baby	car
2.	table	boy
3.	pig	baby
4.	car	table
5.	boy	mirror
6.	mirror	car
7.	boy	pig
8.	baby	table
9.	car	boy
10.	table	pig
11.	mirror	baby
12.	pig	car
13.	table	mirror
14.	baby	boy
15.	mirror	pig

The headset was reversed and 1–15 presented again, this time originally left-ear items going to the right ear and originally right-ear items going to the left ear.

9. On 6/3/73 words were presented dichotically four at a time—two pairs at a time, separated by 0.5 seconds.

Test Stimuli for 6/3/73

a. *Warm-ups*

table	baby
boy	car
pig	table
baby	mirror
car	pig

b. *Dichotic Pairs (presented two at a time)*

	Left ear	Right ear
1.	car	mirror
2.	boy	pig
3.	car	pig
4.	baby	table
5.	boy	mirror
6.	pig	table
7.	car	boy
8.	mirror	pig
9.	baby	pig
10.	mirror	table
11.	table	boy
12.	baby	car
13.	mirror	baby
14.	boy	car
15.	table	car
16.	boy	baby

The headphones were switched and the stimuli presented again, this time originally left-ear items going to the right ear and originally right-ear items going to the left ear. The test was repeated after two administrations of the environmental sounds test.

B. Environmental Sounds

1. On 8/2/72, 8/16/72, and 6/3/73 single pairs of environmental sounds were presented dichotically. On 6/3/73 these same stimuli were also presented four at a time (two pairs at a time, separated by 0.5 seconds).

2. The environmental sounds stimuli consisted of sounds made by the following items in Genie's environment: toy chimpanzee, telephone, car horn, water running, piano.

3. The response array consisted of color photographs of the actual objects making the sounds on tape; all the objects were from Genie's foster home, and their sounds were part of Genie's daily home life.

4. Genie was instructed to point to the pictures corresponding to what she heard.

5. Warm-ups consisted of the stimuli presented monaurally.

6. 8/2/73, 8/16/73, 6/3/73—Twenty Single Pairs of Environmental Sounds.

Test Stimuli

a. *Warm-up (sounds repeated after first presentation)*
   telephone
   piano
   chimp
   water
   horn

7. *Dichotic Pairs*

	Left ear	Right ear
1.	piano	water
2.	horn	piano
3.	horn	chimp
4.	water	telephone
5.	telephone	piano
6.	water	horn
7.	chimp	telephone
8.	water	chimp
9.	telephone	horn
10.	chimp	piano

The headphones were reversed and items 1–10 repeated, this time originally left-ear items going to the right ear, and originally right-ear items going to the left ear.

8. On 6/3/73, a second Environmental Sounds test was administered, where the environmental sounds were presented four at a time, two pairs at a time. For this test, an additional test stimulus, a guitar, was added and a color photo of a guitar in Genie's home environment was added to the array. Twenty-eight pairs were presented. There was a dichotic warm-up as well as a monaural warm-up.

a. *Warm-ups*
   (1) *Monaural warm-ups: set of six sounds repeated*
      telephone
      piano
      chimp
      water
      guitar
      horn

   (2) *Dichotic Warm-ups*

Left ear	Right ear
horn	piano
water	telephone

Left ear	Right ear
guitar	horn
piano	chimp
water	guitar

b. *Test Stimuli (Double Dichotic Pairs)*

	Left ear	Right ear
1.	guitar	horn
2.	telephone	water
3.	piano	chimp
4.	water	guitar
5.	telephone	chimp
6.	piano	horn
7.	horn	telephone
8.	water	piano
9.	guitar	telephone
10.	chimp	water
11.	horn	chimp
12.	telephone	piano
13.	chimp	guitar
14.	water	horn

The headphones were reversed and items 1–14 repeated, this time originally left-ear items going to the right ear, and originally right-ear items going to the left ear.

II. TACHISTOSCOPIC TESTS

A. Dot Location

1. The stimulus grids were $2\frac{1}{2} \times 2\frac{1}{2}$ inch square with the fixation point at the center of the grid.

2. The fixation point was a star.

3. The response grid was 10×10 inch square, and Genie used a wooden pointer to indicate her response.

4. (a) Beginning instructions were: *Ready? Look at the star.*
    (b) The stimulus dot was then flashed onto the T-scope screen.
    (c) The response instructions were: *Show me where the dot was. Where was the dot?*

5. Each stimulus was flashed for 30 msecs.

6. The intensity of the stimulus field was -4.96, and the intensity of the blank field was 7.4.

7. The numbers in the test items in Figure A.1 refer to the following squares in the grid.

1	2	3	4
5	6	7	8
9	10	11	12
13	14	15	16

8. At each test session there were 64 trials, 32 right-hand responses, 32 left-hand responses. The trials consisted of a set of 16 stimuli presented four times.

9. The test stimuli were (refer to Figure A.1):

1.	10	9.	14
2.	4	10.	2
3.	6	11.	15
4.	16	12.	5
5.	3	13.	7
6.	9	14.	8
7.	13	15.	11
8.	12	16.	1

B. Rhyming

1. Stimuli consisted of 15 pictures of objects, the names of which were all familiar to Genie. The names comprised five rhyming triplets:

   (a) pear–bear–chair
   (b) hat–cat–bat
   (c) tie–eye–pie
   (d) bee–key–tree
   (e) toes–nose–rose

2. The response array consisted of three picture choices, one of which rhymed with the test stimulus.

3. Stimulus and response pictures were approximately $1\frac{1}{2}$ inch square, white on black drawings.

4. Each pictured object occurred as both stimulus and response array choices, and all possible combinations were used.

5. Position of the correct choice in the response array was randomized, as was the order of stimuli.

6. There were 60 test trials, 30 flashed to the right visual field, 30 to the left visual field. A set of 30 (15 to the left, 15 to the right) was repeated to comprise the 60 trials.

7. Stimulus duration was 75 msecs.

8. The fixation point was a star.
9. Instructions were as follows:
   Look at the star. Ready? (Stimulus was then flashed.) *Point to the one that rhymes with what you saw. Which one rhymes with what you saw?*
10. Genie used a wooden pointer and pointed with her right hand the first 30 trials, and with her left hand the second 30 trials.
11. Before beginning, Genie had to correctly identify each test picture by naming it aloud.

Test Items:

Stimulus	Visual field	Response choices (in left to right order)
1. cat	right (R)	bat, pie, hose
2. tie	left (L)	bear, eye, bee
3. bat	R	hat, rose, tree
4. bear	L	rose, tree, chair
5. hose	L	bat, tie, rose
6. key	L	chair, tree, toes
7. hat	L	bear, eye, cat
8. tree	R	hose, bee, pie
9. bee	R	tie, key, rose
10. eye	L	hat, pie, chair
11. eye	R	cat, rose, tie
12. pear	R	hose, bear, cat
13. key	R	bee, pie, hose
14. bear	R	hat, pear, toes
15. tie	R	hose, pie, chair
16. bat	L	cat, eye, toes
17. rose	R	toes, pear, pie
18. pear	L	tie, bat, chair
19. pie	R	tie, pear, rose
20. cat	L	rose, hat, tie
21. toes	R	eye, hose, key
22. chair	L	pear, toes, hat
23. chair	R	hose, key, bear
24. hose	R	toes, key, eye
25. rose	L	tie, bear, hose
26. tree	L	rose, chair, key
27. toes	L	cat, pear, rose
28. hat	R	chair, bat, key

Stimulus	Visual field	Response choices (in left to right order)
29. pie	L	bear, eye, toes
30. bee	L	tree, hat, chair
31. cat	R	rose, hat, pear
32. tie	L	hat, hose, pie
33. bat	R	cat, eye, toes
34. bear	L	hat, pear, toes
35. hose	L	toes, key, eye
36. key	L	bee, pear, hose
37. hat	L	chair, bat, pie
38. tree	R	rose, chair, key
39. bee	R	tree, hat, chair
40. eye	L	pear, rose, tie
41. eye	R	hat, pie, chair
42. pear	R	tree, chair, rose
43. key	R	chair, tree, hat
44. bear	R	rose, tree, chair
45. tie	R	pear, eye, toes
46. bat	L	tie, hat, rose
47. rose	R	tie, hose, bee
48. pear	L	hose, bear, cat
49. pie	R	bear, eye, toes
50. cat	L	bat, hose, chair
51. toes	R	pie, pear, rose
52. chair	L	hose, key, bear
53. chair	R	pear, toes, hat
54. hose	R	bat, tie, rose
55. rose	L	cat, toes, pie
56. tree	L	cat, hose, bee
57. toes	L	hose, chair, key
58. hat	R	eye, cat, bee
59. pie	L	tie, pear, rose
60. bee	L	tie, key, rose

APPENDIX III

Excerpt from Kent (1972)

EXCERPT FROM "EIGHT MONTHS IN THE HOSPITAL" BY DR. JAMES KENT (1972)

Affectively, Genie also changed considerably at the Rehabilitation Center. At first we found that the most spontaneous and sustained affective reactions could be elicited when materials she was involved with were dropped or broken. If this behavior was accepted and it was made clear that she was free to repeat it without disapproval, she entered quickly into a ritual play during which she would eventually destroy the object. The nervous, tense laughter first associated with these episodes gradually changed to a relaxed and infectious laugh that would sometimes double her up and bring tears to her eyes. She would often accompany her own actions with cries of "stop it"—burst out laughing and repeat the action. However, despite the teasing and humorous quality to these interactions, the repetitive nature of the activities, the "stop it" phrase, and the kind of release she seemed to gain in voice volume and gross motor freedom suggests to us that these interactions were attempts at active mastery of formerly traumatic situations.

In general, Genie's pleasurable affects became more differentiated, ranging from a quiet smile, such as when praised, to whoops of delight, such as when greeting a familiar figure. The tense laughter became associated only with anxiety-provoking situations, and even in those circumstances became less frequent.

With respect to expressions of anger, these changed also, but less so in their quality. They tended to remain voiceless—sometimes with a strangled sound expressed with mouth wide open as though screaming—and self-directed. What did change was their frequency, their explicability, and their duration. Initially they were frequent, often with no stimulus we understood, but she was easily diverted by a competing stimulus. As time passed, their frequency diminished and they tended to occur only around events that would normally be frustrating to any youngster. However, as her own capacity for symbolic ideational activity grew, so did the duration of her anger reactions. Within about 6 months of her admission, she was capable of sulking for a whole morning because she wasn't included in a bus trip with the rest of the children. This was a vast change from the child we saw during the first month who could be diverted from a tantrum in a twinkling by presenting her with a balloon or a necklace—two of her favorite items.

In general, during her time at Rehab, Genie was not observed to turn her anger to any instrumental use, i.e., she would not attack the object of her frustration. She would on occasion destroy something of her own, but in no case did we observe that it was the object which was actually frustrating her.

One of the few exceptions to this general observation was an occasion several months following admission, when Genie was observed to making hitting gestures at a new but perfectly innocuous patient. Genie was known to hit, but only adults whom she felt safe with, and then only in teasing situations. Making aggressive overtures to another patient was so out of character that we were baffled—until the teacher provided what we think was the missing link: The new patient was weating a dress that was part of the Rehab clothing store but which was formerly one that Genie wore frequently.

It was characteristic of Genie to hoard valued articles—not only her own possessions (including occasional feces), but also encyclopedias from the Rehab library, paper cups, and other odds and ends—and to be quite angry if her pile of treasures was disturbed. But articles of clothing were something she paid scant attention to at this time, thus her upset at seeing another patient wearing one of her old dresses was taken by us to indicate that Genie's sense of self was growing to include not only those things she valued intrinsically, but also things which had acquired value simply because they were hers at one time.

In her relationship with others, including her mother, Genie grew enormously. Although from the beginning she seemed to welcome and be curious about all of her visitors, she gave no affective sign when the visitors left. It was nearly a month before she showed with a fleeting facial expression that the termination of my daily visits had any significance, and nearly another month before she gave a sign that she wanted the visits to continue. In that latter instance she would begin to grab my hand when I said I was going and pull me to sit down. She later became more elaborate and persistent in her efforts to prevent favorite visitors from leaving, but it was of interest to us that in general she relinquished the people close to her with considerably less overt sign that one would expect from the ecstatic greeting we received on arrival.

Genie's relationship with her mother was an exception to this general observation. Nevertheless, Genie changed within a few months from a youngster who minimally differentiated people to a youngster who had several favorites—all adults incidentally, as she never showed more than curiosity about other children—persons whom she would seek out regularly for help, for affectionate teasing, or just to be close to. It is interesting, though, that Genie rarely approached any of us—or anyone else—for solace when distressed. She would receive it when offered, but not actively seek it out, except in the form of protection, as when she would see a dog, an animal she was especially terrified of. One of the exceptions to this general observation occurred when the earthquake struck. It was early in the AM, and Genie ran to the kitchen to be with the cooks, two people of whom she was very fond.

As Genie became more attached to familiar figures and acquainted with her hospital environment, she became increasingly restless and fearful in strange places. This was in marked contrast to her initial reaction to a novel surround, which she would approach readily and with great curiosity. This avoidance of the unfamiliar route on our daily car drives on excursions to near-by stores, she would scoot over in the seat, grab my hand, and begin worriedly scanning the new surrounding.

During this time Genie's relationship with her mother also underwent a considerable change. As we first observed it, Genie seemed less interested in her mother than in many of the other hospital staff. She would comply with her mother's requests to sit on her lap, but she remained still and aloof, and was noted at least to have an angry outburst of scratching and spitting as soon as she could escape. Genie's mother seemed not to be aware of this noticeable lack of warmth; on the contrary, she remarked once after such an episode that Genie seemed to "like me today."

At the time we speculated that Genie was beginning to express some of the anger for the years of deprivation, and her mother was the most familiar association with this. Anyway, we considered it important that Genie have regular and frequent contact with her mother. This was her only real link to her past and we felt that it should be maintained to give Genie a better chance both to come to terms with her own history and to see it as having some continuity with her present.

As time went on, Genie and her mother both changed in their responsiveness to each other. The changes in Genie's mother we attributed in part to her release from her own isolation and fear for her safety, and in part to the efforts of our chief psychiatric social-worker, an extremely skilled psychotherapist who had a deep concern for the mother. Genie's mother became more spontaneous and appropriate with Genie, and Genie, as her relationship deepened with others, became more responsive and relaxed with her mother. Indeed, she began to look forward to the mother's visits with obvious delight, and most interesting is the fact that following the second of the mother's twice weekly visits, Genie began regularly to have a temper tantrum. We are inclined to think that it was [the] mother's leaving that angered Genie, although she separated without obvious distress and the reaction never occurred after the first of the weekly visits. We are also now inclined to think that Genie's reaction to her mother during the first weeks of her hospitalization should be explained partly in terms of her anger at being abandoned by her in the hospital, a reaction we take for granted in normal children but failed to consider in our initial thinking about this peculiar child.

APPENDIX IV

Sketches by Genie

In the following pages, a few of Genie's drawings are presented. For the first few years after her emergence from isolation, Genie drew only upon request. In the last few years, however, Genie has turned to drawing as a way of dealing with and expressing her thoughts, feelings, and fantasies. Some of the drawings are representative of situations or objects that were frequently referred to in her speech. Since Genie herself often labels situations with sentences, I have used some of Genie's own sentences to partially caption some of the pictures.

Genie's drawing of a human figure (12/22/71). Note the lack of either trunk (if lines represent arms) or arms (if lines represent trunk), and legs, ears, hair, clothes, and so forth. Contrast this primitive figure with the detail she produced when asked, at an earlier time (11/8/71), to draw "a cat eating," "a dog eating." The animals have a well defined trunk and head, four legs, and other features. The tongue, one eye, and tail are in keeping with a profile view, a fairly sophisticated perspective.

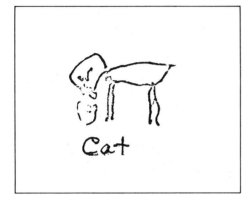

A drawing of Genie in a dentist's chair made in the fall of 1976. Note the dental drill on the upper left. Genie was infatuated with her dentist and often had sexual fantasies about him.

"I want Curtiss play piano." This picture depicts a favorite pastime of ours—me playing, Genie standing by the piano transfixed, almost hypnotized. I always play classical music. My few attempts to play something other than classical music have met with her removing my hands from the piano and placing a book that she knows contains classical music in front of me. This picture was drawn in early 1975.

"Swimming pool like Judy." Genie (on the right) and a friend. The drawing also shows the friend's car and a swimming pool (summer, 1972).

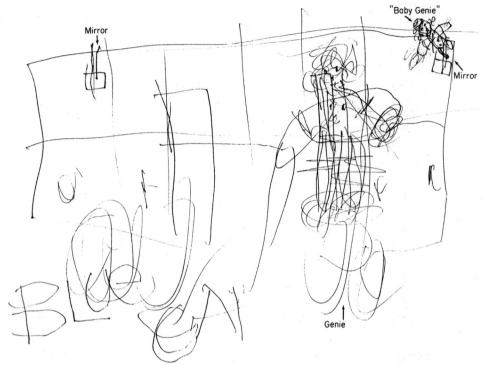

"Mike have blue car." (Mike is the name given to Genie's foster brother). This was drawn in 1976, although it had been almost 5 years since she had seen this car. At the top right, she has drawn the car mirror and a picture of "Baby Genie" (her words) with her legs wrapped around the mirror. Earlier, cars simply meant freedom and excursions for Genie, and she drew only the car itself. Later, her fascination with cars included their mirrors (masturbatory objects for her) and the power of driving a car (drivers and steering wheels). There is another depiction of herself (at the steering wheel) and another mirror drawn at the rear of the car. Note also the car door. The words "Blue Car" were printed from dictation.

REFERENCES

Anderson, S. R. 1975. *The organization of phonology.* New York: Academic Press.

Ayres, J. 1972. *Southern California sensory integration tests.* Western Psychological Services

Bailey, N., Madden, C., & Krashen, S. 1974. Is there a "natural sequence" in adult second language learning? *Language Learning, 24,* 235–243.

Baltaxe, C. A., & Simmons, J. Q. III. 1975. Language in childhood psychosis: A review. *Journal of Speech and Hearing Disorders 40,* 439–458.

Bellugi, U., & Brown, R. 1964. (Eds.) *The acquisition of language. Monographs of the society for research in child development,* 29.

Benton, A. L., Levin, H. S., & Varney, N. R. 1973. Tactile perception of direction in normal subjects. *Neurology, 23,* 1248–1250.

Benton, A. L., Van Allen, M. W., deS. Hamsher, K., & Levin, H. S. 1975. *Test of Facial Recognition.* Department of Neurology, University of Iowa Hospitals, Iowa City.

Berlin, C. I., Lowe-Bell, S. S., Hughes, L. F., & Berlin, H. L. 1972. *Dichotic right-ear advantage in males and females—ages 5–13.* Paper presented at the 84th meeting of the Acoustical Society of America, Miami Beach, Florida.

Berlin, C. I., Hughes, S., Lowe-Bell, S., & Berlin, H. 1973. Dichotic right-ear advantage in children 5 to 13. *Cortex, 9,* 393–402.

Berry, M., & Talbott, R. 1966. *Exploratory test of grammar.* Rockford, Illinois: Author.

Bever, T. G. 1970. The cognitive basis of linguistic structures. In J. Hayes (Ed.), *Cognition and the development of language.* Cambridge, Massachusetts: M.I.T. Press.

Bever, T. G., Fodor, J. A., & Weksel, W. 1965. On the acquisition of syntax: A critique of "contextual generalization." *Psychological Review, 72,* 467–482.

Bloom, L. 1970. *Language development: Form and function in emerging grammars.* Cambridge, Massachusetts: M.I.T. Press.

Bloom, L. 1971. Why not pivot grammar? *Journal of Speech and Hearing Disorders, 36,* 40–50.

Bloom, L. 1973. *One word at a time: The use of single word utterances before syntax.* The Hague: Mouton.

Bloom, L. 1974. Talking, understanding, and thinking. In R. L. Schiefelbusch & L. L. Lloyd (Eds.), *Language perspectives—acquisition, retardation, and intervention.* Baltimore: University Park Press.

Bogen, J., Dezure, R., Tenhouten, W., & Marsh, J. 1972. The other side of the brain IV. The A/P ratio. Bulletin of Los Angeles Neurological Society, *37,* 49–61.

Bowerman, M. 1973. *Early syntactic development: A cross-linguistic study with special reference to Finnish.* London: Cambridge University Press.

Braine, M. D. S. 1963. The ontogeny of English phrase structure: the first phase. *Language, 39,* 1–13.

Brown, R. 1968. Development of wh-questions in child speech. *Journal of Verbal Learning and Verbal Behavior, 7,* 279–290.

Brown, R. 1973. *A first language: The early stages.* Cambridge, Massachusetts: Harvard University Press.

Brown, R., & Bellugi, U. 1964. Three processes in the child's acquisition of syntax. *Harvard Educational Review, 34,* 133–151.

Brown, R., Cazden, C., & Bellugi, U. 1969. The child's grammar from I to III. In J. P. Hill (Ed.), *Minnesota Symposia on Child Psychology.* Minneapolis: University of Minnesota Press, Vol. II, 28–73.

Brown, W., Marsh, J., & Smith, J. 1973. Contextual meaning effects on speech-evoked potentials. *Behavioral Biology, 9,* 755–761.

Carmon, A., & Benton, A. L. 1969. Tactile perception of direction and number in patients with unilateral cerebral disease. *Neurology, 19,* 525–532.

Carmon, A., & Nachson, I. 1971. Effect of unilateral brain-damage on perception of temporal order. *Cortex*, *5*, 63–68.

Carrow, E. 1968. The development of auditory comprehension of language structure in children. *Journal of Speech and Hearing Disorders*, *33*, 99–111.

Carrow, E. 1969. *Auditory test for language comprehension*. Austin: Southwest Educational Development Corporation.

Cedergren, H., & Sankoff, D. 1974. Variable rules: Performance as a statistical reflection of competence. *Language*, *50*, 333–355.

Chomsky, N. 1967. The general properties of language. In C. H. Millikan & F. L. Darley (Eds.), *Brain mechanisms underlying speech and language*. New York: Grune & Stratton. Pp. 73–88.

Chomsky, N. 1975. *Reflections on language*. New York: Pantheon Books.

Clark, E. V. 1971. On the acquisition of the meaning of *before* and *after*. *Journal of Verbal Learning and Verbal Behavior*, *10*, 266–275.

Clark, E. V. 1973. What's in a word? On the child's acquisition of semantics in his first language. In T. E. Moore (Ed.), *Cognitive development and the acquisition of language*. New York: Academic Press.

Clark, E. V. 1974. Some aspects of the conceptual basis for first language acquisition. In R. L. Schiefelbusch & L. L. Lloyd (Eds.), *Language perspectives—acquisition, retardation, and intervention*. Baltimore: University Park Press.

Coker, P. 1975. *On the acquisition of temporal terms*. Paper presented at the Stanford Child Language Research Forum, April 5.

Compton, A. J. 1974. Generative studies of children's phonological disorders: A strategy of therapy. In S. Singh (Ed.), *Measurements in hearing, speech, and language*. Baltimore: University Park Press.

Cunningham, M. A. 1966. A five-year study of the language of an autistic child. *Journal of Child Psychology*, *7*, 143–154.

Curry, F. 1968. A comparison of the performance of a right hemispherectomized subject and twenty-five normals on four dichotic listening tasks. *Cortex*, *4.*, 144–153.

Curtiss, S., Fromkin, V., Krashen, S., Rigler, D., & Rigler, M. 1974. The linguistic development of Genie. *Language*, *50*(3).

Denis, M., & Whitaker, H. 1976. Language acquisition following hemidecortication: Linguistic superiority of the left over the right hemisphere. *Brain and Language*, *3*, 404–433.

DeRenzi, E., & Spinnler, H. 1966. Visual recognition in patients with unilateral cerebral disease. *Journal of Nervous and Mental Disease*, *142*, 515–525.

De Villiers, J., & de Villiers, P. 1973. A cross-sectional study of the acquisition of grammatical morphemes in child speech. *Journal of Psycholinguistic Research*, *2*, 267–278.

De Villiers, J., & de Villiers, P. 1973. Development of the use of word order in comprehension. *Journal of Psycholinguistic Research*, *2*, 331–341.

De Villiers, J., & de Villiers, P. 1974. Competence and performance in child language: Are children really competent to judge? *Journal of Child Language*, *1*, 11–22.

Dore, J. 1975. Holophrases, speech acts, and language universals. *Journal of Child Language*, *2*, 21–40.

Dulay, H., & Burt., M. 1973. Natural sequences in child second language acquisition. *Language Learning*, *24*, 37–53.

Efron, R. 1963. Temporal perception, aphasia, and déjà vu. *Brain*, *86*, 403–424.

Eilers, R., Oller, D., & Ellington, J. 1974. The acquisition of word-meaning for dimensional adjectives: The long and short of it. *Journal of Child Language*, *1*, 195–204.

Eisenson, J. 1972. *Aphasia in children*. New York: Harper & Row.

Eisenson, J., & Ingram, D. 1972. Childhood aphasia—an updated concept based on recent research. In *Papers and reports on child development*. Stanford University. Pp. 103–120.

Ervin-Tripp, S. 1970. Discourse agreement: How children answer questions. In J. R. Hayes (Ed.), *Cognition and the development of language*. New York: Wiley.

Fathman, A. 1975. The relationship between age and second language productive ability. *Language Learning*, *25*(2), 245–253

Fay, W. H. 1973. On the echolalia of the blind and of the autistic child. *Journal of Speech and Hearing Disorders*, *38*, 478–489.

Fischer, S. 1973. *Verb inflections in American Sign Language and their acquisition by the deaf child.* Paper presented at the winter meeting of the Linguistic Society of America, San Diego, California.

Fleming, J. A. 1974. The state of the apes. In *Psychology Today*, January, 1974. Pp. 31–46.

Fraser, C., Bellugi, U., & Brown, R. 1963. Control of grammar in imitation, comprehension, and production. *Journal of Verbal Learning and Verbal Behavior*, *2*, 121–135.

Fromkin, V., Krashen, S., Curtiss, S., Rigler, D., & Rigler, M. 1974. The development of language in Genie: A case of language acquisition beyond the critical period. *Brain and Language*, *1*, 81–107.

Gardner, R. A., & Gardner, B. T. 1969. Teaching sign language to a chimpanzee. *Science*, *165*, 664–672.

Gardner, B. T., & Gardner, R. A. 1971. Two-way communication with an infant chimpanzee. In A. M. Schrier & F. Stollnitz (Eds.), *Behavior of nonhuman primates* (Vol. 4). New York: Academic Press. Pp. 117–184.

Gazzaniga, M. 1970. *The bisected brain*. New York: Appleton-Century-Croft.

Gazzaniga, M., & Hillyard, S. 1971. Language and speech capacity of the right hemisphere. *Neuropsychologia*, *9*, 273–280.

Geffen, G., Bradshaw, J. L., & Nettleton, N. C. 1972. Hemispheric assymetry: Verbal and spatial encoding of visual stimuli, *Journal of Experimental Psychology 95*, 25–31.

Graham, J. T., & Graham, L. W. 1971. Language behavior of the mentally retarded: Syntactic characteristics. *American Journal of Mental Deficiency*, *75*, 623–629.

Graham, F. K., & Kendall, B. S. 1960. Memory-for-designs test: Revised general manual. *Perceptual and Motor Skills*. Monograph supplement 2-VIII.

Greenfield, P., Smith, J., & Laufer, B. 1973. *Communication and the beginning of language: The development of semantic structure in one-word speech and beyond*. New York: Academic Press.

Hansen, H. 1972. *The first experiences and the emergence of "Genie."* Paper presented at the 80th Annual Convention of the American Psychological Association, Honolulu, Hawaii, September 1–8.

Harshman, R., Crawford, H. J., & Hecht, E. 1975. Marijuana, cognitive style, and hemispheric dominance. In *The therapeutic aspects of marijuana: A conference at Asilomar, California November 6–7*. PLOG Research.

Heilbrun, A. B., Jr. 1956. Psychological test performance as function of lateral localization of cerebral lesion, *Journal of Comparative and Physiological Psychology*, *49* (February), 10–14.

Held, R., & Bossom, J. 1961. Neonatal deprivation and adult rearrangement: Complimentary techniques for analyzing plastic sensory-motor coordinations. *Journal of Comparative Physiology and Psychology*, *54* (1), 33–37.

Hess, E. 1958. Imprinting in animals. *Scientific American*, *198* (3), 81–90.

Hess, E. 1964. Imprinting in birds. *Science*, *146* (3648), 1128–1139.

Hillier, W. 1954. Total left hemispherectomy for malignant glioma. *Neurology*, *4*, 718–721.

Hooper, J. 1973. *Aspects of natural generative phonology*. Unpublished doctoral dissertation, UCLA.

Ingram, D. 1974. The relationship between comprehension and production. In R. L. Schiefelbusch & L. L. Lloyd (Eds.), *Language perspectives—acquisition, retardation, and intervention*. Baltimore: University Park Press.

Ingram, T. T. S. 1969. Developmental disorders of speech. In *Handbook of clinical neurology, Vol 4: Disorders of speech, perception, and symbolic behavior*. Amsterdam: North-Holland.

Jackson, J. H. 1932. On the nature of the duality of the brain. In J. Taylor (Ed.), *Selected writings of John Hughlings Jackson*. New York: Basic Books.

Jakobsen, R. 1962. *Roman Jakobsen selected writings. I: Phonological studies*. The Hague: Mouton.

Jakobsen, R., & Halle, M. 1956. *Fundamentals of language*. The Hague: Mouton.

Kanner, L. 1943. Autistic disturbances of affective contact, *Nervous Child, 2*, 217–250.

Karlin, I. W., & Strazzulla, M. 1952. Speech and language problems of mentally deficient children. *Journal of Speech and Hearing Disorders, 17*, 286–294.

Keenan, E. O. 1974. Conversational competence in children. *Journal of Child Language, 1*, 163–183.

Keenan, E. O. 1975. *Evolving discourse: The next step*. Paper presented at the Stanford Child Language Research Forum, April 4–5.

Kent, J. 1972. *Eight months in the hospital*. Paper presented at the 80th Annual Convention of the American Psychological Association, Honolulu, Hawaii, September 1–8.

Kimura, D. 1961. Cerebral dominance and the perception of verbal stimuli. *Canadian Journal of Psychology, 15*, 166–171.

Kimura, D. 1963. Speech lateralization in young children as determined by an auditory test. *Journal of Comparative Physiology and Psychology, 56*, 899–902.

Kimura, D. 1967. Functional asymmetry of the brain in dichotic listening. *Cortex, 3*, 163–178.

Kimura, D. 1969. Spatial localization in left and right visual fields. *Canadian Journal of Psychology, 23*, 445–458.

Klima, E. S., & Bellugi, U. 1966. Syntactic regularities in the speech of children. In J. Lyons & R. J. Wales (Eds.), *Psycholinguistics papers*. Edinburgh: Edinburgh University Press.

Knox, C., & Kimura, D. 1970. Cerebral processing of nonverbal sounds in boys and girls. *Neuropsychologia, 8*, 227–237.

Krashen, S. 1972. *Language and the left hemisphere*. Working Papers in Phonetics, UCLA, No. 24.

Krashen, S. 1973. Lateralization, language learning, and the critical period: Some new evidence. *Language Learning, 23*, 63–74.

Krashen, S., & Harshman, R. 1972. *Lateralization and the critical period*. Working Papers in Phonetics, UCLA, No. 23. Pp. 13–21.

Kucazj, S., & Maratsos, M. 1975. On the acquisition of 'front', 'back', and 'side'. *Child Development, 46* (1), 202–210.

Labov, W. 1972. *Sociolinguistic patterns*. Philadelphia: University of Pennsylvania Press.

Lansdell, H. 1968. Effect of extent of temporal lobe ablations on two lateralized defects. *Physiology and Behavior, 3*, 271–273.

Lee, L. 1966. Developmental sentence types: A method for comparing normal and deviant syntactic development. *Journal of Speech and Hearing Disorders, 31*, 311–330.

Lee, L. 1969. *Northwestern syntax screening test*. Evanston, Illinois: Northwestern University Press.

Lehiste, I. 1970. *Suprasegmentals*. Cambridge, Massachusetts: M.I.T. Press.

Lenneberg, E. H. 1962. Understanding language without ability to speak: A case report. *Journal of Abnormal Social Psychology, 65*, 419–425.

Lenneberg, E. H. 1967. *Biological foundations of language*. New York: Wiley.

Lenneberg, E. H., Nichols, I. A., & Rosenberger, E. F. 1964. Primitive stages of language development in mongolism. In D. McK. Rioch & E. A. Weinstein (Eds.), *Disorders of Communication* (Research publications of the Association for research in nervous and mental disease, Vol. 42): Baltimore: Williams & Wilkins. Pp. 119–137.

Leonard, L. B. 1972. What is deviant language? *Journal of Speech and Hearing Disorders, 37*, 427–446.

Levine, S. 1957. Infantile experience and resistance to physiological stress. *Science, 126* (3270), 405.

Levine, S., Alpert, M., & Lewis, G. M. 1958. Differential maturation of an adrenal response to cold stress in rats manipulated in infancy. *Journal of Comparative Physiology and Psychology, 51* (6), 774–777.

Levy, J., Trevarthen, C., & Sperry, R. 1972. Perception of bilateral chimeric figures following hemispheric deconnexion. *Brain, 95,* 61–78.

Limber, J. 1973. The genesis of complex sentences. In T. E. Moore (Ed.), *Cognitive development and the acquisition of language.* New York: Academic Press.

Linden, E. 1974. *Apes, men, and language.* New York Saturday Review Press, E. P. Dutton.

Lord, C. 1974. *Variations in the pattern of acquisition of negation.* Paper presented at the 6th annual Child Language Research Forum, Stanford University, April 5–6.

Luria, A. R. 1966. *Higher cortical functions in man.* New York: Basic Books.

McNeill, D. 1970. *The acquisition of language.* New York: Harper & Row.

Mecham, M. J., Jex, J. L., & Jones, J. D. 1967. *Utah test of language development.* Salt Lake City, Utah: Communication Research Associates.

Menyuk, P. 1964. Comparison of grammar of children with functionally deviant and normal speech. *Journal of Speech and Hearing Disorders, 7,* 109–121.

Menyuk, P. 1968. The role of distinctive features in children's acquisition of phonology. *Journal of Speech and Hearing Disorders, 11,* 138–146.

Menyuk, P. 1969. *Sentences children use.* Cambridge, Massachusetts: M.I.T. Press.

Menyuk, P. 1971. *The acquisition and development of language.* Englewood Cliffs, New Jersey: Prentice-Hall.

Metzig, E., Rosenberg, S., & Ast, M. 1975. Lateral asymmetry in patients with nervous and mental disease. *Neuropsychobiology, 1,* 197–202.

Metzig, E., Rosenberg, S., Ast, M., & Krashen, S. in press. Bipolar manic–depressives and unipolar depressives distinguished by tests of lateral asymmetry.

Miller, W., & Ervin, S. 1964. The development of grammar in child language. In U. Bellugi & R. Brown (Eds.), *Monograph of the Society for Research in Child Development: the acquisition of language, 29* (1), 9–43.

Milner, B., Taylor, L., & Sperry, R. 1968. Lateralized suppression of dichotically presented digits after commissural section in man. *Science, 161,* 184–186.

Molfese, D. 1972. *Cerebral asymmetry in infants, children, and adults: Auditory evoked responses to speech and music stimuli.* Unpublished doctoral dissertation, Pennsylvania State University.

Mooney, C. M. 1957. Age in the development of closure ability in children. *Canadian Journal of Psychology, 11* (4), 219–226.

Morehead, D., & Ingram, D. 1973. The development of base syntax in normal and linguistically deviant children. In *Papers and reports on child language development.* Stanford University.

Moskowitz, A. 1970. The two-year-old stage in the acquisition of English phonology. *Language, 46,* 426–441.

Nebes, R. 1971. Superiority of the minor hemisphere in commissurotomized man for the perception of part–whole relations. *Cortex, 7,* 333–349.

Nebes, R. 1974. Hemispheric specialization in commissurotomized man, *Psychological Bulletin, 81,* 1–14.

Needleman, R. 1974. *Parameters of autistic and aphasic language.* Paper presented at the Annual conference on brain function, UCLA.

Parisi, D., & Antinucci, F. 1970. Lexical competence. In G. Flores d'Arcais & W. Levelt (Eds.), *Advances in Psycholinguistics.* North-Holland: Amsterdam. Pp. 197–210.

Perlmutter, D. M. 1970. The two verbs begin. In R. Jacobs & P. Rosenbaum (Eds.), *Readings in English transformational grammar.* Waltham, Massachusetts: Ginn.

Poeck, L., Kerschensteiner, M., Hartje, W., & Orgass, B. 1973. Impairment in visual recognition of geometric figures in patients with circumscribed retrorolandic brain lesions. *Neuropsychologia, 11,* 311–317.

Raven, J. C. 1951. *Coloured progressive matrices*. Beverly Hill, Western Psychological Services.

Richie, J., & Butler, J. 1964. Performance of retardates on the Memory-for-Designs test. *Journal of Clinical Psychology*, *20*(1), 108–110.

Riesen, A. H. 1947. The development of visual perception in man and chimpanzee. *Science*, *106* (2744), 107–108.

Rondot, P., & Tzavaras, A. 1969. La prosopagnosie après vingt annees d'etudes cliniques et neuropsychologiques. *Journal de Psychologie Normale et Pathologique*, *66*, 133–165.

Rosenzweig, M. R. 1971. Effects of environment on development of brain and behavior. In E. Tobach (Ed.), *Biopsychology of development*. New York: Academic Press.

Russell, C., & Russell, W. M. S. 1971. Language and animal signals. In N. Minnis (Ed.), *Linguistics at large*. New York: Viking Press.

Russo, M., & Vignolo, L. 1967. Visual figure–ground discrimination in patients with unilateral cerebral disease. *Cortex*, *3*, 113–127.

Rutter, M., Greenfeld, D., & Lockyer, L. 1967. A five to fifteen year follow-up study of infantile psychosis: Social and behavioral outcome. *British Journal of Psychiatry*, *113*, 1183–1199.

Sabsay, S. 1975. *Communicative competence among the severely retarded: Some evidence from the conversational interaction of Down's syndrome (Mongoloid) adults*. Paper presented at the winter meeting of the Linguistic Society of America, San Francisco, California.

Salus, P., & Salus, M. 1973. *Language delay and minimal brain dysfunction*. Paper presented at the winter meeting of the Linguistic Society of America, San Diego, California.

Schlesinger, I. M. 1974. Relational concepts underlying language. In R. L. Schiefelbusch & L. L. Lloyd (Eds.), *Language perspectives—acquisition, retardation, and intervention*. Baltimore: University Park Press.

Schvachkin, M. V. 1948. Development of phonemic speech perception in early childhood. (In Russian) *Izvestia Akad. Pedag. Nauk RSFSR*, *13*, 101–132. Translated into English in C. Ferguson & D. Slobin (Eds.), *Studies of child language development*. New York: Holt, Rinehart & Winston, 1973.

Sinclair-de Zwart, H. 1971. Sensori-motor action patterns as a condition for the acquisition of syntax. In R. Huxley & E. Ingram (Eds.), *Language acquisition: Models and methods*. New York: Academic Press.

Singh, J. A. L., & Zingg, R. M. 1942. Wolf-children and feral man. *Archon Books*: London.

Smith, A. 1966. Speech and other functions after left (dominant) hemispherectomy. *Journal of Neurology, Neurosurgery, and Psychiatry*, *29*, 467–471.

Street, R. F. 1931. A gestalt-completion test. *Contributions to Education* No. 481, Columbia University Teachers College, New York.

Teuber, H. L., & Weinstein, S. 1956. Ability to discover hidden figures after cerebral lesions. *A.M.A. Archives of Neurology and Psychology*, *76*, 369–379.

Teuber, H. L., Battersby, W. S., & Bender, M. B. 1960. *Visual field defects after penetrating missile wounds of the brain*. Cambridge, Massachusetts: Harvard University Press.

Thurstone, L. L., & Jeffrey, T. E. 1956. *Closure speed (gestalt completion) test*. The Psychometric Laboratory, University of North Carolina.

Tinbergen, N., & Perdeck, A. C. 1950. On the stimulus situation releasing the begging response in the newly-hatched herring gull chick. *Behavior*, *3*, part 1, 1–39.

Van Lancker, D. 1975. *Heterogeneity in language and speech: Neurolinguistic studies*. Working Papers in Phonetics, UCLA No. 29.

Waryas, C., & Ruder, K. 1974. On the limitations of language comprehension procedures and an alternative. *Journal of Speech and Hearing Development* 39. No. 1.

Witelson, S., & Pallie, W. 1973. Left hemisphere specialization for language in the newborn. *Brain*, *96*, 641–646.

Zaidel, E. 1973. *Linguistic competence and related functions in the right cerebral hemisphere of man following commissurotomy and hemispherectomy.* Unpublished doctoral dissertation, California Institute of Technology.

Zaidel, E. in press. Auditory vocabulary of the right hemisphere following brain bisection or hemidecortication. *Cortex.*

Zaidel, E. 1977. Unilateral auditory language comprehension on the Token test following cerebral commissurotomy and hemispherectomy. *Neuropsychologia,* *15*(1), 1–17.

Zimmerman, I. L., Steiner, V. G., & Evatt, R. L. 1969. *Preschool language manual.* Columbus, Ohio: Charles E. Merrill.

Zollinger, R. 1935. Removal of left cerebral hemisphere. Report of a case. *Archives of Neurology and Psychiatry* (Chicago), *34*, 1055–1064.

Index